61st Congress, 3d Session } SENATE { Document No. 662

REPORTS OF THE IMMIGRATION COMMISSION

DICTIONARY OF RACES OR PEOPLES

Presented by MR. DILLINGHAM

December 5, 1910.—Referred to the Committee on Immigration and ordered to be printed, with illustrations

WASHINGTON
GOVERNMENT PRINTING OFFICE
1911

THE IMMIGRATION COMMISSION.

Senator WILLIAM P. DILLINGHAM, *Chairman*.
Senator HENRY CABOT LODGE.
Senator ASBURY C. LATIMER.[a]
Senator ANSELM J. McLAURIN.[b]
Senator LE ROY PERCY.[c]

Representative BENJAMIN F. HOWELL.
Representative WILLIAM S. BENNET.
Representative JOHN L. BURNETT.
Mr. CHARLES P. NEILL.
Mr. JEREMIAH W. JENKS.
Mr. WILLIAM R. WHEELER.

Secretaries:

MORTON E. CRANE. W. W. HUSBAND.
C. S. ATKINSON.

Chief Statistician:

FRED C. CROXTON.

Extract from act of Congress of February 20, 1907, creating and defining the duties of the Immigration Commission.

That a commission is hereby created, consisting of three Senators, to be appointed by the President of the Senate, and three Members of the House of Representatives, to be appointed by the Speaker of the House of Representatives, and three persons to be appointed by the President of the United States. Said commission shall make full inquiry, examination, and investigation, by subcommittee or otherwise, into the subject of immigration. For the purpose of said inquiry, examination, and investigation said commission is authorized to send for persons and papers, make all necessary travel, either in the United States or any foreign country, and, through the chairman of the commission, or any member thereof, to administer oaths and to examine witnesses and papers respecting all matters pertaining to the subject, and to employ necessary clerical and other assistance. Said commission shall report to Congress the conclusions reached by it, and make such recommendations as in its judgment may seem proper. Such sums of money as may be necessary for the said inquiry, examination, and investigation are hereby appropriated and authorized to be paid out of the "immigrant fund" on the certificate of the chairman of said commission, including all expenses of the commissioners, and a reasonable compensation, to be fixed by the President of the United States, for those members of the commission who are not Members of Congress; * * *.

[a] Died February 20, 1908.
[b] Appointed to succeed Mr. Latimer, February 25, 1908. Died December 22, 1909.
[c] Appointed to succeed Mr. McLaurin. March 16, 1910.

LIST OF REPORTS OF THE IMMIGRATION COMMISSION.

Volumes 1 and 2. Abstracts of Reports of the Immigration Commission, with Conclusions and Recommendations and Views of the Minority. (These volumes include the Commission's complete reports on the following subjects: Immigration Conditions in Hawaii; Immigration and Insanity; Immigrants in Charity Hospitals; Alien Seamen and Stowaways; Contract Labor and Induced and Assisted Immigration; The Greek Padrone System in the United States; Peonage.) (S. Doc. No. 747, 61st Cong., 3d sess.)

Volume 3. Statistical Review of Immigration, 1819-1910—Distribution of Immigrants, 1850-1900. (S. Doc. No. 756, 61st Cong., 3d sess.)

Volume 4. Emigration Conditions in Europe. (S. Doc. No. 748, 61st Cong., 3d sess.)

Volume 5. Dictionary of Races or Peoples. (S. Doc. No. 662, 61st Cong., 3d sess.)

Volumes 6 and 7. Immigrants in Industries: Pt. 1, Bituminous Coal Mining. (S. Doc. No. 633, 61st Cong., 2d sess.)

Volumes 8 and 9. Immigrants in Industries: Pt. 2, Iron and Steel Manufacturing. (S. Doc. No. 633, 61st Cong., 2d sess.)

Volume 10. Immigrants in Industries: Pt. 3, Cotton Goods Manufacturing in the North Atlantic States—Pt. 4, Woolen and Worsted Goods Manufacturing. (S. Doc. No. 633, 61st Cong., 2d sess.)

Volume 11. Immigrants in Industries: Pt. 5, Silk Goods Manufacturing and Dyeing—Pt. 6, Clothing Manufacturing—Pt. 7, Collar, Cuff, and Shirt Manufacturing. (S. Doc. No. 633, 61st Cong., 2d sess.)

Volume 12. Immigrants in Industries: Pt. 8, Leather Manufacturing—Pt. 9, Boot and Shoe Manufacturing—Pt. 10, Glove Manufacturing. (S. Doc. No. 633, 61st Cong., 2d sess.)

Volume 13. Immigrants in Industries: Pt. 11, Slaughtering and Meat Packing. (S. Doc. No. 633, 61st Cong., 2d sess.)

Volume 14. Immigrants in Industries: Pt. 12, Glass Manufacturing—Pt. 13, Agricultural Implement and Vehicle Manufacturing. (S. Doc. No. 633, 61st Cong., 2d sess.)

Volume 15. Immigrants in Industries: Pt. 14, Cigar and Tobacco Manufacturing—Pt. 15, Furniture Manufacturing—Pt. 16, Sugar Refining. (S. Doc. No. 633, 61st Cong., 2d sess.)

Volume 16. Immigrants in Industries: Pt. 17, Copper Mining and Smelting—Pt. 18, Iron Ore Mining—Pt. 19, Anthracite Coal Mining—Pt. 20, Oil Refining. (S. Doc. No. 633, 61st Cong., 2d sess.)

Volume 17. Immigrants in Industries: Pt. 21, Diversified Industries, Vol. I. (S. Doc. No. 633, 61st Cong., 2d sess.)

Volume 18. Immigrants in Industries: Pt. 21, Diversified Industries, Vol. II—Pt. 22, The Floating Immigrant Labor Supply. (S. Doc. No. 633, 61st Cong., 2d sess.)

Volumes 19 and 20. Immigrants in Industries: Pt. 23, Summary Report on Immigrants in Manufacturing and Mining. (S. Doc. No. 633, 61st Cong., 2d sess.)

Volumes 21 and 22. Immigrants in Industries: Pt. 24, Recent Immigrants in Agriculture. (S. Doc. No. 633, 61st Cong., 2d sess.)

Volumes 23-25. Immigrants in Industries: Pt. 25, Japanese and Other Immigrant Races in the Pacific Coast and Rocky Mountain States. (S. Doc. No. 633, 61st Cong., 2d sess.)

Volumes 26 and 27. Immigrants in Cities. (S. Doc. No. 338, 61st Cong., 2d sess.)

Volume 28. Occupations of the First and Second Generations of Immigrants in the United States—Fecundity of Immigrant Women. (S. Doc. No. 282, 61st Cong., 2d sess.)

Volumes 29-33. The Children of Immigrants in Schools. (S. Doc. No. 749, 61st Cong., 3d sess.)

Volumes 34 and 35. Immigrants as Charity Seekers. (S. Doc. No. 665, 61st Cong., 3d sess.)

Volume 36. Immigration and Crime. (S. Doc. No. 750, 61st Cong., 3d sess.)

Volume 37. Steerage Conditions—Importation and Harboring of Women for Immoral Purposes—Immigrant Homes and Aid Societies—Immigrant Banks. (S. Doc. No. 753, 61st Cong., 3d sess.)

Volume 38. Changes in Bodily Form of Descendants of Immigrants. (S. Doc. No. 208, 61st Cong., 2d sess.)

Volume 39. Federal Immigration Legislation—Digest of Immigration Decisions—Steerage Legislation, 1819-1908—State Immigration and Alien Laws. (S. Doc. No. 758, 61st Cong., 3d sess.)

Volume 40. The Immigration Situation in Other Countries: Canada—Australia—New Zealand—Argentina—Brazil. (S. Doc. No. 761, 61st Cong., 3d sess.)

Volume 41. Statements and Recommendations Submitted by Societies and Organizations Interested in the Subject of Immigration. (S. Doc. No. 764, 61st Cong., 3d sess.)

Volume 42. Index of Reports of the Immigration Commission. (S. Doc. No. 785, 61st Cong., 3d sess.)

LETTER OF TRANSMITTAL.

THE IMMIGRATION COMMISSION,
Washington, D. C., December 5, 1910.

To the Sixty-first Congress:

I have the honor to transmit herewith, on behalf of the Immigration Commission, a report entitled " Dictionary of Races or Peoples," which was prepared for the Commission by Dr. Daniel Folkmar, assisted by Dr. Elnora C. Folkmar.

Respectfully,

WILLIAM P. DILLINGHAM,
Chairman.

CONTENTS.

LIST OF TABLES.

MAPS.

DICTIONARY OF RACES OR PEOPLES.

INTRODUCTORY.

Since eastern Europe became an important source of immigration many new ethnical factors have been added to the population of the United States. Early in the Commission's investigations among these newer immigrants it became apparent that the true racial status of many of them was imperfectly understood even in communities where they were most numerous, and the difficulties encountered in properly classifying the many ethnical names that were employed to designate various races or peoples suggested the preparation of a volume that would promote a better knowledge of the numerous elements included in the present immigrant movement.

While this " dictionary " treats of more than six hundred subjects, covering all the important and many of the obscure branches or divisions of the human family, it is intended primarily as a discussion of the various races and peoples indigenous to the countries furnishing the present immigration movement to the United States, or which may become sources of future immigration.

Until 1899, when the Bureau of Immigration first classified arriving immigrants according to the race or people to which they belonged, practically all population statistics respecting the foreign-born in the United States were recorded only by country of birth. Previous to the adoption of the improved method of recording immigration statistics the Bureau of the Census had attempted in some instances to distinguish among the various east European peoples in the population, and as a result of this effort reports of recent censuses include more or less accurate data relative to the Polish and Bohemian elements in the population. In the first-mentioned case this grouping is accomplished by regarding for census purposes the former Kingdom of Poland as a geographical entity instead of Provinces of Austria, Prussia, and Russia, as Poland has been politically for more than a century. In the same way Bohemia is considered as a geographical unit instead of a part of Austria. With these exceptions, however, census reports make no distinction between the many important ethnical factors to be found among natives of eastern European countries resident in the United States.

Poland and Bohemia also appear as " countries of birth " in earlier immigration statistics, but when the movement of population from Austria-Hungary, Russia, Turkey, and the Balkan States to the United States assumed large proportions the old method of recording arrivals only by the country of their nativity was of little value in determining the ethnical status of such immigrants, and the Bureau of Immigration finally adopted the racial classification. The bureau recognizes 45 races or peoples among immigrants coming to the United States, and of these 36 are indigenous to Europe. This classification was adopted by the Immigration Commission in collecting and compiling data respecting the foreign-born in this country, and it is also made the principal basis of the dictionary of races or peoples. No work of this nature has before been published in the English language, although related works have been printed in the French, German, and other languages.[a] The present work, moreover, differs essentially from previous publications of the same nature in that it is written primarily with reference to the subject of immigration and is for the convenience of students of that subject rather than for the ethnologist. Therefore, in addition to a more strictly ethnological discussion of the various immigrant races and peoples, careful attention has been given to their numerical and geographical distribution, as well as their relative importance in the movement of population to the United States and other immigrant-receiving countries.

In the preparation of the dictionary it was neither the plan of the Commission nor the purpose of the author to attempt an original discussion of anthropology or ethnology, but rather to bring together from the most reliable sources such existing data as it was believed would be useful in promoting a better understanding of the many different racial elements that are being added to the population of the United States through immigration.

In the more strictly ethnological topics of definition and division, or classification of races or peoples according to their languages, their physical characteristics, and such other marks as would show their relationship to one another, and in determining their geographical habitats, an effort has been made to present the view most generally accepted among ethnologists, or, in case of radical and important differences of opinion, to present the rival views. It need not be explained, in view of the vastness of the ethnographical field and the present imperfect state of the science, that mistakes are inevitable in

[a] Since writing this dictionary Matsumura's excellent Gazetteer of Ethnology, published in Japan in 1908, has come to hand. As its name indicates, it is not a dictionary, but it more nearly covers the field than any other single volume in the English language.

a work of this nature. It is not to be regarded as written for the ethnologist, but for the student of immigration; for the one who wants in convenient form an approximately correct statement as to the ethnical status of immigrant races or peoples, their languages, their numbers, and the countries from which they come.

In determining the population and geographical distribution of races and their various divisions, reference was had to the census reports and other official publications of foreign countries, as well as to standard works of history and travel, and the publications of foreign geographical and other scientific societies. On pages 8 to 12 of this introduction is a selected bibliography of general works upon the subject under consideration, and a list of a few of the authorities that were consulted in its preparation.

The number of the chief divisions or basic races of mankind is more in dispute at the present time than when Linnæus proposed to classify them into 4, or Blumenbach into 5, great races. Some writers have reduced the number of such basic races to 3, while others have proposed 15, 29, or even 63. In preparing this dictionary, however, the author deemed it reasonable to follow the classification employed by Blumenbach, which school geographies have made most familiar to Americans, viz, the Caucasian, Ethiopian, Mongolian, Malay, and American, or, as familiarly called, the white, black, yellow, brown, and red races.

The sciences of anthropology and ethnology are not far enough advanced to be in agreement upon many questions that arise in such a study. The use of this classification as the basis for the present work is perhaps entirely justified by the generally prevailing custom in the United States, but there is equal justification in the fact that recent writers, such as Keane and the American authority Brinton, have returned to practically the earlier classifications.[a]

These authorities have also been closely followed by the author of the dictionary in separating the many subdivisions of the five great races one from another according to the languages they speak, and in grouping them into stocks upon the same basis. In other words, the primary classification of mankind into five grand divisions may be made upon physical or somatological grounds, while the subdivision of these into a multitude of smaller " races " or peoples is made largely upon a linguistic basis.[b] The practical arguments for adopting such a classification are unanswerable. It is not merely because it is most convenient and natural to call a man English, Irish, or German according to the language spoken by him or by his ancestors

[a] See p. 6 for some of these classifications.

[b] See classification on p. 5.

in the old home; this is also the classification that has the sanction of law in immigration statistics and in the censuses of foreign countries.[a] In no other way can figures be found that are comparable as to population, immigration, and distribution of immigrants. While it is well to find a classification by physical characteristics insisted upon in the able works of Ripley, Deniker, and others, it is manifestly impracticable to use such a classification in immigration work or in a census. The immigrant inspector or the enumerator in the field may easily ascertain the mother tongue of an individual, but he has neither the time nor the training to determine whether that individual is dolichocephalic or brachycephalic in type. He may not even know that these terms refer to the shape of the head and are considered to be of fundamental importance by the school of ethnologists just referred to. Finally, it may be that neither the ethnical nor the linguistic school has reached the ultimate word, but that a more natural and acceptable classification of peoples will be based in the future upon continuity of descent among the members of a race or of a stock, whether such genetic relationship be established by somatological, linguistic, sociological, or historical evidence, or by all combined.

The classification of races or peoples adopted for convenience by the author of the dictionary is presented on the page opposite.

[a] See further discussion of the principles of classification and of technical terms in article "English," pp. 54–57.

COMPARATIVE CLASSIFICATION OF IMMIGRANT RACES OR PEOPLES.

Based on Brinton (cf. Keane).			People.	Ripley's races, with other corresponding terms.
Race.	Stock.	Group.		
			Scandinavian:	
			Danish	I. TEUTONIC.
			Norwegian	
			Swedish	
		Teutonic	German (N. part)	H. Europæus (Lapouge).
			Dutch	Nordic (Deniker).
			English (part)	Dolicho-leptorhine (Kohlmann).
			Flemish	Germanic (English writers).
		Lettic	Lithuanian	Reihengräber (German writers).
			Scotch (part)	Kymric (French writers).
		Celtic	Irish (part)	
			Welsh	Part Alpine.
			Russian	
			Polish	
			Czech:	
			Bohemian	II. ALPINE (OR CELTIC).
			Moravian	
			Servian	H. Alpinus (Lapouge).
			Croatian	Occidental (Deniker).
	Aryan	Slavonic	Montenegrin	Disentis (German writers).
			Slovak	Celto-Slavic (French writers).
			Slovenian	Lappanoid (Pruner-Bey).
Caucasian			Ruthenian	Sarmatian (von Hölder).
			Dalmatian	Arvernian (Beddoe).
			Herzegovinian	
			Bosnian	
		Illyric	Albanian	
		Armenic	Armenian	
			French	Part Alpine.
			Italian (part)	Part Mediterranean.
			Roumanian	III. MEDITERRANEAN.
		Italic	Spanish	H. Meridionalis (Lapouge).
			Spanish-American	Atlanto-Mediterranean and Ibero-Insular (Deniker).
			Mexican, etc	
			Portuguese	Iberian (English writers).
		Hellenic	Greek	Ligurian (Italian writers).
		Iranic	Hindu	Part Mediterranean.
			Gypsy	Part Teutonic.
		Arabic	Arabian	
	Semitic	Chaldaic	Hebrew	Part Mediterranean.
			Syrian	
	Caucasic		Caucasus peoples	Doubtful.
	Euskaric		Basque	
			Finnish	
			Lappish	
		Finnic	Magyar	
	Sibiric		Bulgarian (part)	
		Tataric	Turkish, Cossack, etc.	
Mongolian		Japanese	Japanese, Korean	
		Mongolic	Kalmuk	
			Chinese	
	Sinitic	Chinese	East Indian (part, i. e., Indo-Chinese).	
Malay			Pacific Islander (part).	
			East Indian (part)	
Ethiopian			Negro	
American (Indian).			American Indian	

SOME CLASSIFICATIONS OF THE GRAND DIVISIONS OF MANKIND.

[For purposes of comparison, the order followed is that of Deniker's remarkable and often misunderstood scheme. It will be seen at once that the larger groups of races recognized by him are more like the grand divisions of other writers than has been commonly supposed. Accuracy of detail has been sacrificed to secure greater clearness in the comparison of groups. Blumenbach's classification, for instance, having been published in 1775, is naturally indefinite as to some of the ethnical groups established since his day and found in Deniker's list, such as "Dravidian" or "Aino." His term "Malay" includes all the Pacific Islanders, who are now distributed among Keane's Mongol, Caucasic, and Negro races.]

Keane (after Linnæus).	Blumenbach.	Deniker.	Huxley.	Flower (cf. Quatrefages).
		1. Bushman.		
		2. Negrito.	1. Negroid.	
		3. Negro.		
1. Negro (except 5).	2. Ethiopian (except 4, 6).	4. Melanesian.		1. Ethiopian (except 5)
		5. Ethiopian (Abyssinian, etc.).		
		6. Australian.	2. Australoid (except part of 5).	
		7. Dravidian.		
		8. Assyroid.		
		9. Indo-Afghan.		
		10. Arab (Semite).	5. Melanochroid (with part of 5).	
		11. Berber.		
		12. Littoral European.		3. Caucasic (with 5).
4. Caucasic (with 5).	1. Caucasian (except 19, 20).	13. Ibero-Insular.		
		14. Western European.		
		15. Adriatic.		
		16. Northern European.	4. Xanthochroid (with part of 27).	
		17. Eastern European.		
		18. Aino.		
		19. Polynesian.		
		20. Indonesian.		
		21. South American.		
3. American.	5. American.	22. North American.		
		23. Central American.		
		24. Patagonian.	3. Mongoloid (except part of 27).	2. Mongol.
		25. Eskimo.		
		26. Lapp.		
2. Mongol.	3. Mongolian.	27. Ugrian.		
		28. Turco-Tatar.		
	4. Malay [a]	29. Mongol (incl. Malay).		

[a] Includes Nos. 4, 6, 19, 20, and a part of 29.

One feature of the dictionary which is of particular interest in a study of immigration is the data showing the numerical extent and geographical distribution of the various immigrant races or peoples. No reliable compilation of this nature was available and its preparation required much research. The data are of value as suggesting the possibilities of future immigration, and also as showing the rate of immigration among the various races at the present time. In some cases, notably those of the Slovaks and Hebrews, where there is a high rate of emigration to the United States, it is conceivable that the movement may become normal or, indeed, that it may cease through an exhaustion of the home supply. On the other hand, in the case of the Russians, Germans, Italians, and certain other peoples the population is so great that although the volume of emigration may be large the rate is low and the supply is practically inexhaustible.

The estimated numerical strength of each of the principal races or peoples in Europe, and the immigration movement of such races from Europe to the United States in the fiscal year 1907, when immigration reached its greatest height, and also the average annual movement for the twelve years ending June 30, 1910, are shown in the table which follows. Reliable data respecting the number of Turks and Syrians in Europe are not available, and consequently these races are omitted. With these exceptions, however, the table includes all European races or peoples which in the years specified contributed more than 2,000 immigrants to the movement to the United States.

Estimated population of certain races in Europe, compared to immigration of such races from Europe to the United States in 1907, and also to the average annual immigration for the 12 years ending June 30, 1910.

Race or people.	Estimated population in Europe.	Immigrants to the United States from Europe.			
		Total number, 1907.	Average annual number, 12 years, 1899–1910.	Number per 1,000 estimated population based on—	
				Total number, 1907.	Average annual number, 12 years, 1899–1910.
Slovak	2,250,000	41,870	31,272	18.6	13.9
Hebrew	8,000,000	146,409	88,232	18.3	11.0
Croatian and Slovenian	3,600,000	47,317	27,704	13.1	7.7
Italian, South	20,000,000	238,469	157,300	11.9	7.9
Norwegian [a]	2,311,000	22,043	17,204	9.5	7.4
Irish [b]	4,500,000	37,715	35,086	8.4	7.8
Polish	17,000,000	137,147	78,528	8.1	4.6
Magyar	8,000,000	59,677	27,848	7.5	3.5
Greek	6,000,000	44,240	17,162	7.4	2.9
Lithuanian	4,000,000	25,764	14,538	6.4	3.6
Ruthenian [c]	3,900,000	23,751	12,059	6.1	3.1
Dalmatian, Bosnian, and Herzegovinian	1,573,000	7,289	2,601	4.6	1.7
Finnish (Western)	3,700,000	14,471	12,436	3.9	3.4
Swedish [d]	5,727,000	21,950	24,463	3.8	4.3
Italian, North	14,500,000	50,510	30,453	3.5	2.1
Bulgarian, Servian, and Montenegrin	9,000,000	26,866	7,872	3.0	.8
Danish [e]	2,700,000	7,163	5,831	2.7	2.2
Bohemian and Moravian	6,000,000	13,507	8,301	2.3	1.4
Portuguese	5,000,000	9,232	5,919	1.8	1.2
Roumanian	10,000,000	19,016	6,782	1.9	.7
English and Scotch [f]	35,300,000	61,797	37,882	1.7	1.1
Welsh [g]	1,700,000	2,560	1,619	1.5	1.0
German	72,200,000	91,059	61,253	1.3	.8
Dutch and Flemish	9,000,000	12,124	7,045	1.3	.8
Armenian [h]	5,000,000	2,273	2,127	.5	.4
Spanish	20,000,000	5,948	2,451	.3	.1
French	39,000,000	8,774	6,671	.3	.2
Russian (including Ruthenian or Little Russian of Russia)	77,200,000	16,652	6,751	.2	([i])

[a] The population figures represent the total population of Norway, and the immigration figures the total number of Scandinavians, mostly Norwegians, coming from Norway.

[b] The population figures represent the total population of Ireland, and the immigration figures the total number of Irish coming from Europe.

[c] The population figures represent the number of Ruthenians in Austria-Hungary, and the immigration figures the number of Ruthenians coming from Austria-Hungary.

[d] The population figures represent the total population of Sweden and the population of Swedes in Russia (Finland), and the immigration figures the total number of Scandinavians, mostly Swedes, coming from Sweden and Russia.

[e] The population figures represent the total population of Denmark, and the immigration figures the total number of Scandinavians, mostly Danes, coming from Denmark.

[f] The population figures represent the total population of England and Scotland, and the immigration figures the total number of English and Scotch coming from Europe.

[g] The population figures represent the total population of Wales, and the immigration figures the total number of Welsh coming from Europe.

[h] Includes Armenian population in Asia and Armenians coming from Asia.

[i] Less than 1 per 10,000.

As previously stated, the dictionary treats of more than 600 subjects, but particular attention is paid to the races or peoples appearing in the classification used for statistical purposes by the Bureau of Immigration and Naturalization, the chief racial stocks represented among immigrants, and some of the ethnical or political terms most commonly used to designate immigrants. The races or peoples recorded by the bureau in the order of their numerical importance as immigrants to the United States for the twelve years ending June 30, 1910, with the number admitted during that period, are as follows:

Race or people	Number	Race or people	Number
1. Italian, South	1,911,933	21. Dutch and Flemish	87,658
2. Hebrew	1,074,442	22. Russian	83,574
3. Polish	949,064	23. Roumanian	82,704
4. German	754,375	24. Portuguese	72,897
5. Scandinavian	586,306	25. Syrian	56,909
6. Irish	439,724	26. Spanish	51,051
7. English	408,614	27. Cuban	44,211
8. Slovak	377,527	28. Mexican	41,914
9. Italian, North	372,668	29. African (black)	33,630
10. Magyar	338,151	30. Dalmatian, Bosnian, and Herzegovinian	31,696
11. Croatian and Slovenian	335,543	31. Armenian	26,498
12. Greek	216,962	32. Chinese	22,590
13. Lithuanian	175,258	33. Welsh	20,752
14. Finnish	151,774	34. Turkish	12,954
15. Japanese	148,729	35. West Indian (except Cuban)	11,569
16. Ruthenian (Russniak)	147,375	36. Spanish American	10,669
17. Scotch	136,842	37. Korean	7,790
18. French	115,783	38. East Indian	5,786
19. Bohemian and Moravian	100,189	39. Pacific Islander	357
20. Bulgarian, Servian, and Montenegrin	97,391		

It will be noted that in several instances the bureau classifies certain races or peoples together. In such instances separate immigration statistics are not available, but in this dictionary each race or people above enumerated is treated separately.

By courtesy of D. Appleton & Co., the publishers, and Prof. William Z. Ripley, the author, several maps from Ripley's "The Races of Europe" have been reproduced in the dictionary.

SELECTED BIBLIOGRAPHY OF GENERAL WORKS.[a]

1. ETHNOLOGY AND ANTHROPOLOGY.

The anthropologist who has been chiefly followed in the classification adopted is the American, Brinton. See:

Brinton, Daniel G. Races and Peoples. New York. 1890.

Brinton, D. G. Anthropology and Ethnology. (In Vol. I of) The Iconographic Encyclopedia. Philadelphia. 1886.

Brinton, D. G. The American Race. New York. 1891.

[a] No attempt can be made to mention the special publications consulted—far more numerous than those indicated—which pertain only to a particular race, people, or country.

Keane has generally supplemented Brinton where the latter is not quite up to date:

Keane, A. H. Ethnology. Cambridge. 1901.

Keane, A. H. Man, Past and Present. Cambridge. 1899.

Keane, A. H. (Six volumes of) Stanford's Compendium of Geography and Travel. London. 1896–1901.

The linguistic classifications of these two authors have been checked up by the somatological classifications of:

Deniker, J. The Races of Man. London. 1900.

Ripley, William Z. The Races of Europe. New York. 1899.

Sergi, G. The Mediterranean Race: a study of the origin of European peoples. (English edition.) London. 1901.

Sergi, G. Specie e varieta umane. Turin. 1900.

Since immigrant races or peoples are classified on the basis of language, frequent reference has been necessary to such works on linguistics as the following:

Lefèvre, André. Race and Language. London. 1894. (In) The International Scientific Series (Vol. 76).

Hovelacque, Abel. The Science of Language. (Trans.) London. 1877. (In) The Library of Contemporary Science.

Whitney, W. D. Language and the Study of Language. 6th ed. New York. 1901.

Müller, Max. The Science of Language. 2 vols. New York. 1891.

The following have been mainly used on general questions, as those of classification, or when detailed information was lacking in the foregoing:

Ratzel, Friedrich. The History of Mankind. (English edition.) London. 1897.

Waitz, Theodor. Anthropologie der Naturvölker. 6 vols. Leipzig. 1859–1872.

Müller, Friedrich. Allgemeine Ethnographie. 2. Auflage. Wien. 1879.

Peschel, Oscar F. Völkerkunde. 7. Auflage. Leipzig. 1897.

Quatrefages, A. de. Histoire générale des races humaines. Paris. 1889.

Quatrefages, A. de. The Human Species. 2d ed. London. 1881. (In) International Scientific Series (Vol. 26).

Prichard, James C. The Natural History of Man. 3d ed. London. 1848.

Prichard, James C. Researches into the Physical History of Mankind. 3d ed. London. 1836–1847. 5 vols.

Prichard, James C. Ethnographical Maps. 2d ed. London. 1851.

Latham, Robert G. Descriptive Ethnology. London. 1859. 3 vols.

Latham, Robert G. The Natural History of the Varieties of Man. London. 1850.

In anthropology, strictly speaking, one must also consult:

Topinard, P. Eléments d'Anthropologie générale. Paris. 1885.

Tylor, Edward B. Anthropology. New York. 1904. (In) The International Scientific Series (Vol. 62).

There are only four[a] special dictionaries which systematically cover the subject of races and peoples, and of these only the first named is of much value to the student of the present day:

Handwörterbuch der Zoologie, Anthropologie und Ethnologie. Herausgegeben von Prof. Dr. Gustav Jäger unter Mitwirkung von . . . F. von Hellwald (etc.). Breslau. 1880–1900. 8 vols.

Dictionnaire des Sciences anthropologiques. Paris. 1889. Publié sous la direction de Ad. Bertillon (etc., etc. A group of distinguished ethnologists cooperated in the preparation of this work. Now rather old).

Galtés, Pio. Diccionario Etnográfico-Anthropológico. Barcelona. 1894. 12°. (Small, and contains many errors.)

Dictionnaire d'Ethnographie moderne. 1853. Paris. (1 vol. of) Nouvelle Encyclopédie Théologique. (Of merely historical interest.)

Space can not be taken to mention all the ethnological and other scientific journals to be consulted in such a work as the present. Worthy of especial mention for the bibliographies they contain are:

Archiv für Anthropologie. Braunschweig. 1866–. (See its bibliography:) "Verzeichniss der anthropologischen Literatur" (pp. 1–169, etc.).

American Anthropologist. New York. 1888–.

Finally, the best ethnographical maps covering the whole field are those of:

Gerland, Georg. Atlas der Völkerkunde. (In) Berghaus (Herm.) Physikalischer Atlas. Gotha. 1892.

2. GEOGRAPHY OF RACES.

Ethnography is most intimately connected with the work of general geographers, some of whom have made contributions of prime importance to this science. Geographical journals and yearbooks, which, like books of travel and description, are too numerous to be mentioned here, are among the best sources of information to the ethnologist. The geographical works most consulted are:

Reclus, Elisée. Nouvelle géographie universelle; la terre et les hommes. Paris. 1876–1894. (English edition) The Earth and its Inhabitants. London. 1876–1894. (Indispensable. The English edition is edited in part by Keane.)

Stanford's Compendium of Geography and Travel. New Issue. London. 1893–1899. 7 vols. (See earlier edition for other volumes by Keane.)

Hettner, Alfred. Grundzüge der Länderkunde. 1. Band. Europa. Leipzig. 1907–. (As a sample of similar systematic works.)

Mill, Hugh R. (editor). The International Geography. 3d ed. London. 1909. (Ditto. Important, though in one volume.)

3. STATISTICS OF POPULATION, BY RACE.

Original sources entirely distinct from the above-noted lines of research must be consulted here. Such are, first, the official censuses of the few countries that make a count of the population by race. Those found most necessary to the present work are the censuses and

[a] Matsumura's Gazetteer has since appeared. (See note, p. 2.)

statistical yearbooks of Russia, Hungary, Austria, Servia, Finland, Germany, Switzerland, and India.

Compendiums needed for constant reference, mainly confined to census returns, are:

The Statesman's Year-Book. Edited by J. S. Keltie. London. 1908. (Annual.)

Almanach de Gotha. Gotha. 1908. (Annual.)

Die Bevölkerung der Erde. (In) Petermanns Mitteilungen. Ergänzungsbände. Gotha. Nr. 163 (1909). Europa; Nr. 135 (1909). Asien (etc.); Nr. 146 (1904). Amerika, Afrika (etc.).

Otto Hübner's Geographisch-statistische Tabellen. Published by Fr. v. Juraschek. Frankfurt. 1909. (Revised annually.)

Perhaps the most competent estimates of population by race, where censuses of such do not exist, are found in:

Brachelli, H. F. (Revised by F. von Juraschek.) Die Staaten Europas. 5th ed. Leipzig. 1907. (Recent, but not complete, even for Europe.)

Hickmann, A. L. Geographisch-Statistischer Universal-Taschen-Atlas. Wien. 1909. (English edition.) Geographical-Statistic Universal Pocket Atlas. London. (1907) (The most complete in appearance, but full of serious errors.)

Fircks, A. von. Bevölkerungslehre und Bevölkerungspolitik. Leipzig. 1898. (In) Hand- und Lehrbuch der Staatswissenchaften (by K. Frankenstein, etc.). (Population given in per cents only.)

Balbi, Adriano. Atlas ethnographique du globe. Paris. 1826. (Also) Introduction à l'atlas. Paris. 1826. 416 pp. (Too old, of course, to be of service, but a fine example of what is needed at the present time brought down to date.)

Kolb, G. F. Handbuch der vergleichenden statistik. Zürich. 1857. (English edition) The Condition of Nations. London. 1880. (A similar remark applies.)

4. STATISTICS OF IMMIGRATION AND EMIGRATION.

Some of the censuses just mentioned devote many pages to statistics of the emigration to foreign countries. Good examples are those of Austria, Hungary, Italy, Servia, and Finland.

Some American publications to be consulted are:

Commissioner-General of Immigration, Annual Reports. Washington. (Used in preparing each article of the dictionary.)

Industrial Commission, Reports. Vol. XV. On Immigration . . . and on Education. Washington. 1901.

Hall, Prescott F. Immigration. New York. 1906.

Smith, Richmond Mayo-. Emigration and Immigration. New York. 1890. (See also other works by Professor Smith.)

Commons, John R. Races and Immigrants in America. New York. 1907.

5. GENERAL WORKS OF REFERENCE.

The encyclopedias, gazetteers, and dictionaries most consulted for bibliographical references and otherwise, and followed generally in spelling, are:

The New International Encyclopædia. New York. 1907.

The Encyclopædia Britannica. 10th ed. London. 1902.

The Encyclopedia Americana. New York. 1907.

Brockhaus Konversations-Lexikon. 14th ed. Leipzig. 1896.
Meyers Konversations-Lexikon. 6th ed. Leipzig. 1909.
La Grande Encyclopédie. Paris. 1886–1902.
The Century Dictionary. New York. 1904.
Standard Dictionary. New York. 1907.
Lippincott's Gazetteer of the World. Philadelphia. 1906.
Longman's Gazetteer of the World. London. 1908.
Ritter's Geographisch-Statistisches Lexikon. 9th ed. Leipzig. 1905.

6. BIBLIOGRAPHIES.

Of general bibliographical assistance, besides the helps already mentioned and the card catalogues and other aids at hand in the Library of Congress, may be mentioned:

Bibliographie der Sozial-wissenschaften. Berlin. 1907. (Annual. Helpful in statistical references.)

International Catalogue of Scientific Literature. Fifth year. London. 1907. (Annual. Full in special ethnology.)

Geographisches Jahrbuch. Vol. XXXI. Gotha. 1908. (Annual. Full in special ethnology.)

RACES OR PEOPLES.

A.

ABYSSINIAN. (See *Semitic-Hamitic.*)

ADERBAIJAN TURK. A name applied to certain Turks of Persia. (See *Tataric.*)

ADRIATIC race. (See *Caucasian.*)

AEROEMOYRET. Same as **Evremeiseti.** (See *Finnish.*)

AFGHAN or **PATHAN.** The native Iranic race or people of Afghanistan, from which the country takes its name; Caucasian in physical type and Mohammedan in religion; related in language (Pashto) to the Persians and to the northern Hindus (see); commonly known in India as "Pathan." Of the 5,000,000 inhabitants (estimated) of Afghanistan, only one-third are Afghans. More than 500,000 are Hindus and about that number are Tajiks, that is, Persians. As in Persia, there is a great variety of other races or peoples in Afghanistan, Turko-Tataric, Mongolic, and Aryan. They do not come to America, so far as is known.

AFRICAN (black). (See *Negro.*)

AFSHAR. A nomadic Turkish tribe of Persia related to the Osmanlis. (See these and *Tataric.*)

AINO. A primitive Caucasian-like people in Japan, now numbering less than 20,000. (See *Japanese, Caucasian,* and *Mongolian.*)

AISSORE or **AYSSORE.** (See *Assyrian* and *Syrian.*)

ALBANIAN (native name, **Skipetar**; ancient name, **Illyrian**; called by Turks **Arnaut**). The native and aboriginal race or people of Albania or western Turkey. Unlike most of the so-called European "races," this is a distinct race physically and not merely linguistically. It has the smallest population of any independent division of the Aryans in Europe and does not even appear by name in immigration statistics.

The Albanians are perhaps less known in a scientific way than any other European people, unless it be certain tribes of the Caucasus. Not only is their classification uncertain in the newer science of physical anthropology, philologists also are still disagreed as to their place in the Indo-European family. (See article *Aryan.*) Misled by the Greek loan-words in it, scholars first classified Albanian as a Hellenic dialect. Others as vainly have tried to place it in the Italic division or in the Slavic. It appears to be really one of the eight or nine distinct branches of the Aryan family tree. It is the most backward in cultivation of all. It hardly has a literature. Like the neighboring Servian or Croatian (see), it labors under the misfortune of being written in different alphabets, in both the Greek and the Latin, according to the religion prevalent in each locality. It is not surprising that the rate of illiteracy is one of the highest in Europe.

From a physical point of view, a more favorable judgment can be awarded Albanians. Tall and muscular, of rather blond and regular features, the Albanian is clearly Caucasian, although subject to a race Mongolian in origin, the Turk. (See articles on these.) Yet in one respect he resembles the Asiatic type; he has one of the broadest heads not only of Europe but of the world. The face is broad, in sharp contrast with the long, oval face of the pure Greek type, which adjoins the

Albanian on the south. It is this combination of "giantism" and hyperbrachycephaly, that makes the race physically distinct and seems to warrant Deniker in giving it a separate name, the "Adriatic" or "Dinaric." It resembles most the "Celtic" or "Alpine" race, and is so placed by some. But the type is taller: the northern Albanians, like the Montenegrins, rival the Scotch and the Norwegians in stature.

The Albanians are to-day a mixed race, as is every European people. From northern Albania the type shades off in every direction, most rapidly on the south, where it borders on the long-headed, darker, and shorter Mediterranean type. On the east, and especially on the north, it merges into the great wave of Slavic invasion, nearly as broad-headed as the Albanian in type but considerably shorter. The Turks are so few in number in European Turkey and have assimilated so little with the Albanians that they have had but little influence in the composition of the race. Indeed, it is not the Turkish race that incloses the Albanians on the east, but the Bulgarians of Turkey. On the southeast is a small Roumanian population, the Tsintsars. (See corresponding articles.)

No line can be drawn as to physical type between those Albanians who inhabit the northern border of Albania and the Serbo-Croatian peoples that adjoin them; that is, the Montenegrins, the Dalmatians, the Bosnians, and the southern Serbs. (See all these in article *Croatian.*) The same "Adriatic" type can be followed parallel with the sea until it merges into the "Alpine" type among the Friulans or Ladins, non-Italian Latins of the Italian border. To speak more precisely, the extremely high cephalic index of 89 has been found at Scutari, near the northern border of Albania, and the same (88) even in Epirus, where most of the people are Greeks. The average height is about 5 feet 7 inches, although on the Herzegovinian border it reaches 5 feet 9 inches.

The Albanians go under many different names. Skipetar and Arnaut are equivalents of Albanian. All mean "highlander." (Compare the *Alb* in *Albanian* with *Alp.*) Until about the fifteenth century they were not called Albanians but Illyrians, or even Macedonians. From them came the name of the ancient Roman province of Illyricum, embracing Epirus and parts of Macedonia, and of Napoleon's "Illyrian Provinces;" and from these latter came the name Illyrian, wrongly appropriated by all the Serbo-Croatians (Slavs) early in the last century. As already indicated, all the Slavs of the Balkan Peninsula made their settlements during the middle ages. The Albanians, or Illyrians proper, previously occupied the entire country north to the Danube.

The names of the less important dialects and tribes need not be considered. Some of them are temporary; that is, dependent upon the tribal system of government which still obtains. The Gegs and the Tosks, however, are to be sharply distinguished. The Gegs, including the Malliesors and the Mirdites, are the northern Albanians; while the Tosks, including the Yapides, are those living in Epirus on the south. The Gegs are mainly Mohammedans and Roman Catholics using the Latin alphabet; the Tosks are also in part Mohammedan, but mainly Orthodox, like their neighbors, the Greeks, whose religion, civilization, and even language they have in great part adopted. The northern Gegs are more rude and warlike and generally herdsmen; the Tosks, more civilized and settled agriculturists. The Gegs are taller and more truly Albanian in type; the Tosks, darker and more like the modern Greeks.

The Albanians' main distinction in history is the persistence with which they have kept their independence. Even the Turkish rule in Albania has been but nominal ever since the Moslems first overran the Peninsula in the fifteenth century. It is felt only in the larger towns. They are brave, but turbulent in spirit—warriors rather than workers. Even their own tribes are at enmity among themselves and tribal and family feuds are common.

Albania, somewhat indefinite in its boundaries, is but a small country, less than 300 miles long by 40 broad. It embraces the Turkish vilayets of Scutari and Janina and a part of Monastir. In the wider sense it includes ancient Epirus and a part of Macedonia. There are also Turks and Greeks settled in Albania, and even Roumanians (Tsintsars) in the southeast; but the basis of the population is Albanian.

No census of Albanians has ever been taken. They probably number 1,500,000; some say 2,000,000. There are also some 250,000 in the eastern part of Greece and 90,000 in southern Italy and Sicily, where they established colonies centuries ago. The number in the Austro-Hungarian provinces north of Albania is still less. In Monastir they number only about 12,000. In religion the Albanians are said to be about equally divided among the Moslem, the Catholic, and the Greek faiths. Somewhat careful religious statistics have been privately collected for the greater portion of Albania, as follows:

Vilayets.	Mohammedan.	Catholic.	Orthodox.	Jewish.	Total.
Scutari	133,965	81,997	6,642	....	222,604
Janina	228,346	267,317		3,439	499,102
Total	362,311	355,956		3,439	721,706

In total population Albanians rank below almost all the "races" of Europe. They perhaps outnumber the Slovenians of Austria and are half as numerous as the Norwegians, the Danes, or the Western Finns. But since they have emigrated extensively to Greece and to Italy and the rate of immigration to America on the part of their northern neighbors, the Croatians and Slovenians, is one of the highest in Europe, it would appear probable that the Albanians also are to be reckoned with as a factor of American immigration. Thus far they have not been counted separately by the Bureau of Immigration. Some of them as immigrants are called Greeks because they speak that language; others, Turks because the Mohammedan Albanians often call themselves Turks; others appear in the column of "Other peoples." In this column we find about 2,000 in 1907, 1,300 of whom came from Turkey in Europe. The number of Greeks reported from the same country was 7,000; the number of Turks, 1,100.

ALGERIAN. A native of Algiers. A geographical, not an ethnological term. About two-thirds of the population of 3,000,000 are Berbers and one-third are Arabs. (See these and *Moor.*)

ALPINE race. (See *Aryan* and *Caucasian.*

ALSATIAN. A native of Alsace, in Germany, formerly a part of France. A geographical term. Alsatians are counted in immigration statistics as either French or German (see) according to the language they speak.

ALTAIC. (1) Same as **Ural-Altaic** (see) or, better, (2) the division which includes the Tataric, Mongolic, and Tungusic stocks. (See *Turkish.*)

ANATOLIAN TURK. A Turk (see) living in Anatolia, that is, Asia Minor. A geographical term.

ANDALUSIAN. A native of the province of Andalusia. (See *Spanish.*) Not a racial name.

ANGLO-SAXON race. Same as **English** (see).

ANNAMESE. The principal race or people of the former empire of Annam, now known as French Indo-China and including Annam, Tonking, and Cochin-China. The Annamese are Indo-Chinese (see), a division of the Sinitic branch of the Mongolian race (see). They show some infusion of Malay blood. In culture and religion they resemble the Chinese. Their population is estimated at about 14,000,000, including 7,000,000 Tonkinese.

ARABIAN. One of the three great groups of the Semitic branch of the Caucasian race. The Arabians are related to the Hebrews and include Arabs proper and the wandering Bedouin tribes of the desert. (See *Semitic-Hamitic.*) They have long since spread out from the country that bears their name and settled in distant portions of Africa and Asia, as well as penetrated into Europe. They have given their language, through the Koran, to the vaster populations of Mohammedan faith. They are not to be confounded with the Turks (see), who are Mongolian, Tatar, in origin and speech, rather than Caucasian. Neither are they closely related to the Syrians (see), who are Christians and Aryans, not Semites; nor even to the Berbers and the modern Moors of north Africa, who are Hamitic rather than Semitic in origin. Yet Syrians and Moors alike have long used the Arabic tongue.

The Arab population of Arabia is between 3,500,000 and 5,000,000. Still more live in northern Africa. Very few come to the United States. The Immigration Bureau classifies them under "Other peoples," which included only 236 individuals in all from Asiatic peoples in 1907.

ARAGONESE. A native of Aragon. (See *Spanish.*)

ARAMAIC or **ARAMEAN.** One of the Chaldean group of Semitic languages. It includes the *Syro-Chaldean* as spoken by the Ayssores. (See these terms and especially *Assyrian.*)

ARMENIAN (called by themselves **Haik**). The Aryan race or people of Armenia, in Asiatic Turkey. Linguistically the Armenians are more nearly related to the Aryans of Europe than to their Asiatic neighbors, the Syrians, Arabs, and Hebrews (Semites), and especially the Turks and Kurds, the inveterate enemies of the Armenians. In language the latter are more European than are the Magyars, the Finns, or the Basques of Europe. The nearest relatives of the Armenic tongue are the other members of the Indo-Iranic group of Aryan languages, which includes the Persian, the Hindi, and the Gypsy. In religion the Armenians differ from all the above-named peoples excepting the Syrians in that they are Christian. They boast a church as old as that of Rome. To add to the ethnical confusion they are related physically to the Turks, although they exceed these, as they do almost all peoples, in the remarkable shortness and height of their heads. The flattening of the back of the head is noticeable at once in most Armenians. It can only be compared to the flattened occiput of the Malay, often noticed in Filipinos. (See articles on the above races.)

Only a fraction of the Armenians are found in their own country, Armenia; perhaps 650,000 out of a total variously estimated at from 3,000,000 to 5,000,000. Over 1,000,000 live in Russia, in the Transcaucasus (only 30,000 in Ciscaucasia); 400,000 in European Turkey; 100,000 in Persia; about 15,000 in or near Hungary; and 6,000 in India and Africa. Perhaps half their number still live in different parts of the Turkish dominions. Large numbers of those who have migrated did so because of the persecutions of the Turks and Kurds directed against them. Their rate of immigration is very low, about 1 per 2,000 of population. They stand among the smallest in number of our immigrant races or peoples, only 2,644 arriving in 1907, and 26,498 during the 12 years 1899–1910, but form noticeable colonies, especially in New York and Massachusetts. These two States receive nearly two-thirds of their number.

ARMORIC or **ARMORICAN.** Same as **Breton** (see).

ARNAUT. Same as **Albanian** (see).

AROMUNI or **ARAMANI.** Same as **Tsintsar.** (See *Roumanian.*)

ARYAN, INDO-EUROPEAN, INDO-GERMANIC, INDO-CELTIC, CELTO-GERMANIC, JAPHETIC, or **SANSCRITIC.** The family of inflected languages spoken by all the races or peoples of western Europe (with the exception of the Basques) and throughout eastern Europe and southern Asia, with some exceptions, as far as eastern India.

Since four-fifths of our immigrants are of Aryan stock and their racial relationships to each other are determined by their languages, the student of immigration will need some acquaintance with the results of philology as regards the ordinary groupings of the Aryan tongues. Upon this, he will find, depends the distinction, for example, between Slovak and Czech (Bohemian), or the relationship of the Lithuanian to the Russian and the Old Prussian, or the very existence of Croatian, Slovenian, Bosnian, and Herzegovinian, as distinct "races" among our immigrants from the Balkan States. (See articles on these and *Slav* for details.)

The Aryan is the most important family of all inflected languages. The Semitic-Hamitic (see) is the only other division of them. The only other type of languages found in Europe is the agglutinative (see *Ural-Altaic, Finnish, Turkish, Magyar*); and the only remaining forms of speech in the world are the monosyllabic (see *Chinese*) and the polysynthetic (see *Indian, American*).

It will be seen that the words "Aryan," "Indo-European," and the like are linguistic rather than ethnological. Yet there has been much written, especially among the earlier philologists, about an "Aryan race." Although no longer strictly scientific, this expression will sometimes be used, for convenience, in this dictionary to designate the group of peoples originally speaking Aryan tongues.

It must be admitted that there is greater diversity between eastern and western Aryans than there is, for instance, between the Aryan Greeks on the one hand and the Semitic Jews or Turanian "Hungarians" and Finns on the other. As different as the latter are in language from ourselves, they share more fully our modern science, literature, and civilization and they acquire more readily our tongue than does the Aryan Hindu or Persian. Physically, also, they have become more like ourselves than are the darker and Asiaticized Hindus.

As a matter of fact, there are at least three races, anthropologically speaking, instead of one in western Europe. They are, as Ripley and others have shown, the "Teutonic" or "Nordic" (tall, blond, and long-headed), the "Alpine" (broad-headed), and the "Mediterranean" (brunette and long-headed). Huxley long ago marked out in this field two distinct physical races, the "Xanthochroid" and the "Melanochroid," or light and dark Caucasians (see). The Aryan, the German, the French, and the Italian are "races" from a linguistic point of view that combine dissimilar portions of physical races. Yet, as has been shown in the Introductory, such use of words is unavoidable (see p. 3).

More questionable are innovations in the use of these terms to fit some social theory. De Lapouge, for instance, limits the use of the word "Aryan" to the blond, long-headed, or Teutonic race; and an active social propaganda in Germany is built upon this supposed identification of races. Yet Sergi, as an Italian, holds that the original Aryans were dark and of Mediterranean rather than of Teutonic stock.

Turning now to a less doubtful use of terms, it is safe to divide the Caucasian grand division of mankind on the basis of language into the Aryan, Semitic, Hamite, Caucasic, and Euskaric stocks (see these). The last two possess agglutinative languages and are confined to the small areas of the Caucasus Mountains and the Pyrenees. The word "Indo-European" is preferable to "Aryan" in scientific usage. Germans are more inclined to use the term "Indo-Germanic," and to use "Aryan" in the sense of "Indo-Iranian;" that is, to designate the eastern group of Indo-European languages.

The Aryan "races" comprise nearly half the population of the earth, say 700,000,000 out of a total of 1,500,000,000. Of course, a great multitude of these are Asiatic Aryans, the most of whom are crowded into India. Still, the Aryans of Europe are nearly double the Aryans of Asia in number, 520,000,000 as against 280,000,000. This European stock also outnumbers the Chinese, the greatest homogeneous population beyond all exception in the world.

The Aryan stock is divided as follows by Hickmann:

Races.	*European population.*
Teutonic (German, English, Scandinavian, etc.)	131,000,000
Slavonic (Russian, Polish, Bohemian, etc.)	127,200,000
Italic (French, Spanish, etc.)	107,300,000
Hellenic	4,400,000
Lettic (including Lithuanian)	4,000,000
Celtic (Scotch, Irish, Welsh)	3,200,000
Illyric	1,500,000
Armenic	300,000
Indo-Iranic (Hindu, etc.)	300,000

(See other details in Introductory table, p. 5.)

These comprise practically all Europeans with the exception of the Magyars of Hungary, the Turks of Turkey, various Finno-Tataric peoples of eastern and northern Russia and of Lapland, and the Caucasus peoples. Turkish Armenia, in Asia, and the greater part of the countries eastward to the Ganges, also are Aryan, excluding the large Dravidian territory (see) in southern and central India.

Of American immigrants, as has been said, four-fifths are still Aryan, in spite of the largely increasing numbers of non-Aryans now arriving from eastern Europe—Hebrews, Magyars, Finns, and Turks. (See details of Aryan immigration under each race and in article *Caucasian.*)

ASHKENAZIM. The northern or German-Polish Jews, as distinguished from the southern or Spanish-Portuguese Jews, called Sephardim. They form about 90 per cent of the Jewish race. (See *Hebrew.*)

ASIATIC race. (See *Mongolian.*)

ASSAMESE. A subdivision of the Indo-Aryan Hindus (see) living in Assam, the easternmost province of India proper. Their language, the Assamese, is spoken by 1,350,000 persons.

ASSYRIAN, ASSYROID, AYSSORE, KALDANI (CHALDEAN), SYRO-CHALDEAN, NESTORIAN, EAST SYRIAN. All these names have been applied to a small population living in the northwestern angle of Persia, near the borders of Turkey and Russia, and especially about Lake Urmia. Some of them on coming to the United States as immigrants insist that they are not Syrians, but Assyrians. It is believed that they are more properly to be considered as East Syrians and, therefore, contained in the "Syrian" race or people of the Bureau of Immigration, although so good an authority as Deniker holds that they belong to an entirely distinct race, which he calls the "Assyroid." In any case, they belong to the Syrian stock (Semites) linguistically.

It will be convenient to discuss briefly at this point the Assyrian and Assyroid races and then the relation of the Ayssores to these.

ASSYRIAN AND ASSYROID.

The Assyrian is an ancient language, extinct for at least 2,000 years. No people to-day can claim pure physical descent from this stock. The arid region occupied by the early Assyrian empire has been swept by one civilization after another. Their ancient Semitic speech was largely replaced by that of conquering Medes and Persians and, later, of Mohammedan hosts. It finally disappeared after the Babylonians and Chaldeans, who used a Semitic tongue, replaced the Assyrians in Mesopotamia. Turkish, Persian, Kurdish, and Arabian blood has been added to the ancestral stock of the modern "Assyrians." Reclus says: "The Assyrians and Chaldeans were either exterminated, or else absorbed in the victorious races, forfeiting name, speech, and the very consciousness of their race."

The Assyroid was first added by Deniker to his list of the distinct races of the earth; and he says that "it is not found pure in any population, but it counts a sufficient number of representatives to give a character to entire populations, such as the Hadjemi-Persians, the Ayssores, certain Kurdish tribes, and some Armenians and Jews." Even Deniker, it will be noted, does not claim that there is any longer an Assyrian race, either physically or linguistically, while even his cognate Assyroid is not found pure. It is sufficient to say that practically all other ethnologists divide Deniker's "Assyroids" between the Aryan and Semitic-Hamitic branches of the Caucasian race.

THE AYSSORES.

The Ayssores, therefore, are not Assyrians, either physically or linguistically. The Bureau of Immigration has classified races according to the languages they speak, and practically all ethnologists proceed upon the same principle. A scientific definition of the Ayssores, therefore, would seem to be: That branch of the Aramaic division of the Chaldean group of Semitic peoples (Caucasian) which is located farthest to the northeast, and especially about Lake Urmia in Persia. They are called "Syro-Chaldeans" in the Russian census. Their own language not only is that which was spoken commonly in Palestine in the time of Christ, but other dialects of it are still found on the eastern border of Syria. It is, however, often called a missionary language, since it has been revived and kept alive largely by Protestant missionaries. The Ayssores, like most Syrians, now speak Arabic. It is apparently due to the enthusiasm of Archbishop Benson over a people speaking the language of Christ, rather than as a result of any scientific demonstration, that these people have been misnamed "Assyrian," "Chaldean," "Nestorian," and even "Armenian." The people have been proud to accept and defend the title given them as representatives of the ancient Assyrians.

The "Assyrians" are more backward in civilization than the western Syrians, having been more sorely pressed to maintain their very existence against the surrounding Mohammedan population, and especially the Kurds. Some of them, like their neighbors, the Armenians, have sought refuge on Russian soil. The Russian census shows 5,000 of them located in Transcaucasia. Their entire population is so small that it is of no significance as a source of immigration. Although constituting a few distinct communities in the United States, their number is lost sight of in the general mass of Syrian immigration (see).

AUSTAFRICAN. (See *Negro.*)

AUSTRALIAN. Any inhabitant of Australia. Not a racial name. Immigrants from Australia, of whom there are very few, are listed in immigration statistics as "English," "Irish," etc., according to their mother tongue. (See articles on these.) The name Australian is also applied by ethnologists to the black natives of Australia. (See *Negro.*)

AUSTRIAN. Not a race name and not used by the Bureau of Immigration. It has no significance as to physical race or language. There is no Austrian race in the sense in which we use the terms French, German, Italian, Hebrew, or Bohemian "race." The term "Austrian" simply means an inhabitant or native of Austria. Austria contains more different races or peoples than any other country of Europe except Russia. Germans form the largest ethnical group in Austria; Magyars, the largest of Hungary. The following table shows the diversity of races or peoples represented by large populations in Austria-Hungary and the relative proportion which the Austro-Hungarian section of these races contributes to the immigration from Europe to the United States. For further details see articles on each of these races, as *German, Hebrew, Polish, Bohemian, Slovenian.*

Population of Austria-Hungary, and immigration to the United States from Austria-Hungary and from Europe, in 1907, by race.

Chief races or peoples.	Population in 1900.		Immigration to United States.		
	Austria.	Hungary, including Croatia and Slavonia.	Immigrants from Europe in 1907.	Immigrants from Austria-Hungary in 1907.	Per cent from Austria-Hungary.
German	9,171,000	2,135,000	91,000	40,500	44.5
Bohemian and Moravian	a 5,955,000	....	13,500	13,400	99.3
Slovak		2,020,000	41,900	41,800	99.7
Polish	4,259,000	....	137,100	59,700	43.5
Ruthenian	3,375,000	429,000	23,900	23,700	99.1
Slovenian	1,193,000	99,000	47,300	47,100	99.6
Croatian	711,000	1,679,000			
Servian		1,052,000	b 26,900	b 6,200	23.0
Roumanian	231,000	2,799,000	19,000	18,400	96.9
Magyar	10,000	8,742,000	59,700	59,600	99.8
Italian and Ladin	727,000	27,000	288,900	1,500	.5
Others	....	272,000	450,300	27,600	6.1
Total	c 25,632,000	19,254,000	1,199,500	338,500	28.2
Hebrew d	1,225,000	851,000	146,000	18,900	12.9

a Including Slovak.
b Including Bulgarian and Montenegrin.
c Excluding 518,000 foreigners, of whom over half are Magyars.
d Counted as German, etc., in language, but as Jews in the census of religions.

AUVERGNAT. A native of Auvergne, formerly a province of central France. (See *French.*)

AVARO-ANDIAN. (See *Caucasus peoples.*)

AYSSORE. A small modern Asiatic people sometimes wrongly called *Assyrian* (see).

AZERBEIDJIAN TURK. Same as **Aderbaijan.** (See *Tataric.*)

B.

BALTIC. A name sometimes given to the Lettic (see) group of languages.

BASHKIR. One of the largest Tatar peoples (see) of Russia.

BASQUE (synonyms: **Euskarian** and, formerly, **Iberian** as to language). The people originally speaking the Basque language, the sole non-Aryan language of western Europe. But few now live in the old province of southwestern France, Gascony, formerly called "Vasconia" after them; about 500,000 still remain on the other side of the Pyrenees in northwestern Spain. They are a fragment, perhaps the only distinct remnant, of the pre-Aryan race of Europe. Recent researches connect them, not with the Mongolian Finns (see) as formerly, but with the Hamitic (Caucasian) Berbers of northern Africa. They are not now easily distinguishable in physical appearance from their Spanish or French neighbors, although many still speak the strange Basque tongue. The latter is not inflected, like most European (Aryan) languages, but agglutinative, like the typical languages of northern Asia.

Basques are counted in with Spanish or French by the Bureau of Immigration in case they speak these languages. It is known, however, that but few are coming to the States, although they go in considerable numbers as workers to the Panama Canal Zone. It is said that 200,000 Basques have emigrated to South America during the last half century.

BAVARIAN. A native of Bavaria, in Germany. Not an ethnological term. (See *German.*)

BEDOUIN. A wandering Arab (see).

BELGIAN. A native or citizen of Belgium. Not the name of a race and not used by the Bureau of Immigration. Southern Belgians are for the most part Walloons (see), that is, French (see), and northern Belgians are Flemish. (See *Dutch and Flemish.*)

BELSAN. (See *Ruthenian.*)

BELUCHI, BALUCH, or **BILOCH.** The native Iranic (Caucasian) people of Baluchistan. Of no significance in immigration. (Cf. *Afghan, Persian, Hindu.*)

BENGALESE or **BENGALI.** The principal race or people of Bengal, British India. Their language, a modern Hindu tongue, the Bengali, is spoken by nearly 45,000,000 persons. The broad head of the Bengalese is thought to be due to Mongolian admixture. (See *Hindu.*)

BERBER. The most important native race or people of northwestern Africa; of Hamitic (Caucasian) origin. (See *Semitic-Hamitic* and *Moor.*) They number at least 7,000,000 in Morocco and Algeria and 500,000 in Tunis and Tripoli. Not known as immigrants.

BERKIN. An Istrian division of the Slovenian race (see).

BESSERMAN. A small tribe of Eastern Finns (see).

BHIL. A name given to a people of India of Dravidian physical stock (see), but now speaking a Hindu dialect (see). The Indian census reports 760,000 persons speaking the Bhil dialects. Their religion is a form of animism requiring neither priest nor temple.

BICOL or **VICOL.** (See *Filipino.*)

BIELOCHROVAT, KRAKUS, or **CRAKOWIAK.** Names applied to a subdivision of the Poles (see).

BIELO-RUSSIAN. The term used by Russians themselves to designate White Russian. (See *Russian.*)

BIRMAN. Same as **Burmese** (see).

BISAYAN. Same as **Visayan.** (See *Filipino.*)

BLACK race. (See *Negro.*)

BLACK RUSSIAN. (See *Russian.*)

BLATACI. (See *Bohemian and Moravian.*)

BOER. A white person of Dutch (see) descent, especially in the Transvaal.

BOHEMIAN and MORAVIAN (CZECH). It will be convenient to discuss these races or peoples in one article. They are counted together by the Bureau of Immigration.

Czech or **Tsekh** is best defined as the westernmost race or linguistic division of the Slavic (with the exception of the Wendish fragment in Germany); or, as the race or people residing mainly in Bohemia and Moravia, but partly also in Hungary.

Bohemian is the westernmost division or dialect of the Czech and the principal people or language found in Bohemia.

Moravian is that division of the Czech found in Moravia; that is, between the Bohemians and the Slovaks.

Other definitions different from the above can be referred to good authority, but are confusing and will be mentioned only at this point. Thus, some authors reverse the meanings of Czech and Bohemian, making Bohemian the name of the division which includes the Czech, the Moravian, and the Slovak. (See, for example, Keane's classification in article *Slav*, although his usage varies.) The term "Moravian Brethren" is also frequently used in a religious sense as the name of a well-known sect which is akin to "Bohemian Brethren." Finally, "Bohemian" in the current literary or artistic sense means one of unconventional or Gypsylike habits. It comes perhaps from "Bohémien," the French word for "Gypsy." Gypsies were once ignorantly supposed to come from Bohemia.

The Czech is most nearly related to the Polish and Wendish languages, which, with it, constitute the so-called Western Division of Slavic languages. "Czech" generally covers also the Slovak (see), which in the Austrian census is not separated from the Bohemian and Moravian. Although the total Czech population is rather small, about 8,200,000, Czechs, in 1907, stood sixth in rank as to the number of immigrants to the United States.

BOHEMIAN.

The Bohemian people appears on the ethnological even more than on the political map as a peninsula intruding far into German territory, for Bohemia is nearly cut off from Moravia by Germans of lower Austria pressing in from the south and Germans of Prussia pushing down from the north. One-third of the population of Bohemia itself is composed of Germans, who inclose the Moravians on every side except the east. In early times the domain of the Western Slavs extended farther, not only into Germany nearly as far as Berlin, but on the south far beyond Vienna, into Carinthia. Here another intruding race, Mongol in origin—the Magyar—has divided the Western Slavs from the Croatians and other Southern Slavs.

The long contact of the Bohemians with the Germans has profoundly modified their civilization, if not their physical type and even their language. They are the most nearly like western Europeans of all the Slavs. It may be fairly said that they are the most advanced of all. This is in great part due to their native endowment as Slavs. Their weight of brain is said to be greater than that of any other people in Europe. At the same time the eastern Bohemians and Moravians are among the most broad-headed—that is, Slavic or "Eastern"—in physical type. They do not show the Asiatic element, Finnic or Tataric, found in the Russians, but they show a Teutonic admixture in their being of greater height than most Slavs and often in the presence of a blond element among them.

Although the Bohemians and the Moravians form but a minute fraction of the great Slavic stock, less than 2 per cent, they have contributed not a little to its history. They were practically the first Slavs to come under the influence of western civilization. Cyril and Methodius, apostles to the Slavs, gave them their alphabet. Since the eighth century they have had a literature of their own, which until the Hussite war was the most important of all Slavic literatures. Huss, the Bohemian, a century before Luther, sounded the first note of religious freedom in Europe. To Comenius, the Moravian, are due the beginnings of modern education in Europe. During the long years of German Catholic rule the use of the Bohemian language was proscribed. To-day it is again flourishing.

While the Germans and the Bohemians have been strenuous rivals in this corner of Austria, it is due to their joint efforts that Bohemia is now "the brightest jewel in the Austrian crown." Its natural wealth and the industry of its inhabitants have made it the richest province of the monarchy. The Bohemians, like the Slavs in general, are preeminently a nation of agriculturists, but they also excel as miners and as craftsmen. In religion all but 5 per cent are Roman Catholic. In art they are leaders; as musicians they are unsurpassed. They are equally renowned in the political and in the military service of the monarchy.

The ordinary ethnological details require but little space in this article. There are no subdivisions of the Bohemians to be described. Their physical and linguistic characters are sufficiently described in the article on the Slavs with the exception of what is noted here. Their alphabet is like our own, with added diacritical marks. Formerly they used the German type. While their native language is a barrier to full entrance into the current of western thought, the common use of German has supplemented it. Their population and immigration figures are given on the page following.

MORAVIAN.

Neither need much space be given to their brothers on the east, the Moravians. Their ethnical type is much the same, although we find here more dialectal variation and, on the east, transitional types that approach the Slovaks or the Poles. The Moravians speak the same language as the Bohemians, notwithstanding some difference in dialects. Both divisions are, therefore, to be considered as constituting but one race in a classification of European races. The division into two is political, geographical, and historical, rather than ethnical. Like the Bohemians, the Moravians are surrounded only by Germans and their Czechish kinsmen—excepting the Leks, or Waterpolaks, in the northeastern corner of their territory. Some consider these last to be Poles; others, Moravians. The Walachs, who live on the Slovak border in the Carpathians, are more properly a division of the Moravians, although some call them Slovaks (see). They are divided into the Javorins, the Pasekarsches, and the Zalerzaks. The Horaks live in the western mountains of Moravia; the Hanaks about the center, on the river Hanna. The latter include the Blataci, the Moravcici, and the Zabecaci. The Opovans and the Podhoraks also are Moravians. The breadth of the head increases among the Czechs as we leave the German border on the west, reaching among the Hanaks the remarkable index, for Europe, of 86.

Czech population of Austria-Hungary.

	Bohemia.	Moravia.	Silesia.	Hungary.	Miscellaneous.	Total.
Total for 1900	3,930,093	1,727,270	146,265	2,002,165	169,245	7,975,038
Total for 1851	2,621,450	1,264,027	88,068	1,704,312	176,401	5,854,258
Bohemians	2,621,450				14,377	2,635,827
Moravians		1,190,150	88,068			1,278,218
Slovaks		73,877		1,704,312	35,324	1,813,513
Czechs in army					126,700	126,700

Outside of Austria-Hungary there are at the present time probably less than 200,000 Czechs in Europe, making a total of about 8,200,000 for the race.

The foregoing table gives the Czech population of Austria-Hungary in 1900, and also shows the famous distribution by races, as estimated by Czörnig from the census of 1851, as similar details can not be found in the most recent census. Including the Slovaks the total Czech population of Europe about equals the total of Magyars or of Jews. The Bohemians alone constitute about half the entire number, or 4,000,000, and therefore about equal in numbers the Lithuanians or the Dutch.

As immigrants the Czechs come to America at about the same rate per 1,000 of population as the Lithuanians or the Ruthenians of Austria-Hungary; that is, more rapidly than most Slavic races, although only one-third so rapidly as the Hebrews. The high rate of Czech immigration is mainly due to the Slovaks, whose rate of immigration according to population is the highest of any race or people. The Bohemians and Moravians, on the other hand, come at the very low rate of less than 2 per 1,000 of population. With less than a third of the Czech population, the Slovaks sent 377,527 immigrants to the United States in the twelve years 1899–1910, as against 100,189 Bohemians and Moravians combined. In other words, the small Slovak people stands eighth among immigrant races in annual arrivals, while the Bohemians and Moravians stand about eighteenth. During the period mentioned, 301,078 of the Slovaks and 64,519 of the Bohemians and Moravians admitted to the United States went to the States of New York, Pennsylvania, Ohio, and Illinois.

BOHEMIAN BRETHREN. (See *Bohemian and Moravian.*)

BOHÉMIEN. The name by which Gypsies (see) are known in France.

BOIKO. A subdivision of the Red Russian branch of the Ruthenians (see).

BOLIVIAN. (See *Spanish American.*)

BOSNIAN. A political division of the Serbo-Croatians. (See *Croatian.*)

BRAHMAN. Not the name of a race. A member of the sacerdotal or priestly caste of the Hindus (see). The Brahmans number about 15,000,000 and are found throughout India.

BRAZILIAN. Any white native of Brazil. There are about 6,000,000 whites in Brazil, nearly one-half of whom are foreign-born. Of the latter over 1,000,000 are Italian, 800,000 Portuguese, 300,000 German, and 100,000 Spanish (see these). Immigrants from Brazil, of whom there are very few, are classed by the Bureau of Immigration according to the mother tongue. (See *Spanish American.*)

BRETON or **ARMORICAN.** The most southern and only continental branch of the Celtic group of the Aryan family. It is located in Brittany, in the northwestern part of France. The Bretons belong, with the Welsh, to the Cymric division of Celtic (see) peoples. Their language, the Breton, in its early form resembled the Cornish (see), now extinct. It was carried to Armorica, in France, by emigrants from Britain, who gave the name of Brittany to the new country and their language to the inhabitants. Their language now contains many French elements. It, like the Welsh, is at the present time the native language of about 1,000,000 persons, but it possesses much less vitality than Welsh (see), for it has practically no literature and is being rapidly supplanted by French. The latter is now the language of the cultured and is taught in all the schools of Brittany. There are four distinct dialects of Breton—the Léonarde, the Trécorien, the Cornouaillère, and the Vanneteuse.

Physically the Bretons, like most modern peoples, are a mixed stock. Yet those of the interior are distinctly Alpine in type; are short in stature, round-headed, brunette, and have dark-blue eyes. They resemble the Auvergnats and the Savoyards of southern France and the Swiss of the Alps. There has been, however, considerable infusion of Teutonic blood, especially in the coast districts, where the people are taller, longer-headed, and resemble the inhabitants of Normandy. (See *French.*) This Celtic-speaking people of the Continent is thus seen to have little ethnic relationship to the Celts of the British Isles, who are distinctly long-headed and tall; in fact, are among the tallest of all Europe. (See *Irish, Scotch,* and *Welsh.*)

The manners and customs of Brittany resemble those of other remote parts of France, and present, indeed, a very fair likeness of mediæval France. The inhabitants revere the ancient dolmens and cromlechs, and cling tenaciously to many pagan customs.

Bretons do not appear in immigration statistics, but are probably counted as French, with whom they bear a close ethnic relation. The latter race or people is considered to be three-fifths "Celtic" ("Alpine") in origin, and is placed in the "Keltic division" by the Bureau of Immigration.

BRITISH, BRITON. (See *English.*)

BROWN race. (See *Malay.*)

BUGAN. A name applied to Ruthenians (see) living on the Bug.

BUKOWINIAN. A geographical, not a racial, term. Any native of the duchy of Bukowina in eastern Austria. The Bukowinians represent three very different linguistic divisions of the Aryan family—Slavs, Latins, and Teutons. The population numbers 730,000, of whom over 40 per cent are Ruthenians, about 32 per cent are Roumanians, and nearly 22 per cent are Germans; less than 5 per cent are Poles. (See these.) In religious affiliations they present equally great variations—70 per cent are of the Orthodox (Greek) faith, about 12 per cent are Catholics, and over 13 per cent are Jews.

BULGARIAN. The native race or people of Bulgaria, belonging linguistically to the Eastern branch of the Slavs, and therefore Aryan; supposed to be Finnic (Mongolian) in origin, although now European (Caucasian) in physical type. It is probably the most numerous people in European Turkey also; but its numbers are small compared with those of other

Slavic races or peoples, and thus far its rate of immigration to America is quite low.

The Bulgarians and their neighbors on the north, the Roumanians, are among the rare races that are physically of one stock and linguistically of another. Both possess adopted languages. While the Bulgarians appear to be Asiatics by origin who have adopted a Slavic speech, the Roumanians (see) are Slavs who have adopted a Latin language. Since language is the test in a systematic classification of European races, as explained in the Introductory (see), this is the chief point that need be discussed in an article on the Bulgarians; and there can be no doubt as to the position occupied by this tongue. The Bulgarian belongs in the Southeastern division of Slavic languages, and in many respects stands between Russian and the Serbo-Croatian dialects. (See articles on these, and especially *Slav.*) It so closely resembles the latter as to give the Servian linguist excuse for representing most of the Bulgarians of Turkey to be Servians. Yet, in an important sense, it is the predecessor of both Russian and Servian. The Old Bulgarian was the earliest of the Slavic languages to be written and persists even to this day in the liturgy of the Orthodox church under the name of Church Slavonic. Its alphabet, the Cyrillic, is the oldest form of all modern Slavic alphabets, although some hold that an alphabet of similar appearance, the Glagolitic, antedates it among the western Slovenians.

Although Bulgaria possesses the oldest Slavic literature, it dates back but little over 1,000 years. It was not until the ninth century that Cyril and Methodius, apostles to the Slavs, put it into written form. Apparently only a century or two before this the Bulgarians spoke a Finnish language, which they brought into Europe with them from Asia. While they adopted the language of the Slavs, whom they conquered and organized politically, they were themselves swallowed up in the Slavic population. They lost not only their ancient language but their physical type. While they are the most truly Asiatic in origin of all the Slavs, they are Europeanized in appearance and character. In some respects their life is more civilized and settled than that of some of the Slavs farther west, as in Montenegro and Dalmatia. They are not only less warriors in spirit than these, but are more settled as agriculturists. Yet they seem to feel that they do not belong to the civilization of Europe, properly speaking, for they say of one who visits the countries farther west that he "goes to Europe."

The question concerning the physical type of the Bulgarians is more difficult to solve. Less scientific work has been put upon this portion of Europe than most sections, and there is still doubt as to the movements of the race in prehistoric times and therefore as to their place of origin. There can be little doubt, however, that two physical types are found on opposite sides of Bulgaria. While those of the west are distinctly broad-headed, those on the east are, at least in part, as distinctly long-headed. The western Bulgarians are predominantly, it would appear, of the same Slavic type as their neighboring kinsmen, the Serbo-Croatians. The Albanians (see), who adjoin them on the southwest, are similarly very broad-headed, but are taller than the true Slavs. The explanation of the long-headed type in the east is not so simple. Some think it indicates the early Finnic origin. Others might argue that it is Italic, or at least "Mediterranean," for there is no doubt this element is predominant amongst the eastern Roumanians who adjoin them.

Bulgarian.

Bulgarians of the eastern type are predominantly brunette, with dark hair, although it is said that 40 per cent have light eyes. The race is rather low in stature and stockily built, but no distinctly Mongolian feature remains, unless it be the high cheek bones and rather narrow eyes which are common amongst them. It must be assumed that the present Bulgarians have assimilated Turkish, Greek, and Roumanian elements as well as Slavic. This is true even of their language as well as of their blood. The Bulgarian is, in fact, the most corrupt of all Slavic languages at the present time. Although it possessed the first Slavic literature, it now has almost none; and what it has, has been developed within the last century.

Of Bulgarian dialects the most important to mention is the so-called Macedonian. Some have claimed that there is an independent Macedonian language and therefore race or people. But this would appear to be one of the patriotic misrepresentations not unknown amongst the partisan philologists of this region. The other chief dialects are the Rhodopian and the Southern Thracian or the Upper and Lower Moesian. The well-known Pomaks are the Mohammedan Bulgarians, a fine type physically. Less than 20 per cent of the Bulgarians are Mohammedans; three-fourths are of the Orthodox faith. Bulgarians themselves contemptuously call the mongrel people of the coast "Gagaous."

There would appear to be little doubt that the Bulgars came through southern Russia to their present home in the time of the early migrations of the middle ages. Some records locate them in the second century on the river Volga, from which they appear to have taken their name. In fact, a country called "Greater Bulgaria" was known there as late as the tenth century. If the common supposition be correct, the Bulgarians are most nearly related in origin to the Magyars of Hungary and the Finns of northern Russia. After these they are nearest of kin to the Turks, who have long lived amongst them as rulers. But Turks and Finns alike are but branches of the great Ural-Altaic family, which had its origin in northern Asia, probably in Mongolia. (See articles on these.)

The career of the Bulgarians thenceforward is well known. They were for a time the most dreaded foes of the Eastern Empire. They played the part in the east that the Teutons did in the west—first as the enemies of the higher civilization, then as its allies and protectors against the barbarians living beyond; finally as an independent and powerful people. In the tenth century the Kingdom of Bulgaria covered the most of what is now European Turkey and Macedonia. The Bulgarians were practically independent from 678 A. D. to 1392 A. D., when they were brought under subjection to the Turk; and within the last generation Bulgaria has again obtained its independence from Turkey, and more recently has received an added slice of Turkish territory—that portion south of the Balkan Mountains, known as East Roumelia. Previously Bulgaria was limited to the region between the Balkans and the Danube, with the exception of the Roumanian district lying between the lower Danube and the Black Sea, which is called the Dobruja. On the west, as already intimated, Bulgaria is bounded by Servia; on the southwest, by Turkey.

The Bulgarians occupy a territory at least one-half larger than Bulgaria itself. The most of this lies south of Bulgaria, in Turkey proper, especially in central Turkey, extending westward to Albania. In fact, all of central Turkey is Bulgarian in population down to the Ægean Sea, excepting a narrow strip along the coast, and this is occupied, not by the Turks, but by Greeks. It is not commonly understood that the Turks form but a small minority of the population of European Turkey; some say but one-seventh of it. A census has never been taken. Of course they are scattered everywhere in an official capacity, as the Greeks are widely scattered as traders. And there are other races or peoples in the portion of Turkey that in population is predominantly Bulgarian. Especially in Macedonia is this list of races increased by the addition of Serbs and other southern Slavs, of Albanians, and even of Roumanians, in considerable numbers. The last named, under the designation of Tsintsars, or Kutzo-Vlachs, extend in a rather compact body from southwestern Macedonia southward well into central Greece.

Putting the geography of the Bulgarian people in another way, it covers the eastern third of the Balkan Peninsula. The western third is Serbo-Croatian; the southern third, Greek and Albanian. All this has been carved out of the older Turkish Empire; most, excepting Greece, in the partition of 1878. Bulgaria itself contains nearly 500,000 Turks, including quite compact settlements in the southern part of East Roumelia and in the northeastern part of Bulgaria near the Black Sea. There are also considerable numbers of Gypsies, Roumanians, Greeks, and Spanish Jews—from 30,000 to 90,000 of each. The Bulgarians themselves number 3,200,000 (census of 1905) in Bulgaria. The total population is 4,000,000. The total number of Bulgarians in Europe has been estimated variously at from 4,000,000 to 5,000,000. Of these, there are probably 1,000,000 in Turkey. To-day they are found in but small numbers elsewhere. The Russian census gives 170,000.

So far as concerns American immigration, the Bulgarians would seem of less consequence than most other Slavs as regards either their present or their future rate of movement. The rate of immigration per 1,000 of population appears to put them below nearly all other Slavs, excepting the Bohemians and the Russians. In 1907 this rate was 3 per 1,000 for the Bulgarians, combined with the Servians and Montenegrins, from whom they can not be separated in immigration statistics. As compared with these, the related Croatian-Slovenian group came to America at the rate of 13 per 1,000 in that year, while the Slovaks with the Hebrews led with a rate of 18 per 1,000. The number of Bulgarians is too small to permit of even such a temporary flood of immigration as characterizes the Hebrews or the Irish. Bulgarians, Servians, and Montenegrins, like other Slavs, go mainly to States where unskilled labor is most in demand. In the twelve years 1899–1910, 97,391 immigrants of these races were admitted to the United States. Of these 22,476 went to Pennsylvania, 18,467 to Illinois, 15,197 to Ohio, and 9,942 to New York.

BURMESE. The native race or people of British Burma. Unlike the other peoples of India, who are Caucasian in stock, with a dark Dravidian element in the south, the Burmese are Mongolian in origin, forming part linguistically of the Indo-Chinese group (see) of Farther India. If any came to the United States they would properly be classed as East Indian (see). The population of Burma numbers 10,000,000.

BURUT. Same as **Kara-Kirghiz.** (See *Kirghiz.*)

C.

CAGAYAN or **IBANAG.** (See *Filipino.*)

CALABRIAN. A native of the southernmost province of the Italian Peninsula. A geographical term. Calabrians and Sicilians are prominent factors in the recent great tide of immigration which puts the South Italian in the lead of all incoming races. They have not been counted by provinces in immigration statistics.

CALMUCK. Same as **Kalmuk** (see).

CAMBODIAN or **KAMBOJAN.** Any native of Cambodia. (See *Khmer* and *Indo-Chinese.*)

CANAANITIC. (See *Semitic-Hamitic.*)

CANADIAN. A geographical, not a racial, designation. Immigrants from Canada are classified under French, English, Scotch, Irish, etc. (see). The Canadian population has not become sufficiently homogeneous to allow us to speak of a Canadian race. From 1886 to 1906 the Bureau of Immigration did not attempt to record the number of immigrants entering the United States from Canada. The increase in the Canadian-born population in the United States in various census years, however, shows that the movement has been continuous and comparatively large. The report of the Commissioner-General of Immigration shows that 51,941 immigrants were admitted to the United States from Canada in 1909. Of the total number admitted 12,850 were recorded as French (practically all so-called French Canadians), 10,708 as English, 4,819 as Scotch, 4,332 as Italian, 3,950 as Irish, and 3,031 as German. Among the immigrants admitted from Canada in recent years have been a considerable number of south and east Europeans who have settled in Canada and later came to the United States. Canadians are not recorded as immigrants when they enter the United States for "temporary sojourn" only.

The following table, compiled from the Canada Year Book, 1908, shows the composition of Canada's population by race or descent in the census years mentioned:

Population of Canada, by race or origin, census years 1871, 1881, and 1901.

Race or origin.	1871.	1881.	1901.	Per cent of total. 1871.	1881.	1901.
English	706,369	881,301	1,260,899	20.3	20.4	23.5
Irish	846,414	957,403	988,721	24.3	22.1	18.4
Scotch	549,946	699,863	800,154	15.8	16.2	14.9
Other British	7,773	9,947	13,421	.2	.2	.2
Total British	2,110,502	2,548,514	3,063,195	60.5	58.9	57.0
Austro-Hungarian	....	....	18,178	....	....	.3
Chinese and Japanese	....	4,383	22,050	....	.1	.4
Dutch	29,662	30,412	33,845	.9	.7	.6
French	1,082,940	1,298,929	1,649,371	31.1	30.0	30.7
German	202,991	254,319	310,501	5.8	5.9	5.8
Indian and half-breed	23,037	108,547	127,932	.7	2.5	2.4
Italian	1,035	1,849	10,834	(a)	(a)	.2
Jewish	125	667	16,131	(a)	(a)	.3
Negro	21,496	21,394	17,437	.6	.5	.3
Scandinavian	1,623	5,223	31,042	(a)	.1	.6
Russian	607	1,227	28,621	(a)	(a)	.5
Other races	4,182	8,540	10,639	.1	.2	.2
Not specified	7,561	40,806	31,539	.2	.9	.6
Grand total	3,485,761	4,324,810	5,371,315	100.0	100.0	100.0

a Less than 0.05 per cent.

CANADIAN FRENCH. (See *French Canadian.*)

CANARESE or **KANARESE.** A Dravidian tribe (see) of southwestern India; not referring to the Canary Islands.

CANTONESE. The Chinese (see) inhabitants of Canton and the surrounding territory. Not an ethnical term.

CARINTHIAN. (See *Slovenian* and *German.*)

CARNIOLAN. Same as **Krainer.** (See *Slovenian.*)

CASHMIRIAN. Same as **Kashmiri.** (See *Hindu.*)

CASTILIAN. A native of Castile, the former kingdom which gave its name to the Castilian or Spanish language. Not an ethnographical term. In immigration statistics listed as Spanish (see).

CATALAN. The race or people of Catalonia, the eastern division of Spain. They extend somewhat north over the line into France. Their language resembles the Provençal of France (see *French*) more than it does the Castilian of Spain. Castilians can not understand Catalans as easily as they understand Portuguese. For convenience the Catalans are counted as Spanish (see).

CAUCASIAN, CAUCASIC, EUROPEAN, EURAFRICAN, or **WHITE race.** (See *xanthochroi* and *melanochroi* races, p. 31.) The name given by Blumenbach in 1795 to the white race or grand division of mankind as distinguished from the Ethiopian, Mongolian, American, and Malay races (see these). The term is now defined more suitably for our purposes in a broader sense by Brinton and Keane, namely, to include all races, which, although dark in color or aberrant in other directions, are, when considered from all points of view, felt to be more like the white race than like any of the four other races just mentioned. Thus the dark Gallas of eastern Africa are included, partly on linguistic grounds, partly because they have the regular features of the Caucasian; the Berbers of northern Africa because of the markedly blond and regular features found amongst them; the dark Hindus and other peoples of India still more emphatically because of their possessing an Aryan speech, relating them still more closely to the white race, as well as because of their physical type; and possibly the Polynesians, Indonesians, and Ainos of the Pacific because of their physical characteristics, although in this discussion these will be excluded from the definition. (See *Pacific Islander.*) The general opinion is that the Dravidians and Veddahs, south of the Aryan Hindus in India, are not Caucasian. They do not possess an Aryan tongue; and physically they more nearly approach the Negro.

It will be seen from the above that the Caucasian race was by no means originally confined to Europe. It has long covered the northern third of Africa and practically all of southern Asia to the borders of Farther India. Although called the "European" race, it more likely had its origin in Asia or even in Africa than in Europe. Because of the latter theory, Brinton calls it the "Eurafrican" race. It does not even now fill certain large sections of Europe. The Mongolian race not only occupies the most of eastern and northern Russia but northern Scandinavia and the greater part of Finland, while the dominant races of Turkey, of Roumania, and even of Hungary are Mongolian in origin.

Although the white race would be supposed to be the one best understood, it is really the one about which there is the most fundamental and sometimes violent discussion. The word "Caucasian," for instance, is in nearly as bad repute as "Aryan" at the present time amongst ethnologists. Yet, as Keane has said of the former term, both words may be preserved with conventional meanings as are many of the early terms of natural history, although the early ideas associated with their use be discarded. While the word "Caucasian" has reference mainly to physical characters, "Aryan" will be used here as applying strictly to linguistic groupings. As explained in the introduction (p. 4), such use is general and practically unavoidable in immigration statistics and in European censuses. The English seldom use the word "Caucasian" in the narrower sense as designating only the peoples of the Caucasus Mountains. (See *Caucasus peoples.*)

The Caucasian is the only grand division of mankind which possesses inflected languages. In two of its minor divisions, the Caucasic and Euskaric, are also found agglutinative tongues. The scope of the word "Caucasian" may be better indicated by naming the subdivisions of the race. The following is substantially agreed upon by both Brinton and Keane, if the doubtful Polynesians and Ainos of the latter be discarded. The larger linguistic divisions or "stocks" are the Aryan, Caucasic, Euskaric, Semitic, and Hamitic. (See articles on these terms and classification in Introductory.) Both authors combine the two last named under the term "South Mediterranean," a stock located south and east of this great sea. Brinton applies the term "North Mediterranean" to all the rest, while Keane prefers to use the terms "North Mediterranean," "North European," "Iranic," and "Indic" as equivalent to Brinton's term "Aryan." Brinton divides the Aryans into the Teutonic, Lettic, Celtic, Slavonic, Armenic, Iranic, Illyric, Italic, and Hellenic groups. (See these.)

Passing now from the classification found most convenient in immigration topics, other schemes that are much discussed should be referred to here. Forty years ago Huxley replaced the word "Caucasian" by two terms: "Xanthochroi," meaning the blond race, and "Melanochroi," or the brunette portion of the Caucasian race. Ripley has summed up in a masterly manner all the physical classifications made since that of Huxley. He shows that the great consensus of opinion thus far favors the distinction of three great races in Europe, which he calls the "Teutonic," the "Alpine," and the "Mediterranean." An attempt has been made in the introduction to correlate these terms with the more common linguistic classification of Brinton. (See table on p. 5.) As is pointed out (p. 4), Ripley's classification is impracticable in immigration statistics and in censuses of races, and therefore it need not be given extended discussion here. Moreover, it appears probable that his classification must be largely modified by the studies of Deniker, now in progress. The latter has added to the three classical races of Europe the "Atlanto-Mediterranean," the "Oriental," and the "Adriatic," with possibly three or four other "subraces." Ripley has practically admitted the existence of the Adriatic as a distinct race. (See *Albanian.*) Deniker has wisely given as an alternative classification to that of his physical types a classification of "peoples" based on linguistic grounds which may be profitably compared, in a discussion of each immigrant race, with those of Brinton and Keane here adopted (as in Introductory, table on p. 6).

In population the Caucasian race leads the world, with about 800,000,000 souls. Nearly 300,000,000 of these, however, are of darker branches of the race, and live in Asia, 220,000,000 of them being Aryans of India. The Mongolian race numbers, perhaps, 200,000,000 less than the Caucasian, although extending far into Europe, as above noted. Asia, both Mongolian and Caucasian, has a population of nearly 900,000,000, as against the 400,000,000 inhabitants of Europe. Fully nine-tenths, or 750,000,000, of the Caucasian population of the world is Indo-European, or Aryan. (The population of various Caucasian "races" or peoples will be found in the respective articles relating to each.)

Nearly all the immigrants that come to the United States are from Europe; that is, about 1,200,000 out of 1,285,000 in 1907. About the same proportion is Caucasian. Indeed, 75,000 of the 100,000 counted here at the most as Mongolian are such only in origin and language; they are Finns, Magyars, and Turks who have become Europeanized. Ripley has divided the European immigrants of 1907 as follows:

European immigration to the United States, 1907, by races specified.

Races.	Number.	Per cent.
Mediterranean (or Atlanto-Mediterranean and Ibero-Insular)	330,000	25
Slavic	330,000	25
Alpine (or Celtic)	194,000	16⅔
Teutonic (or Baltic, or Northern)	194,000	16⅔
Jewish	146,000	12½

The names just written resemble those used by the Bureau of Immigration for the grand divisions of European races, excepting that the Bureau counts the Jewish in the Slavic division, and puts Magyars, Turks, and Armenians under the heading "All others." As thus divided, the immigrants of 1907 were:

Races.	Number.	Per cent.
Iberic	283,000	28
Slavic	409,000	37
Keltic	116,000	11
Teutonic	214,000	19

(See *Slav* for detailed comparisons among the 16 leading immigrant races included in the above.)

The most interesting fact in immigration is the sudden and astounding recent change in the character of the immigration. While up to 1880 it was almost entirely from northwestern Europe, or, in other words, was composed of races or peoples which now constitute the older American stock, immigration comes mainly at the present time from southern and southeastern Europe; that is, chiefly from Italian, Hebrew, and Slavic stocks that differ widely from the American in language, character, and political institutions. This reversal in the character of immigration was effected in twenty years, between 1882 and 1902, as shown by the following per cents of the total immigration of those years:

Immigration to the United States.	1882.	1902.
	Per cent.	*Per cent.*
From western Europe	87	22
From southern and eastern Europe	13	78

Western European immigration as here understood does not include the small immigration from the Spanish Peninsula. The per cents of 1902 have remained about the same since then. The above facts may be represented in another form as follows:

In twenty years the immigration from western Europe has decreased 75 per cent (from 563,000 to 137,000); that from southern and eastern Europe has increased 475 per cent (from 84,000 to 486,000).

Taking each at its highest tide, the annual immigration from western Europe was, twenty-five years ago (in 1882), 563,000; that from southern and eastern Europe is now (in 1907) 971,000.

The newer type of immigration has thus reached in a single year nearly 1,000,000 out of a total immigration from all countries of 1,285,000.

CAUCASUS PEOPLES, CAUCASIAN. The group of native races or peoples peculiar to the Caucasus, as the Russian territory, Caucasia, is sometimes called; not found elsewhere. More exactly defined on linguistic grounds, they constitute one of the four distinct divisions of the white race; that is, they are a non-Aryan stock, which, with the Aryan, the Semitic, and the Euskaric stocks, make up the great Caucasian or White division of mankind. It is, of course, confusing and objectionable to use the term "Caucasian" in the narrowest sense, as is sometimes done, to designate only the peoples of the Caucasus. This term was first used by Blumenbach, who applied it to the Caucasian division of mankind because he considered a Georgian of Caucasia the most perfect and ideal specimen of the white race. A full discussion of the Caucasus peoples can hardly be undertaken in this dictionary. It is not only the most difficult problem in European ethnology, but these peoples are at present of little importance in an immigration study. The population is small. Their names do not appear in immigration statistics.

So far as a general view of the non-Aryans of the Caucasus can be given in a few words, they may be said to mediate in most particulars between Europeans and Asiatics, as would be expected from their geographical location. "Nowhere else in the world probably," says Ripley, "is so heterogeneous a lot of people, languages, and religions gathered together in one place as along the chain of the Caucasus Mountains." While this statement covers the Mongolian population of the Caucasus as well as the Caucasus peoples proper, it is true that the latter are greatly mixed in physical stock and most diverse in type. The blond type of Europe is lacking, it is true, but some western Georgians are long-headed, like northern races. The prevailing head form, however, is broader than that of the Russian, although the latter is broad-headed for a European. In stature the non-Aryans are generally tall and of robust physique.

As divided on a linguistic basis, there are at least 50 tribes in this region with an area no larger than that of Spain. Ripley gives the number of dialects as 68, including at least one that is Aryan, the Osset. The Caucasus languages proper are more

Caucasus peoples.

Asiatic than European in type, for they are agglutinative, not inflected like the Aryan and Semitic tongues. Yet they are not related to any linguistic family of Asia or of any other part of the world. The civilization of the region is backward, due in part to its inaccessible nature. The people have figured but little in history except as independent and almost unconquerable mountaineers. After long years of warfare they were finally brought into subjection by the Russian Government. But the spirit of the most populous race, the Circassian, or Cherkess, was not yet broken. Four-fifths of the entire population of half a million removed en masse into Asiatic Turkey, although they received but scant welcome from their Mohammedan brethren. Their territory has since been occupied by Russians. A scattered remnant remains. In religion, the Kartvelians or Georgians are Greek, or Orthodox. Most of the remaining Caucasus tribes are Mohammedan, although some of the intruding tribes are still really pagan. The law of the vendetta, that is, of blood for blood, reigns among the mountaineers.

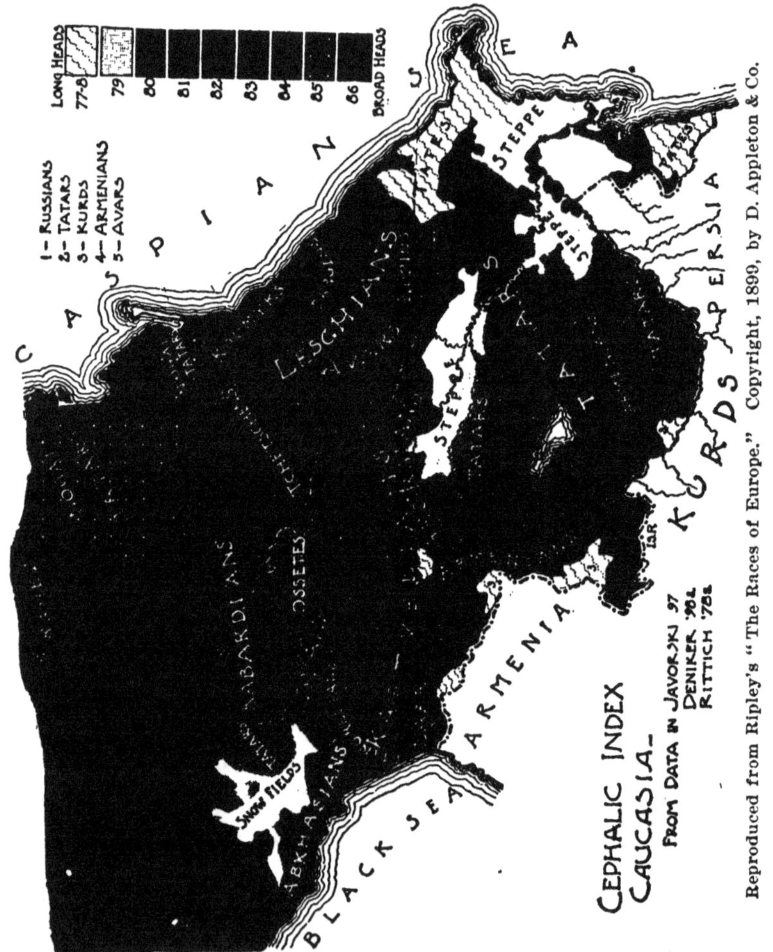

Reproduced from Ripley's "The Races of Europe." Copyright, 1899, by D. Appleton & Co.

A word on the geography of the Caucasus may well precede any discussion of the divisions of its population. Caucasia, called in Russian "Kavkaz," is an administrative division of lieutenancy of the Russian Empire lying between the Euxine or Black Sea and the Caspian. It includes two mountain ranges, the Caucasus and a range opposite it in Asia sometimes called "Anti-Caucasus" separated by plains or steppes. Northern Caucasia or Ciscaucasia consists of three provinces lying north of the Caucasus Mountains; Transcaucasia, of six provinces lying south, together with Daghestan lying north on the Caspian side. All south of the Caucasus Mountains is, properly speaking, in Asia, although the Russians, in their steady advance toward the south, prefer to call it Europe. In the following table the line between the eastern and the western provinces is drawn somewhat arbitrarily to indicate racial groupings. Erivan is more properly a southern than an eastern province, since its population of Armenians, Kurds, and Ayssores is only an extension of that lying farther south in Turkey and Persia.

Races or peoples in the Caucasus.

[Distribution of each by provinces is indicated in per cents.]

Races or peoples.	Population.	Western part of—			Eastern part of—						
		Northern Caucasia.	Transcaucasia.		Northern Caucasia.		Transcaucasia.				
		Kuban.	Kutais.	Kars.	Stavropol.	Terek.	Tiflis.	Daghestan.	Baku.	Elizabethpol.	Erivan.
Kartvelian:											
Georgian	821,720		41				57				
Imeretian	273,184		99								
Mingrelian	239,615		99								
Svanetian	15,756		99								
Total	1,350,275										
Other Caucasian:											
Chechenz	226,496					98					
Avaro-Andian	212,680							74			
Kurin	159,213							59	30		
Darguin	130,209							92			
Kabard	98,538					85					
Kasi-Kumyk, etc	90,880							84			
Abkhasian	72,103		84								
Ingush	47,409					99					
Circassian	43,332	89									
Udin	7,100									99	
Kist	413						72				
Total	1,088,373										
Turko-Tatar:											
Tatar	1,509,785								32	35	
Osmanli-Turk	139,419		33	46							
Kumyk	83,389					38		61			
Nogai	64,048				30	58					
Karapapakh	29,902			99							
Karatchai	27,222			98							
Turkoman	24,522				66						
Other Turko-Tatar	1,621										
Total	1,879,908										

Races or peoples in the Caucasus—Continued.

Races or peoples.	Population.	Western part of—			Eastern part of—						
		Northern Caucasia.	Transcaucasia.		Northern Caucasia.		Transcaucasia.				
		Kuban.	Kutais.	Kars.	Stavropol.	Terek.	Tiflis.	Daghestan.	Baku.	Elizabethpol.	Erivan.
Aryan:											
Russian—											
Great Russian	1,829,793	45			25						
Little Russian	1,305,463	69									
White Russian	19,642	63									
Other Aryan—											
Osset	171,127					56	39				
Armenian	1,118,094									26	40
Kurd	99,836										49
Tat	95,056								95		
Talych	35,291								99		
Ayssore	5,286						28				54
Other	221,834										
Total	4,901,412										
Hebrew	40,498		15			15		15	20		
Other	28,898										
Grand total	9,289,364										

Of the 9,000,000 inhabitants of Caucasia, the table shows that only about one-fourth, or a little over 2,000,000, are Caucasus peoples, properly speaking. Their Russian conquerors constitute already the largest homogeneous population of the Caucasus (3,000,000) and are located mainly in the dispossessed territory of the Circassians on the Black Sea. The Tatars stand third numerically (1,500,000). They are largely Russified, and located for the most part on the Caspian side of Transcaucasia. They and their Turko-Tatar kinsmen appear more widely distributed throughout Caucasia than the Caucasus peoples themselves, and number three-fourths of the population of the latter. Like the Armenians, some of them are merely extensions of larger populations in Asia. The Armenians, though but recently immigrated into Caucasia from the troublous districts of Turkey, already number over 1,000,000. They, with the remaining Asiatic Aryans in Caucasia, about equal in number the Turko-Tatars; that is, equal three-fourths of the Caucasus peoples proper. (See the appropriate articles for discussion of all the preceding races found in Caucasia.)

Reviewed by geographical regions, Transcaucasia is mainly Kartvelian or Georgian in the west, Armenian in the center, and "Other Caucasian" in the east, while northern Caucasia is mainly Russian in the west and "Other Caucasian" in the east. The Turko-Tatars and 40,000 Hebrews are scattered throughout both divisions. The chief center of population of each ethnical division noted in the foregoing table is computed upon the Russian census of 1897. Compared with the chief emigrating races or peoples of Europe the number of Caucasus peoples proper is small, and if they did emigrate to the United States the movement would be of little importance numerically. The few that do come to this country are probably

 Caucasus peoples.

counted as Russians when they speak Russian, or otherwise are included among the "Other peoples" of the immigration tables.

The following classification of Keane is more complete from a linguistic point of view and agrees in the main with that of Hovelacque:

I. SOUTHERN DIVISION (HOVELACQUE'S "SOUTHERN").

[Kartveli stock.]

Race or people.	Location.	Population.
Georgian	East of Mesk range to Tiflis district	1,150,000
Imerian, Rachan	Imeria (Imeritia)	
Mingrelian, Gurian, Lechgum	Mingrelia	
Laz	Lazistan	
Svan	Upper Ingur and Tskhenis valleys	
Pshav, Khevsur	Sources of Alazan and Yora	

II. WESTERN DIVISION (HOVELACQUE'S "CHERKESSIAN").

Race or people.	Location.	Population.
Cherkess: Ubych, Shapsuch, Dshiget	Left bank Kuban	188,000
Abkhasian	Coast of Euxine, north of Ingur River	
Kabard	North and east of Elbruz	

III. EASTERN DIVISION (HOVELACQUE'S "KISTIAN" AND "LESGHIAN").

Race or people.	Location.	Population.
Chechenz: Ingush, Galgai, Kist, Tush, Karabulak	Right bank, Upper and Middle Terek	170,000
Lesghian: Avar, Kazi-Kumykh, Andi, Dargo, Dido, Duodez, Ude, Kubachi, Kurini	Daghestan	540,000

IV. CENTRAL DIVISION.

Race or people.	Location.	Population.
Oss or Ossetian	Both slopes of Great Caucasus about Kazbek	127,000

The above terminology does not quite agree with the figures of the last census. Thus, the Kabards are put into the Western Division, although they are located mainly in the eastern part of Transcaucasia; and Hovelacque puts the Western and the Eastern divisions together into what he calls the Northern Division, while the census shows that more than one-half of these tribes are centered in the south; that is, in Transcaucasia. Finally, the census is correct in considering the Ossets as Aryans instead of as a division of the Caucasus peoples proper.

Space can not be taken to speak of the physical and social characteristics of each of these subdivisions, nor to fully identify all the tribal names mentioned by different writers. The following additional list may, however, be regarded as approximately correct:

KARTVELIAN OR KARTHLI.

Gruzian or Georgian proper.

CHERKESS OR CIRCASSIAN.

Abadzeh, Alaz, Adighe (Natukai, etc.), Abasa, Absne, or Asega.

CHECHENZ, KIST, OR KISLI.

Itchkerian or Mountain Chechenz, Mosok (Tush), Lamur (Ingush).

LESGHIAN.

Kurin.—Tsakhur (Tabassauran, etc.).

Kazi-Kumyk or Lak.—Agul, Budukh, Khinalugh.

Dargo.—Hyrkelin.

Avar.—Maarulal (name Avars give themselves), Bagulal, Khunzakh, Khindalal, Baktlin.

Other Lesghian.—Chek, Muchadar or Rotul, Usmei, Kaitak, Karatin, Akhvak, Akusha, Ideri, Chamalal, Khvarchin, Kapuchin, Gunzal, Botlikhtz, Artchin, Khaidak, Tzakhur, Tzesa or Tzunta (Dido), Kuanal (Andi), Agbukhan (Kubachi).

Iron, As, and Alan are other names of the Ossets, and therefore not of Caucasus peoples strictly speaking. The Ossets include the Digorians, the Tagaurs, the Kurtatines, and the Alaghirs.

Finally the term Circassian is used in three senses: (1) Properly as equivalent of Cherkess; (2) often as covering the entire Western Division (above); and (3) wrongly to include also the Eastern. The map on page 34, taken from Ripley, while primarily intended to show the cephalic index of the region, also indicates the location of the principal Caucasus peoples.

CELTIC or **KELTIC**. The westernmost branch of Aryan or Indo-European languages. It is divided into two chief groups, with several subdivisions, as shown in the following table from Keane:

I. GAEDHELIC (GAELIC).

Irish, Old and Modern.
Erse, or Gaelic of the Scottish Highlands.
Manx, of the Isle of Man.

II. KYMRIC.

Old Gaulish, extinct.
Kymraeg, or Welsh.
Cornish, extinct.
Brezonek, or Low Breton.

Irish, because of its more extensive literature and greater antiquity, is considered to be the chief branch of the Gaelic group. Modern Erse or Scotch is thought to be a more recent dialect of Irish. (See *Scotch.*) Manx is the dialect spoken by a small number of persons in the Isle of Man. Welsh is the best preserved of the Cymric group. It has a literature nearly if not quite as rich as that of Irish, and is spoken by a larger population than any other Celtic language found in the British Isles. (See *Welsh.*) Low Breton, or Armorican, is the speech found in Lower Brittany, in France. It is spoken by nearly two-thirds as many persons as are all other Celtic dialects combined. (See *Breton.*) No Celtic language has a current literature of any extent. Each succeeding census shows a decrease in the number of persons who speak a Celtic tongue. In few places is a Celtic language taught in the schools. Everywhere these languages are being supplanted by English or French.

The term "Celtic" is used in different senses by the philologist and the anthropologist. The former includes in it all peoples originally speaking a Celtic language. The latter has used the term to designate a broad-headed physical type called "Alpine" by Ripley. As shown elsewhere (see *Caucasian*), there are three great physical races in Europe which Ripley calls "Teutonic," "Alpine" ("Celtic"), and "Mediterranean." The first named is tall, long-headed, and blond, and comprises most of the northern races of Europe. The last named is short, long-headed, and very brunette, and includes the races living on the shores of the sea whose name it bears. The "Celtic" is of medium stature, broad-headed, and rather brunette. The eyes are more often gray and the hair brown, though all variations are found, due to admixtures with the Teutons and the Mediterraneans living on either side of them. (For other names for this type, see table in Introductory.) This "Celtic" race seems to have had its main center of dissemination in the highlands of the Alps of midwestern Europe.

Since the Celtic-speaking races, with the exception of the Breton, are not, as was once thought, of one and the same physical type, Ripley recommends the dropping of the word "Celtic" as a term to designate a physical stock and the substitution of the word "Alpine" instead. While all Celtic-speaking peoples are mixed races, those of the British Isles are distinctly long-headed and tall, in fact, are among the tallest of all Europe. They are therefore to be classed as Teutonic or "Northern," rather than as Alpine. The Bretons are the only people having a Celtic tongue who are predominatingly of the Alpine physical type. And even they have received much infusion of Teutonic blood, especially in the coast districts.

The Bureau of Immigration places in the "Keltic division" three "races or peoples" that speak a Celtic language—Irish, Scotch, and Welsh—and two that are distinctly of the Alpine or Celtic physical stock, the French and the North Italian. Manx and Breton do not appear by name in immigration statistics. As explained elsewhere (see Introductory and *English*), this dictionary uses the term "Celtic" in the sense of the philologist and the term "Alpine" to designate the so-called "Celtic" physical stock.

Celtic-speaking peoples are found in the western part of Ireland; in the mountains of Scotland and Wales; in Monmouthshire, England, which borders on Wales; in the Isle of Man; and in the western part of Brittany. It is impossible to give the population of the Celtic race—that is, of those whose ancestral language was Celtic—since most of its members now speak English or French only. The census of 1901 of the United Kingdom reports 1,806,000 who can speak a Celtic tongue. Hickmann estimates the total Celtic population of Europe at only 3,200,000 and that of the world at 9,200,000. However much others may increase this number, the Celtic population of the world is insignificant when compared with that of other branches of the Indo-European family, as Teutonic 131,000,000, Romance or Italic 107,300,000, and Slavonic 127,200,000.

Nevertheless, despite their small population, the Celtic races formed, until the recent change in the tide of immigration to America, a very important element. (For further details and immigration figures, see articles *Irish*, *Scotch*, *Welsh*, and *Breton*.)

CELTO-GERMANIC. Same as **Aryan** (see).

CENTRAL AMERICAN. All immigrants born in Central America, excepting Spanish Americans (see), are classified by the Bureau of Immigration according to race as Negro (see) or as members of the European or other race or people from which they sprang. (Cf. *Cuban*, *Mexican*.)

CERNAGORIAN or **TSRNAGORTSI.** Same as **Montenegrin.** (See *Croatian*.)

CEYLONESE. Any native of Ceylon; mainly Sinhalese and Tamils (3,200,000); also about 4,000 very primitive aborigines, the Veddahs. (See these and *Caucasian*.)

CHALDEAN. A term used in Brinton's classification (see Introductory and *Semitic-Hamitic*) to designate that group of Semitic languages which includes the Babylonian, the Assyrian, the Canaanitic (Hebrew, etc.), and the Aramaic dialects. (See article on *Syrian* for subdivisions of the Aramaic, and on *Assyrian* for a discussion of the Ayssores, who sometimes call themselves Assyrians.)

CHALDEE or **SYRO-CHALDAIC.** The Aramaic language spoken by the Jews in the time of Christ, said by some to have been brought to Palestine from Babylon after the captivity. Sometimes called also Chaldean (see), although that word is defined according to Brinton as a group term to include the Chaldee and many other languages. The language is now but little used except where revived by missionaries. A dialect is still spoken by the Ayssores. (See *Assyrian* and *Syrian.*)

CHARVAT. (See *Slovak* and *Croatian.*)

CHECH or **CHEKH.** (See *Czech* in article *Bohemian and Moravian.*)

CHEREMISS or **CHERMISSIAN.** A division of the Eastern Finns (see).

CHERKASI, CIRCASSIAN (see) or **CHERKESS.** (See *Caucasus peoples* and *Ruthenian.*)

CHERNOMORISH. A division of the Cossacks (see) of the Dneiper; that is, a subdivision of the Little Russians. (See *Ruthenian.*)

CHINESE. The race or people inhabiting China proper. Linguistically, one of the Sinitic groups of the Mongolian or Asiatic race. The name Chinese is also applied, erroneously from an ethnical standpoint, to all the natives of the Chinese Empire, including China proper; that is, to the entire Sibiric group. These are, on the northeast the Manchus, on the north the Mongols, on the west the tribes of Turkestan and of Tibet. The name does not properly apply to the other Sinitic peoples—the Cochin-Chinese and the Annamese of the French colonies and the Burmese of the British colonies, all of whom border on China on the south, and southwest. (See *East Indian.*) The people of Manchuria and of Mongolia are not so nearly related linguistically to the Chinese as they are to the Japanese (see). All these "Sibiric" peoples have agglutinative languages, while the Chinese is isolating and monosyllabic, being more nearly related to the languages stretching from Tibet southeast to the Malay Peninsula.

The Chinese physical type is well known—yellowish in color, with slanting eyes, high cheek bones, black hair, and a flat face. The eye is more properly described as having the "Mongolic fold" at the inner angle. This mark is found to some extent in all Mongolian peoples, in the Japanese, and now and then in individuals of the European branches of this race in Russia and Austria-Hungary.

Estimates of the population of China proper run from 270,000,000, an American official estimate, to 400,000,000, a Chinese estimate. The other peoples of the Empire are comparatively small in numbers, the entire Chinese Empire having a population of from 330,000,000 to 430,000,000. The Chinese are spreading rapidly over the countries toward the south, replacing the Malay to a great extent as a land-owning class in the Malay Peninsula and other portions of Malaysia, where they already number between 5,000,000 and 7,000,000, including those in the Philippines. In the Americas and Hawaii there are about 140,000. Chinese laborers have been excluded from the United States since 1882. It is estimated that the total emigration of Chinese to the United States has exceeded 200,000, of whom only 90,000 now remain. Still larger numbers, 350,000, have gone to the Dutch East Indies. Adding to these an emigration of 130,000 to Singapore, 120,000 to Peru, and perhaps 30,000 to Australia, there appears a total emigration within fifty years of over 800,000. This number, however, is small when compared with emigration from several European countries during that period. In the twelve years 1899–1910, 22,590 Chinese were admitted to the United States.

No doubt Manchus and others who can not strictly be called Chinese appear as such in United States immigration statistics, especially students and other members of the Manchu families who have long been a ruling caste in China. American law defines the word "Chinese" in a political sense to include all subjects of China. Koreans, Japanese, and East Indians (see these) are counted separately.

CHOROBAT. (See *Croatian* and *Slovak.*)

CHOTSCHER. (See *Chude* under *Finnish.*)

CHUDE. A western subdivision of the Finns (see).

CHUVASH. An important Tataric people (see) in eastern Russia, classified by some among the Finns (see).

CINGALESE. Same as **Sinhalese** (see).

CIRCASSIAN (CHERKASI) or **ADIGHE.** The northwestern group of the Caucasus peoples (see). They call themselves Adighe and are known to Russians and Turks as Cherkess. They speak a non-Aryan tongue. Among the dialectal divisions of the Circassians are the Shapsuch, Ubych, and Dshiget. Some call the Abkasians and Kabardians Circassians. All these groups show more or less admixture of Tataric (Mongolian) intrusive elements. Their women are noted for their beauty and adorn the harems of Turkey and Persia. The Circassians are Mohammedans and are a proud-spirited people. They formerly numbered about 500,000, but nearly four-fifths of them emigrated to Asiatic and European Turkey after the Russian conquest, some forty-five years ago.

COCHIN-CHINESE. (See *Indo-Chinese.*)

COPTS or **KOPTS.** The purest representatives of the ancient Egyptians. (See *Egyptian* and *Semitic-Hamitic.*)

COREAN. (See *Korean.*)

CORNISH. The native race or people of Cornwall, the southwestern county of England. The Cornish, linguistically and physically, is Kymric, a division of the Celtic branch of the Aryan stock. Its nearest relatives are the Welsh and the Breton; next come the Irish, the Manx, and the Gaelic of the Scottish highlands. (See these and *Celtic.*) The people of Cornwall are, therefore, not so nearly related to the English as to the Irish. Yet they are for convenience usually counted as English when they come to this country as immigrants. Their language is now English, the Cornish speech having become extinct a little over a century ago. But the population is the most deeply brunette in Great Britain, being quite the opposite of the typical English. The population of the county is about 320,000.

CORSICAN. A native of the island of Corsica, which has belonged to France since the time of Napoleon, who was born here. The language is an Italian dialect. The population is mixed in race, but is supposed to be at bottom Iberic, thus being related to the early inhabitants of Spain and perhaps to the Berbers of North Africa, with later additions chiefly from Italy and France. The Corsican is almost as dwarfish as his neighbor, the Sardinian (see), being fully 9 inches shorter than the Teutonic average of northern Europe. The population numbers about 300,000.

In spirit the Corsican is independent and revengeful, and the history of the long rule of Genoa in the island was marked by continuous revolt. It is not known to what extent Corsicans come to the United States, as in immigration statistics they are included with immigrants coming from France.

COSSACK or **KAZAK.** (Cf. *Kirghiz-Kazak,* following). This term is used in two very different senses. The first is popular and historical, rather than ethnological, and refers to "the Cossacks of the Don" and others of southern Russian origin, who furnish the famous cavalry of the Czar,

These Cossacks are Russian (Caucasian), rather than Tataric, in race. In its second meaning, strictly ethnological, the word is equivalent to "Kirghiz-Kazak," and refers to the largest race of Central Asia of Tataric (Mongolian) origin. The historical Cossacks, being the best known, may first be briefly discussed; then the real Kazaks, ethnologically speaking. The former may be called the Western or Russian Cossacks; the latter the Eastern or Asiatic Cossacks, or Kazaks proper. The latter spelling of the name is more scientific and preferable when speaking of the Eastern Kazaks. (Cf. *Kirghiz, Korean, Kalmuk.*)

WESTERN COSSACK (OR COSSACK OF THE DON, ETC.).

The historical Cossacks, named, after the portions of southern Russia they first occupied, "Cossacks of the Dnieper" and "Cossacks of the Don," are of mixed race ethnically. Those of the Dnieper are mainly Little Russian—that is, Ruthenian (see) in origin; those of the Don are Great Russian. Some were Polish in origin, as the famous chieftain Mazeppa, the hero of Byron's verse. Others, on the Don, may have been of Tataric origin; at least the name and the form of social organization are Tataric. The name "Kazak" means "rider" or "robber." The Cossacks were both. Their name is to be defined as meaning, not a race, but a mixed Russian population having a certain social organization, communistic and semimilitary in character. These communities probably had their origin toward the close of the middle ages as a result of the desperate and repeated struggles with Asiatic invaders. They had the form of organization best fitted to survive, as it is now the best fitted to protect the Asiatic boundaries of the Empire. Hence Cossack settlements have extended as the Empire enlarged. Emigration has been to Siberia, under government auspices, rather than to the United States. Other races, as the Bashkirs, have become organized on the Cossack plan. The Cossacks of southern Russia who have remained in the old home have devoted themselves more seriously to agricultural pursuits, and, if any come to America, are probably known simply as Ruthenians, or Russians, according to the language they speak. The Zaporog Cossacks were so called in the sixteenth century because they lived "below the cataracts," on the Dnieper. They were Ruthenians.

EASTERN KAZAK (OR KIRGHIZ-KAZAK).

To be defined as the largest Tataric tribe of Central Asia, extending from Lake Balkash on the east to the Volga in Russia; nomadic, Mohammedan, and possessing a relatively pure Turkish speech. Their speech points to this region as being a former home of the Turks of Turkey, although the latter have become, physically, far more Europeanlike than the Kirghiz. Although called Kirghiz by ethnologists, they themselves reserve this term for their kinsmen, the Kara-Kirghiz (see *Kirghiz*), and call themselves simply Kazak. The Russians applied to them the name Kirghiz-Kazak, to distinguish them from the western Cossacks or military communities described above. Some writers claim that the Kirghiz are physically Mongolic but linguistically Tataric. There is no doubt that their features are more Asiatic in type than those of the Tatars of Russia, but this may have come from their frequent intermarriages with Mongolic tribes.

Their civilization is still very primitive. Only the wandering life of herdsmen is possible on the barren steppes

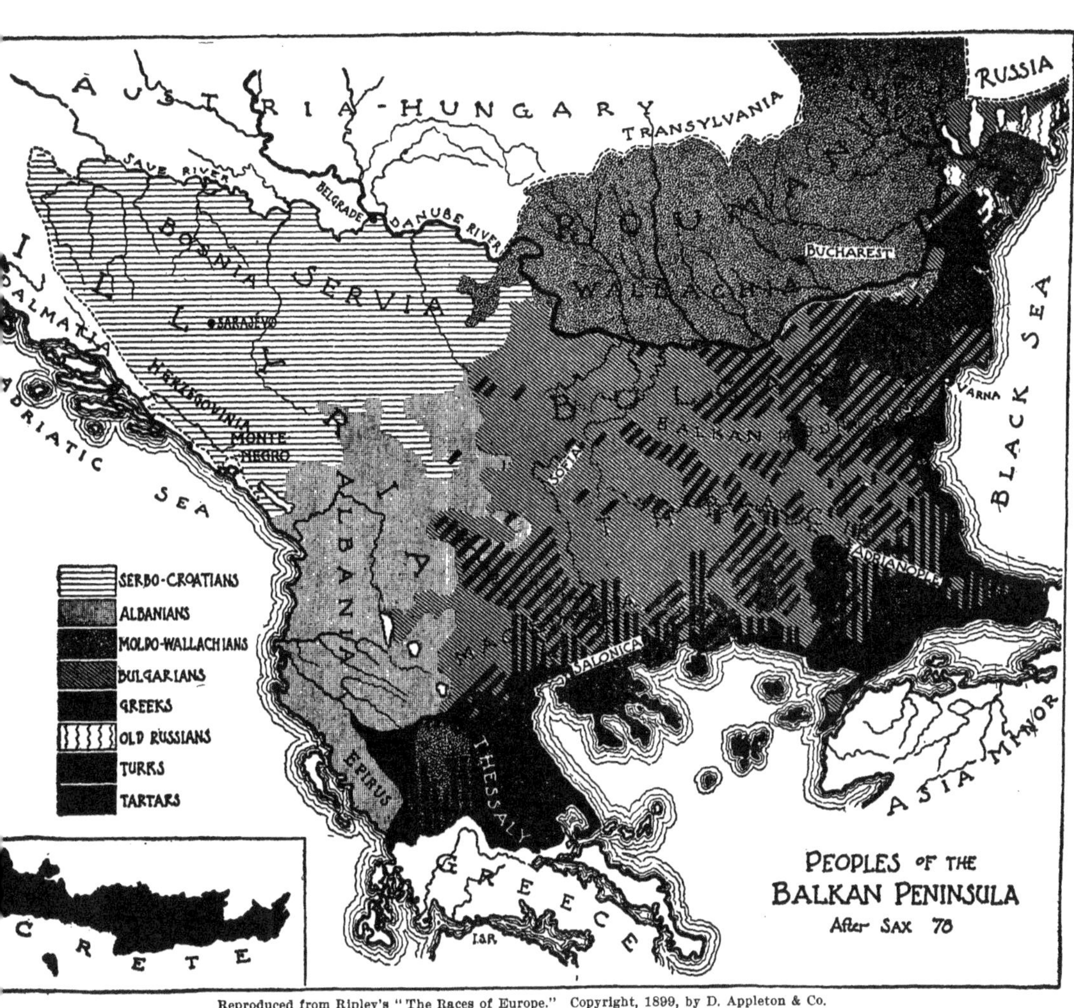

Reproduced from Ripley's "The Races of Europe." Copyright, 1899, by D. Appleton & Co.

60813°—vol 5—11. (To face page 43.)

of Central Asia. The people are unlettered and their religion is often Shamanism rather than the Mohammedanism which they profess. They number 4,000,000, some 260,000 of whom live in the province of Astrakhan, on the northern border of the Caspian Sea, in Russia.

The Kara-Kirghiz of Central Asia are comparatively of little importance. They number only about 100,000. If members of either of these tribes came to America, it would be less confusing to call them "Kirghiz" instead of "Kazak." As has just been shown, the latter term applies to men of various races. (See *Tataric* for other details as to population.)

COSTA RICAN. (See *Spanish American.*)

CRAKUS, KRAKOWIAK, or **BIELOCHROVAT.** Names applied to a subdivision of the Poles (see).

CREOLE. (See *Negro.*)

CRETAN. (See *Greek.*)

CRIMEAN TATAR. A Tatar (see) living in the Crimea, in southern Russia.

CROATIAN or **SERVIAN,** or, better, **SERBO-CROATIAN,** including the so-called **Croatian, Servian, Bosnian, Dalmatian, Herzegovinian,** and **Montenegrin (Tsrnagortsi)** races or peoples. (Related words: *Chroat, Khrobat, Carpath, Khorvat, Horvath,* and *Hervat* or *Hrvat;* also *Serb* or *Srp, Sorb,* and *Sorabian.* Sometimes included, with Magyars and others, in the term *Huns* in American speech. To avoid this name Croatian immigrants sometimes insist that they are *Austrians,* while some call themselves Hervats rather than Croatians.)

The Serbo-Croatian is a distinct and homogeneous race, from a linguistic point of view, and may be defined as the one which, with the closely related Slovenian, constitutes the Southern Division of the Slavic, the linguistic stock which occupies the countries above indicated, including Slavonia. It is not an ethnical unity in physical characters and descent, but a mixed race. It is separated into the above so-called races on political and even religious grounds. It forms an important subject in the present study, for it is typical of the newer flood of immigration from southeastern Europe and contributes largely to it.

GEOGRAPHY OF THE BALKAN PENINSULA.

Definitions of the Serbo-Croatian peoples depend so largely upon political boundaries that a preliminary sketch of the Balkan States will conduce to clearness. The southern part of the Balkan Peninsula is occupied by Greeks, Albanians, and a minority of Turks. All the rest—that is, the greater part—is Slavic. Roughly speaking, the eastern half of the Slavic territory is Bulgarian (see). This race belongs to the Eastern Division of Slavs and occupies the entire region from the Danube south nearly to the Ægean Sea and Constantinople itself. The main range of the Balkan Mountains is in their territory, running eastward to the Black Sea. The Serbo-Croatians are west of the Bulgarians, occupying all the territory to the Adriatic Sea. They are restricted, therefore, to the northwestern part, or about one-third, of the Balkan Peninsula. Once the Empire of Servia covered all the country southward to Greece.

If the northern boundary of the peninsula be considered a line running eastward from the head of the Adriatic to the Black Sea following the Save River to the Danube and down the latter, it will include all the Bulgarians and the Southern Slavs with the exception of the Slovenian territory, northern Croatia, and Slavonia. These will also be included within the limits of the peninsula if its boundary may be fixed a little farther north to the Drave. This article is not concerned further with the countries of Greece, Turkey (including Albania), and Bulgaria (including Eastern Roumelia); nor with Roumania, which lies north of Bulgaria, and therefore outside the limits of the Balkan Peninsula. Ripley, however, includes the Roumanians among the peoples of the Balkan Peninsula, as is shown by the map facing page 43. (See article *Roumanian* for this race or people, kindred in physical type to the Slavic, but possessing a Latin tongue.)

The remaining States constitute Serbo-Croatian territory. The Kingdom of Servia, situated just south of the Danube and the Save, midway between the Black Sea and the Adriatic, is the only independent State amongst them, excepting the small principality of Montenegro. The latter occupies the southern angle of the Serbo-Croatian territory, with Turkey on the southeast and the narrow territory of Dalmatia and the Adriatic on the southwest. The remaining Serbo-Croatian territory belongs to the Austro-Hungarian monarchy. Herzegovina, northwest of Montenegro and similar to it in size, and Bosnia, larger and extending north from Herzegovina to the Save and Slavonia, were attached in 1878; Dalmatia, a narrow strip of coast land between these two States and the Adriatic, is an older possession of Austria. Still farther north are the former kingdoms of Slavonia, lying along the southwestern boundary of Hungary proper, and Croatia, lying farthest to the northwest in the peninsula next to Austria and the Adriatic. These two provinces now form part of the Kingdom of Hungary. All the Southern Slavs—that is, the Serbo-Croatians and the Bulgarians—were subject to Turkey only thirty years ago, excepting those on the northern fringe inhabiting Croatia, Slavonia, and Dalmatia. If, as is sometimes said, these are not Balkan States, all the Balkan Peninsula excepting Greece was then covered by Turkey—as also was Greece itself a century ago.

THE SERBO-CROATIANS IN GENERAL.

Ask a Bosnian his race and he will answer "Turk" if he is a Mohammedan; "Latin" or "Croatian" if a Roman Catholic; and "Servian" if an adherent of the Greek Church. Yet in all these cases the race is the same because the language is the same. The case of the Bosnian is typical of the entire Serbo-Croatian people, which is peculiar amongst all the races or peoples of Europe in appearing to be divided into six or more separate ethnical branches; that is, as many as there are political States if not religions in this region, while the scientist can have no doubt but that all are of one race. Their case resembles that of the Poles, who, since the partition of Poland, make part of three different nationalities; or that of the Germans, constituting to a greater or less degree the German, the Swiss, and the Austrian nationalities. In like manner, Bosnian, Dalmatian, Montenegrin, and Herzegovinian are only names of nationalities or of political groups, while the corresponding race or people is Serbo-Croatian.

Language, as explained in the Introductory, is the necessary basis of all official classifications of European races. It is the one followed by all European censuses of races, and is adopted in this dictionary. The Bureau of Immigration has found it desirable for practical considerations to subdivide and group the Serbo-Croatians as follows: The Servian and Montenegrin are counted with the Bulgarian, the Croatian with the Slovenian, and the Dalmatian, Bosnian, and Herzegovinian are given a separate column. Yet there can be no doubt that the Bulgarians and the Slovenians are outside the Serbo-Croatian race, although they are most closely related to it by language.

The confusion in Serbo-Croatian terminology has its origin in both politics and religion. From a partisan standpoint it has become quite customary to use only provincial names, like Croatian. To recognize the broader racial name would lend weight to the sentiment for Serbo-Croatian consolidation and the political independence of the Serbo-Croatians. Linguistic grounds are sought by others for a broader union embracing the entire northern belt of Balkan States from the Adriatic to the Black Sea, including both the Slovenian territory on one side of the Serbo-Croatians and Bulgaria on the other. Religious rivalries likewise have led to ethnographical fictions. Not only has a fraction of a race like the Bosnians been led to say that they are of three races or peoples when they practically mean three religions; these religions have given them three alphabets for one speech. The Serbo-Croatians of the west, who are Roman Catholic, can not read the publications of the eastern Serbo-Croatians, who are Orthodox, although both have the same language, for the former use the Roman alphabet or sometimes the strange Glagolitic letters, while the latter use the Russian characters fostered by the Greek Church.

The geographical limits of the Serbo-Croatians are not easily determined. They are defined on the north by the Danube and the Drave; that is, by Hungarian and Slovenian territory. On the east, also, they coincide with the boundary between Servia and Bulgaria, except that northeastern Servia is occupied by Roumanians. But as to the southern boundary the wildest and most divergent statements are made by students of the question according to their political bias. Some pro-Servians would claim Macedonia and the greater part of Turkey, even to the Black Sea, to be Servian by language; while it is generally held that the Slavic language found here is Bulgarian. A fair statement would seem to be that northwestern Turkey is Serbo-Croatian, including a narrow strip of northern Albania, as well as the large districts known as Old Servia and Novibazar. The last named lies between Servia and Montenegro. Old Servia is farther southeast. These two Serbo-Croatian districts in Turkey are about as large as Montenegro and Herzegovina.

As thus delimited, the Serbo-Croatians are inclosed on the west by the Adriatic Sea; on the northwest by the closely related Slovenians; on the north by the totally different Magyars or Hungarians, of Mongol origin; on the northeast by a more nearly related people, the Roumanians; on the southeast by distant relatives, the Bulgarians; and on the south by the Albanians, a race differing both in language and physical type from any other in Europe. The region is aptly named the "whirlpool of Europe." The Balkans are the storm center, and the "Eastern question" is always acute. Within a generation European Turkey has lost half of its territory, and several new nations have appeared upon the map of the peninsula. The keen rivalries between nationalities and races have obscured scientific questions and rendered more difficult the classification of peoples.

Even the choice of the term Serbo-Croatian is a comparatively recent expedient to allay national jealousy. The language may as properly be called either Croatian or Servian. It was once called the Illyrian, an ethnical misnomer for which an excuse was sought in political history. But the ancient Illyrians were an entirely different race. (See *Albanian.*) Few traces of them, it is said, can be found among the Slavs now occupying the country. The apostles of the "Illyrian" propaganda would take into their fold Bulgaria on the east and the Slovenians on the west. "Yugo-Slavic"—that is "South Slavic"—is a name more recently adopted by other patriotic Slavs in an attempt to inculcate a feeling of unity among all Serbo-Croatians and Slovenians. It is pan-slavism on a small scale.

The historical and linguistic relations existing between widely separated branches of the Slavs are often indicated or suggested by strange similarities in their names. The terms Slav, Slovak, Slovenian, and Slavonian are discussed in the article on the Slovenian. As there pointed out, Slavonian in the narrowest sense may mean the nationality (not a race) inhabiting the former kingdom of Slavonia. The race or people living there is the Servian or Croatian. Curiously enough, Croat, Hervat, and the related words given at the head of this article are variations of an old word meaning highlands or mountains (cf. *Carpathians*); hence not strictly ethnical terms, although some immigrants insist that Hervat and not Croatian is the proper name of their people. "Horvatok" is the name given Croatians on the Magyar ethnographical map. In like manner as the forms Hervat, Horvath, and even Kharpath come from Hrvat, so such variations as Serb and Sorb came from Srp. In the Serbo-Croatian, as in other Slavic languages, a vowel is not written with this "r." The "h" easily passes into "kh" and "b" into "p" or "v." In these and similar words, therefore, are indicated the ancient relationships existing between widely different divisions of the Slavs; between the Serbs, Croats, or Hervats, and Slovenians or Winds of the Southern Division on the one hand, and, on the other, in the north, the disappearing Sorbs and Wends and the Slovaks, with their forerunners, who left their name in ancient Chrobatia and the Carpathians.

The technicalities of the *stho*, *cha*, and *kay* dialects of the Serbo-Croatian need not be entered into here. In a general way they correspond to: (1) The southern, Servian, or, better, that spoken in Herzegovina, which has become the literary form of the Serbo-Croatian; (2) the western, Croatian, the use of which is gradually receding to the coast of Dalmatia; and (3) that found on the western border of Croatia, which is more properly called a separate language, the Slovenian.

Of the numerous names borne by Serbo-Croatian dialects and divisions of the population only a few need be given here. Some are merely names of political divisions. Thus the "Cernagorians" are simply the Montenegrins, the two words having the same meaning. "Tsrna Gora," in their language, means "black mountain." The Ragusans are the natives of the old city of Ragusa; Dubrovcans is another name for these. Others are the Syrmians, sometimes considered to be a fourth division of the Serbo-Croatians, named after a plain in Croatia-Slavonia; the Cices of Istria, and the Hranicares of the borders. Skipetar is a name applied to the Slavonized Albanians (see) of the coast. An Istrian—that is, a native of Istria—may be of any race; more likely a Serbo-Croatian, Italian, or Slovenian.

The Morlaks, who call themselves "Vlah" or "Wlach," may be, as some claim, Slavonized Roumanians (Wallachs); but if so, the change has been quite complete, for they might be taken to-day as the primitive Servian stock, not only in physical appearance and dialect, but in character and customs. They form a considerable population in northern Dalmatia and adjacent territory, especially in Istria. Reclus says that they are amongst the least advanced peoples of Europe. Certain other names found amongst Serbo-

Croatians really designate social groups rather than distinct races, dialects, or political divisions. Thus the well-known word "Haiduk," meaning originally in the Turkish language something like highwayman or freebooter, was adopted by the Servians in the sense of defender of the home land. Formerly Servians of the best families became Haiduks and pillaged Turkish villages. The Tchetnitsi were a class of these that made a specialty of taking the heads of their slain enemies. The Uskoks were, like them, brigands before they settled down to agricultural pursuits. They fled from Bosnia and Herzegovina to the Montenegrin mountains for protection against the Turks.

The savage manners of the last century are still met with amongst some Serbo-Croatians of to-day. Armed conflicts are not uncommon. Political feuds are especially bitter. Murders resulting from private vendettas occur frequently in some localities. Illiteracy is prevalent and civilization at a low stage in retired districts. Yet some points like Belgrade, the capital of Servia, are centers of literary activity and avid of all that makes up western civilization.

In physical appearance the Serbo-Croatians are quite distinct from other Slavs. In fact, they would seem to be, at bottom, not Slavic, or "Eastern," to use Deniker's terms, but "Adriatic." The latter differs from any other race in Europe in combining unusual stature with unusual breadth of head. Its purest representatives are found a little farther south amongst the Albanians (see), a remnant of the ancient Illyric race, using this word in its proper sense. In northern Albania, and especially in Herzegovina, are found some of the broadest heads in the world, with an average cephalic index of 87. The race is also one of the tallest of Europe, averaging 5 feet 9 inches. This type shades off in every direction, especially on the south, where both the Turks and the Greeks are shorter. The ancient Greeks belong to the long-headed "Mediterranean" race. On the north, the Albanian type is modified by the great Slavic wave of migration that brought with it the present Serbo-Croatian language of the country. But while the average height of the Slav is considerably less, the head is broad, as it is also in the "Alpine" race, farther northwest, into which the Serbo-Croatian type insensibly passes. The type is brunette, but not of the darkest. Although not so strong or stockily built as the tallest men of northern Europe, the Serbo-Croatian is vigorous and well adapted to hard labor. He makes a good workman in America, and goes mainly to the States where unskilled labor is most in demand—Pennsylvania, Illinois, New York, and Ohio.

Distribution of Serbo-Croatians in 1900.

Croatia and Slavonia	2,102,000
Dalmatia	565,000
Bosnia and Herzegovina (estimated)	1,550,000
Servia	2,299,000
Montenegro (estimated)	250,000
Elsewhere (estimated)	1,434,000
Total (estimated)	8,200,000

Population and immigration of Serbo-Croatian and related countries.

Group.	Population (estimated).	Immigration.	
		Number (1907).	Rate per 1,000 of population.
Croatia, Slavonia, and Slovenian territory	3,300,000	47,125	14
Dalmatia, Bosnia, and Herzegovina	2,115,000	7,263	3
Bulgaria, Servia, and Montenegro	7,550,000	11,053	2

The Bulgarian and Slovenian population is necessarily inserted in the above table, although it is not Serbo-Croatian, for otherwise the immigration and population figures could not be compared. As already explained, the Bureau of Immigration groups Bulgarians and Slovenians with the Serbo-Croatian peoples.

Croatian.

It is quite impossible to enter separate figures for the Servians in Turkey, where no census has ever been taken. Some estimates, especially by Servian partisans, place this number at over 500,000; others, as low as 40,000.

The foregoing statistics are significant, considering that the Southern Slavs typify the new character of American immigration that has replaced the tide from northwestern Europe. (See articles *Slav* and *Caucasian* for general comparisons on this point.) The Southern Slavs not only outnumber any other race in the Balkan Peninsula, but they constitute about one-half its population if we add to them the small Albanian population to which they are physically related. The Greeks do not make up one-third of the population, while the Turks are hopelessly in the minority, estimated by some as only one-seventh as many as the Slavs. Its 8,000,000 or 8,200,000 of population puts the Serbo-Croatian race about tenth in rank among all European races as to size. It may, therefore, be reckoned with as a steady and important source of future immigration. In immigration statistics Croatians and Slovenians are counted together. During the twelve years 1899–1910, 335,543 immigrants of these races were admitted to the United States.

At present the Southern Slavic rate of immigration is high only in the most northwestern group, that of Croatia, Slavonia, and the Slovenian territory. In 1907 the Croatian-Slovenian rate of immigration was about 13 per 1,000 of population, exceeding that of any other race or people except two, the Hebrew and the Slovak. There are said to be already 270,000 Croatians in the United States. It is interesting to note that the two Slavic elements of the highest immigration tide come wholly from Austria-Hungary, while the same country stands second only to Russia as the source of Hebrew immigration. At present the immigration rate of the Bulgarians and the Serbo-Croatians living nearest them is rather low. A dozen other races come at a more rapid rate. The Polish and the Irish come nearly three times as fast; the Greeks, neighbors of the Serbs on the south, nearly equal the Irish in their rate of coming. In absolute numbers, the Dalmatia-Bosnia-Herzegovina group, with its small population, stands still farther down the list. The Croatian-Slovenian, on the other hand, stands well toward the top (the ninth) among the larger races or peoples. It sends more immigrants to the United States than any other ethnical group of its size.

THE VARIOUS NATIONALITIES.

The terms "Bosnian," "Dalmatian," "Herzegovinian," and "Montenegrin," as shown above, are not names of races, but rather of nationalities found within the Serbo-Croatian ethnical territory. The same is true, of course, of the Servian, the Croatian, and the Slavonian as nationalities. Further details are necessary concerning each, especially as to their ethnical and religious elements.

Keeping constantly in mind that by the so-called Servian and Croatian races are generally meant only the Orthodox (Greek) and Roman Catholic divisions, respectively, of the one Serbo-Croatian race, the reader will better understand the following statistics from the Austrian and Hungarian censuses of 1900:

Distribution of Serbo-Croatians, by religion.

Geographic divisions.	Catholic.		Orthodox.		Total.	
	Number.	Per cent.	Number.	Per cent.	Number.	Per cent.
Croatia-Slavonia	1,482,353	61.6	607,381	25.4	2,089,734	87.0
Hungary proper	188,552	1.1	434,641	2.6	623,193	3.7

To these may be added the population of Bosnia and Herzegovina, 1,568,092, of whom the 334,142 Roman Catholics may be counted roughly as Croatians and the 673,246 Oriental Orthodox as Servians. But very few of the 548,632 Mohammedans are Turks, although generally calling themselves by that name. It is said that the Bosnian nobility became Mohammedans in order to preserve their feudal rights, but that they differ in more respects than race from Turkish Mohammedans. For instance, they do not practice polygamy.

Of the Servian nationality—that is, of the citizens of Servia—90 per cent are Servian by race and 98 per cent Orthodox in religion. The Roumanians in Servia number only 90,000. The Gypsies come next with half that number. The Roumanians (see), like the Servians, are for the most part Orthodox. While the Turks proper number only 1,000 in Servia, there are 15,000 Mohammedans.

The small independent principality of Montenegro has had no census. It is estimated that nearly 90 per cent of the population of 250,000 are Orthodox. The remainder are Roman Catholics or Mohammedans, the latter being Albanians. In Dalmatia 96 per cent of the population is Serbo-Croatian by race and 84 per cent Roman Catholic in religion. These probably all call themselves "Croatian." Nearly all the rest of the people are Greek (not "United") in religion. Less than 3 per cent of the population are Italians. These live along the coast in cities like Ragusa. There are no Turks in Dalmatia, so far as shown by the census.

In the Hungarian provinces of Croatia and Slavonia, besides the Serbo-Croatian population, which, as shown above, is 87 per cent of the whole, about 5 per cent of the population, or 134,000, are German, and 4 per cent "Hungarian." This is the classification by mother tongue. Classified by religion, all the Servians are "Oriental Greek," while 99 per cent of the "Croatians" are Roman Catholic, as are also 80 per cent of the Germans and Hungarians. No Turks or Mohammedans appear as such by name in the census. Finally, in the Coastland, including Istria, while nearly one-half of the population is Italian, the most of the remainder are Serbo-Croatians (143,000) and Slovenians. Nearly 99 per cent are Catholic.

CUBAN. Defined sufficiently well for the purposes of this dictionary by the Bureau of Immigration and Naturalization: "The term 'Cuban' refers to the Cuban people (not Negroes)." This narrower definition covers, however, only 60 per cent of the population of Cuba—that is, the native whites—for 13 per cent are Negroes, 16 per cent mulattoes, and 10 per cent foreign-born whites. It also excludes Indians. The term is generally used in a wider sense to include all natives of Cuba, regardless of color, especially including those of mixed blood.

In race, therefore, the population of Cuba is mainly composed of pure Spanish stock, contrary to the popular impression, if Catalans and Basques may be called pure Spanish, for these are the most important stocks that have come to the island from Spain. It is also popularly supposed that there is much Indian blood in Cuba, as in Mexico and in the countries farther south. This is not the case, for the sufficient reason that the Indian aborigines were almost entirely killed off in war and at forced labor within fifty years from the landing of Columbus. Negroes to some extent have suffered the same fate, for it is estimated that fully 900,000 were brought to the island as slaves. In 1817 they outnumbered the white population.

The Cuban census of 1907 gives a total population, in round numbers, of 2,000,000, of whom 1,200,000 are native whites, 200,000 foreign-born whites, 270,000 Negroes, 330,000 of mixed race, and 12,000 Chinese. Of the foreign-born whites, 80 per cent are Spaniards and 3 per cent (6,713) Americans. Cuba is therefore distinctly Spanish, or "Latin," in its sympathies and civilization. Comparatively few Cubans have emigrated to the United States—in 1907 only 5,475 (white). Spanish, English, and other foreign-born whites coming from Cuba are not included in this count. The same is true of immigrants from the rest of the West Indies. (See *West Indian*, *Mexican*, *Spanish American*, and *Negro*.) The number of Negroes coming to the United States from Cuba can not be stated, but it is not large, for the total Negro immigration in 1907 was only 5,235, of whom 4,561 were from the West Indies, including Cuba. All aliens coming from Cuba are counted as immigrants, although, in common with persons coming from Canada, Newfoundland, and Mexico, they are for the most part exempted from the head tax.

CYGANY or **TSIGANE**. The Hungarian name for Gypsy (see).

CYMRIC or **KYMRIC**. (See *Celtic*, *Welsh*, and *Breton*.)

CZECH. (See *Bohemian and Moravian*.)

D.

DALMATIAN. A political division of the Serbo-Croatians. (See *Croatian*.)

DANISH. (See *Scandinavian*.)

DOLENCI. A subdivision of the Slovenians (see).

DOM. A wandering tribe of India. (See *Gypsy*.)

DOUKHOBOR. A Russian (see) sect. Not the name of a race.

DRAVIDIAN. The great native stock of southern India, including the Tamils and Telugus, the Munda tribes, such as the Kohls, located farther north, and perhaps the Sinhalese and Veddahs of Ceylon. Though clearly non-Aryan, especially as to language, there is no agreement as to their place in a primary classification of mankind. Their relationship has been variously given as with the Caucasian (southern Hindus), the Mongolian, the African, and the "Australoid" races, and, finally, as independent of all. (*See* articles on these, and *Hindu* and *East Indian*.) They number nearly 60,000,000 in India and 3,000,000 in Ceylon. A good number emigrate as coolies.

DRUSE. A warlike branch of the Syrians (see) inhabiting the mountain regions of the Lebanon and the district of Hauran. They call themselves "Unahidin" (Unitarians).

DUBROVCAN. Same as **Ragusan**. (See *Croatian*.)

DUTCH and FLEMISH (less accurately **Hollander**, **Netherlander**, and **Belgian**). The two westernmost races or peoples on the Continent of Low German or Teutonic origin, the Dutch being the native people of Holland (the Netherlands) and the Flemish that of Flanders—that is, of the western part of Belgium. The Dutch and Flemish languages are intermediate between English on the one hand and German on the other. The chief differences between the Dutch and Flemish are those of political boundaries, customs, and religion, rather than of language or physique. Hollander, Netherlander, and Belgian are names of nationalities and not of races. Holland-Dutch is a term vulgarly used in America to distinguish Dutch from German, while Pennsylvania Dutch is a name wrongly given to the old Pennsylvania German families.

Dutch and Flemish.

DUTCH.

Etymologically Dutch is simply the German "Teutsch"—that is, "Teuton"—and, therefore, might be used as a generic term to include all Germans. But in scientific usage the term is now limited to the people of Low German descent living in the Rhine delta. Germans themselves never extend the word "Deutsch" to the Netherlands. The Dutch or Netherlandish language is derived from Old Saxon, a division of the long extinct Old Low German. The word "Dutch" is sometimes wrongly used, especially in the United States, to mean the German language in all its forms.

Dutch is the literary and national language of Holland; it is also the language of the Dutch colonists in South Africa (Boers), and in the East and West Indies. Besides Dutch, there are other dialects of Low German origin used in Holland: Frisian, Saxon, Friso-Saxon, and Friso-Frankish. Frisian is said to have been the language of the early Teutonic people throughout Holland. It had a literature of its own in the fourteenth century, but has been pressed upon by the Saxon and Frankish until it exists today only as a patois in the province of Friesland and on some of the islands of the coast. Saxon and Friso-Saxon are spoken throughout the eastern and southeastern part of Holland. Friso-Frankish is spoken in Zeeland—that is, the island province north of Belgium, and in the western part of Holland. Dutch is spoken in the provinces of North and South Holland.

Physically, the northern Dutch are for the most part long-headed, oval faced, tallish, and blond. The Frisians also are good examples of this type. Southward in the western part of Holland there is more and more of an admixture of a round-headed brunette element, shorter and stouter than the northern type, which is thought to be descended from the ancient "Alpine" race, with more or less Teutonic admixture. Three-fifths of the people of Holland are Protestants; most of the remainder are Catholics. There are about 100,000 Jews in Holland. In social customs the Dutch show greater affinity to the English than to the German. They have been called the Englishmen of the mainland. Like the English, the Dutch have been great colonizers.

Holland is an independent kingdom. It is now called the Netherlands, a term formerly given to the lowland country comprising both Holland and Belgium. It is one of the smallest countries of Europe, having a superficial area of only 12,000 square miles. Its ethnographical boundaries coincide with its topographical formation: the Frieslanders hold the alluvial plains, the Saxons are confined to sandy tracts, while the lowlands of the delta of the Rhine have a population mixed in origin. The Dutch population of the world has been variously estimated at from 4,000,000 to 6,300,000. The population of Holland itself is 6,000,000, or 1,000,000 less than that of Belgium, and a third more than that of Ireland. Rudler and Chisholm estimate 71 per cent of the population to be Dutch, 14 per cent Frisian, 13 per cent Flemish, and 2 per cent other Low German. There are about 400,000 Boers in South Africa and 75,000 Dutch colonists in the East and West Indies. In Immigration Bureau statistics Dutch and Flemish are counted together. In 1907 there were 6,637 immigrants from Holland, 6,456 of whom are classed as Dutch and Flemish. The rate of Dutch immigration from Holland in that year was but a little over 1 per 1,000 of the population.

FLEMISH.

Philologists differ as to the position of Flemish, linguistically. Some consider it to be a branch of Old Low German, closely akin to Dutch, if not identical with it; others place it as a dialect of Dutch and say that it is now nearly extinct; while still others consider it to be a dialect of equal rank with Frisian and Saxon, but distinct from Dutch. The literary language of the Flemish people is now Dutch.

Physically the Flemish are of the prevailing Dutch type—tallish, blond, and round-faced—the type so often portrayed by Rubens. The Flemish occupy the northern and western provinces of Belgium and the northeastern part of France bordering on Flanders. There are over 3,000,000 in Belgium, 750,000 in Holland, and 200,000 in the northern part of France, making a total of over 4,000,000 Flemish in Europe—that is, about equal to the number of Dutch in Holland.

BELGIAN.

The term Belgian simply means a native or inhabitant of the Kingdom of Belgium. It has no significance as to physical race or language. The Belgian nation is represented by two chief linguistic stocks, a Teutonic (Flemish) which occupies the plains and the coast lands, and a French (Walloon) which occupies the uplands (see these). The two peoples also differ in industries. The Flemings are characteristically tenant farmers; the Walloons are small proprietary farmers, miners, and manufacturers.

Belgium ranks eighteenth in superficial area and eighth in population amongst European countries. It is the most densely populated country in Europe, having a population of over 7,000,000 in an area of 11,300 square miles; that is, of about 600 to the square mile. The Kingdom is not evenly populated, the Flemish provinces being much more densely settled than the Walloon. Of the total number, 42 per cent speak Flemish only and 38 per cent French only, while 12 per cent speak both Flemish and French, and 6 per cent speak Flemish, French, and German. Both French and Flemish are official languages. All public documents are printed in both. Both are taught in the schools. At the University of Ghent the professors lecture in both French and Flemish. The Belgians are for the most part Catholics.

Despite its density of population Belgium is an exception amongst European countries in that it has more immigration than emigration. About 90 per cent of this movement is to and from Holland, France, and Germany. Only an insignificant number come to America, less than 1 per 1,000 of the population.

In 1907 there were 4,162 emigrants from Belgium to the United States, of whom 2,929 are reported by the Bureau of Immigration as Dutch and Flemish. In number of immigrants the Dutch and Flemish taken together stand twenty-first down the list—that is, above the French, but far below all the principal immigrant races or peoples. They go mostly to Michigan, Illinois, New York, and New Jersey.

E.

EASTERN or **ORIENTAL** race. (See *Caucasian.*)

EAST-INDIAN. Any native of the East Indies. The latter is a very broad and vague term which has come down from the time of Columbus, and embraces the vast populations of India, Farther India, and Malaysia; that is, of all the countries sotuh of the Chinese Empire and lying between the Indus on the west and the island of New Guinea on the east. The last-named island falls to the domain, therefore, of the Pacific Islanders (see). Filipinos (see) are Malayan, and therefore East Indian, as thus defined, but are not counted in immigration statistics.

Ethnologically the term "East Indian" has no meaning, although its convenience has perhaps justified its use while immigration to the United States from this part of the world was very small. Geographically it comprises races of the most diverse culture, from the dwarf Negrito of the Philippines, perhaps the lowest race of mankind in degree of civilization, to the European-like Hindu, who uses the Aryan speech (see) and has a civilization older than our own. All the five great races or divisions of mankind, with the exception of the American Indian, are found represented in the East Indies. The great Caucasian population of India has just been mentioned. The inhabitants of Indo-China, Burma, and Siam are Mongolian. Those of the Malay Peninsula and Archipelago are Malay, with a small remnant of a true Ethiopian or black race, the Negritos, scattered here and there. The Bureau of Immigration puts all East Indians into the "Mongolic" grand division.

The population of the four great races found in the East Indies, with the exception of the black race, is immense, certainly over 350,000,000, forming with that of China about half the population of the entire earth. Of all the East Indians, nearly six-sevenths are natives of India, and will claim chief attention here as a probable factor in future immigration. The peoples farther east have shown little tendency to emigrate. Of these, the densest population is that of Java, numbering nearly 30,000,000. Although the oldest in Malay civilization, this people has neither the physical nor the mental energy of its kinsmen, the Filipinos, and, unlike the Hindus, it has shown little or no tendency to emigrate to other countries. The Indo-Chinese of the mainland, like the Malays, have less energy and enterprise than the true Chinese and do not migrate. Their country is not so densely populated. Practically none of these populations, with the exception of the Filipinos, are Christian or greatly influenced by western civilization.

Of the 294,000,000 people of India, including Burma, it is unnecessary in this work to especially consider the non-Aryan multitudes, a population nearly as large as that of the United States. The dark Dravidian element is much the largest of these, numbering 60,000,000. Three-fourths of India, however, is, like ourselves, Aryan—(220,000,000) a population nearly two-thirds as great as that of all Europe. It is this Aryan population of northern India that is generally called Hindu, although the term also applies to a religion or to the people having a certain social organization based upon Brahmanism. (See *Hindu.*) One of the many "Hindu" tongues is Hindi, spoken, with its dialects, by about 100,000,000 persons. About 3,000,000 of these are Christians.

The Caucasian features of the northern Hindus are easily remarked, although they are generally dark. They are often tall, although not so strong, energetic, and aggressive as the Chinese in competition with Europeans. Some have been educated in English schools or colleges in India. All are keen in trade, making good merchants, and perhaps identify themselves with western civilization to a greater degree than do the Chinese.

The population of India is one of the densest of the globe. The people must emigrate or die by the million in the famines that periodically reduce their numbers. The protection of the rest of the world against an Indian flood of migration is their poverty, their inability to provide the cost of transportation, and their lack of initiative.

India has sent out about 20,000 "coolies" or laborers annually in recent years, largely to British colonies in the West Indies and South Africa; in other words, about as large an emigration as that of Russians, Scotch, or

Lithuanians to the United States. A few have been coming recently to British Columbia and the western coast of the United States. In 1908 the total "East Indian" immigration to the United States was 1,700, of whom 1,000 came direct from India and about 700 from Canada. In the twelve years 1899–1910, only 5,786 were admitted. Nearly all went to the States of California and Washington.

EGYPTIAN. In an ethnographical sense, the ancient race or people of Egypt, best represented to-day by the Copts or Fellahs, although those are generally of mixed stock. In a political sense, any native of Egypt. In the present population of Egypt, about 10,000,000, there are many racial elements, mostly Hamitic (Fellahin and Copts) and Semitic (Arabs and Bedouins). The Christian Copts number perhaps 800,000, and still preserve a liturgical form of the ancient Egyptian language. Practically all the remaining population is Mohammedan, including the larger section known as the Fellahin or laborers, who have adopted the Arabic language. Their number has been variously estimated at from 1,000,000 to 5,000,000. Very few Egyptians have found their way to America. (See *Semitic-Hamitic.*)

ENGLISH or **ANGLO-SAXON**; inaccurately **BRITISH**. The principal race or people of England; the westernmost European branch of the Teutonic stock; the race that first spoke the English language.

Of course there is no necessity in this dictionary for discussion of a subject so well understood by all as the character, social institutions, and other qualities of the English as an immigrant people. It may be assumed that all Americans understand the race which has given us our language and laws and political institutions. Yet there may be some doubt as to the ethnical position of the English—as to which of the present components of the mixed English nation are to be considered as unassimilated immigrant elements and which as truly English. If it can be said, as some claim, that the new race now being formed in America is already more German than English, perhaps even more Irish than English, the student of races will realize that clear distinctions need be drawn in the case of so composite a race as that in England. In the case, for instance, of an immigrant from England who comes of Irish or Scotch descent, how long a residence of his ancestry in England entitles him to be called English? The question goes deeper than this, namely, to the determination of what constitutes a race in ethnology. It is perhaps convenient to consider, in discussing a race so well known as the English, the definition and classification of races upon which this dictionary proceeds.

As explained in the Introductory (see), race is determined by language in such phrases as "the races of Europe," but by physical qualities, such as color, hair, and shape of head, when we speak of "the five great races" or grand divisions of mankind. In either case the attempt is made to bring into a common class all who have the same inheritance. But the term "race" is sometimes used in other senses. Thus we may reach wider and wider "races," each including the preceding, as when we speak of the English race, the Teutonic race, the Aryan or Indo-European race, the Caucasian race, and, finally, the human race. Not only is there this popular looseness in the use of the word, but its scientific acceptation in the most exact of studies, namely, in national census taking, is also variable. While in some European censuses race is determined by the mother tongue of the individual, in other countries it is determined by the "language of converse" or "customary language." It is evident that an Irish family that has lived for generations in England would be called Irish by the first test,

English by the second. But how long a residence in England will entitle an Irishman, or a Scotchman, or a French Huguenot, or one of Norman French stock, to be called English if the mother tongue is the test? Evidently this phrase must be interpreted to mean the ancestral or racial language in dealing with a stock which has kept itself quite pure in descent. But since the greater part of the English population of to-day is of mixed origin, a census may adopt the arbitrary rule that the paternal line only shall determine the race, or, what is evidently more difficult and more scientific, it may name the mixed races as such, or consider the race to be determined by the preponderating element in the mixture.

Since all this is merely a matter of definition, so far as consistency in the present dictionary is concerned, the following principles and definitions may be given as those adopted and presumably scientific. In the narrow sense, the race of an immigrant is determined by ancestral language, as above indicated. The historical limit which determines the transition from one race into another as thus defined varies with different races. It will be assumed in this article that the English race is practically one thousand years old, since the essential elements composing it were welded before or soon after the Norman invasion.

Still other definitions will conduce to clearness of thinking. Not only is a distinction to be made between race and nationality, but the terms "English people," "English stock," "English-speaking people," and, consequently, "English language" need definition also. The English nationality includes all native and naturalized citizens of England. It therefore includes members of other races besides Englishmen in the ethnical sense. The term "Englishman" may mean merely one of English nationality. The "English stock" is a loose expression for the English race. A stock in ethnology generally includes several races. The "English-speaking people," as is evident, includes all individuals in all parts of the world who speak the English language. The term "English language" is more capable of exact definition than all the foregoing, for, philologically, it is impossible to confuse it with any other. It is only as old as the English race. The expression "English people" is a loose one. By definition in this dictionary it is the equivalent of the term "the English race," which embraces the English in America; it means also the people of the particular country or nationality, England. "Briton" is a name applied to the ancient race of England, by some supposed to have been of Celtic origin. The word is used at times to mean any native of Great Britain. In this sense it includes different races, as English, Irish, and Welsh. It, or rather "North Briton," is the term by which the Lowland Scotch prefer to be called instead of English. In this dictionary they will be called "Scotch" (see). "British" is a term of nationality rather than of race. It also means the Celtic language spoken by the ancient Britons.

Linguistically, the English are Teutons. Although the English language is very composite, the grammar and the spoken language are still characteristically Anglo-Saxon, that is, Low German, notwithstanding that it has lost many of its inflections. English is closely related to the dialects still spoken in Flanders, in the Netherlands, and on the northern shores of Germany. It is to-day the language of about 126,000,000 individuals living under a score of different governments, among which are two of the greatest nations of the world, the British Empire and the United States of America. No other Indo-European tongue is spoken by so many persons. Russian ranks next with 90,000,000, then German with 76,000,000, Spanish with 50,000,000, French with 46,000,000, and Italian with 33,500,000 (Hickmann).

Physically, as well as linguistically, the English are a very composite product. The prevailing English type is tall, long-headed, and generally blond, although, as Beddoe has pointed out, there is no one type characteristic of all England. He finds what he calls Anglo-Scandinavians and Anglo-Saxons, both Teutonic in type, located in the northern, the eastern, and the southern parts of England; a short, darker type of marked "Celtic" character in the western part, bordering on Wales, and a still darker Celtic type, the Cornish, (see) in Cornwall. The Lowland Scotch (see Scotch), the people living south of the southern firths of Forth and Clyde and on the eastern side of Scotland, are said to be nearly identical in racial character and closely related in their dialect to the people of the northern part of England. It has been variously estimated that the English race is from one-fifth to one-half Scandinavian, if not, in fact, more Scandinavian than Anglo-Saxon. Freeman says "when we set foot on the shores of Scandinavia and northern Germany, we are simply revisiting our ancestral home."

In geographical distribution the English are more widely dispersed than any other people, being found in all parts of the world. No exact figures can be given as to the number of the English. The population of England is about 31,000,000. According to the Canadian census of 1901 there were in Canada 1,260,899 persons of English race or origin. And, as is well known, the English form no small part of the population of the United States.

The English hold high rank as an emigrating and colonizing people. They, with the Irish, Scotch, Germans, and Scandinavians, gave the distinctive character to immigration to the United States prior to 1882. These races from northwestern Europe then formed nearly 90 per cent of the total immigration from Europe. Since then there has been a rapid decrease in the immigration of the Celto-Teutonic peoples, but a still more rapid increase in that from the countries of southeastern Europe, comprising especially Italy, Austria-Hungary, Russia, and Greece. In 1902 the latter countries furnished nearly 80 per cent of our European immigration, while that from northwestern Europe fell to 22 per cent. This change of ratio is not due so much to the falling off of three-fourths of the immigration from northwestern Europe as to the rapid increase in that from southeastern Europe, an increase of nearly fivefold in twenty years, and of over twentyfold in twenty-five years, that is, to 1907.

The United States was until 1900 the favored destination of British emigrants, the total number coming here annually from the United Kingdom being greater than of those going to all other countries combined; but in 1905 the curve of immigration to British North America rose and passed that for the United States. During the twenty years 1883–1903, British emigration to South Africa, Australia, and Canada was about equally divided, seldom rising above 20,000 per year to each, and never above 40,000. For some years past Australasia and South Africa have attracted only about 10,000 to 15,000 annually.

In 1909 there were 39,021 English immigrants to the United States, of whom 26,203 came from the United Kingdom and 10,708 from British North America. In absolute numbers of immigrants the English in 1907 held eighth place down the list of immigrant races and peoples, with a total of 51,126. Their rate of movement is very low, only a little over 1 per 1,000 of the population of England, which is but one-sixth that of the Irish and one-fifteenth that of the Slovak or of the Hebrew. As compared with these races, future immigration from England must relatively increase. The population of the smaller races is so far below that of the English that they can not long continue coming at the present rate.

The English, like the Irish and the Germans, are found in all parts of the United States. The States to which they went in largest numbers in 1909 are: New York (10,439), Massachusetts (4,379), Pennsylvania (2,945), California (2,438), Illinois (2,048).

ESKIMO. The northernmost race or people of America, held to belong to the American race by most American writers, but to the Mongolian by many others. (See these terms.) It differs much in important respects from either of these races, combining characteristics of both. The difficult questions involved need no discussion here. It is but rarely that one of this race has been brought to the United States. The Aleuts of the Bering Sea region resemble Mongolians more than do the Eastern Eskimos, in that they are short-headed. They speak, however, an Eskimo dialect unrelated to any Mongolian tongue. The Eskimo population is variously estimated at from 20,000 to 40,000.

ESTH or **ESTHONIAN.** A division of the Western Finns. (See *Finnish.*)

ETHIOPIAN. A word used in different senses to designate: (1) the entire Negro race (see), (2) a language spoken by a Semitic people of Abyssinia, and (3) the East African Hamites. (See *Semitic-Hamitic.*)

EURAFRICAN. Same as **Caucasian** (see).

EUROPEAN race. A term generally used as equivalent to Caucasian (see). But "*Homo Europæus*" is the name applied by recent writers, following Lapouge, to the tall, blond, and long-headed or "Northern" race of Europe distinguished generally from the "Alpine" and "Mediterranean" races of central and southern Europe. It is also called the "Aryan" race by Lapouge, but includes little more than the Teutonic and Celtic divisions of the Aryans as defined in this dictionary. (See these terms and Introductory.)

EUSKARIC stock. A linguistic division of the Caucasian race at present represented by only the Basques (see) of Spain and France. Their language is of the agglutinative type, the only non-Aryan language of western Europe.

EVREMEISETI. A division of the Western Finns. (See *Finnish.*)

F.

FELLAH. A name given to the peasant class of Egyptians. (See *Egyptian* and *Semitic-Hamitic.*)

FILIPINO or **PHILIPPINE ISLANDER.** A geographical rather than an ethnographical term, meaning any native of the Philippine Islands. It is included, therefore, in the terms "East Indian" and "Mongolic Division," as used by the Bureau of Immigration (see these terms). Filipinos of pure blood are all Malay (called by Keane "Oceanic Mongol"), with the exception of the Negritos and possibly the doubtful "Indonesians."

But few words can be given to them in this dictionary, for they are not considered legally as immigrants upon coming to the United States. The tendency among recent ethnologists in the Philippines is to consider that the pagan Indonesians of the interior are not an "aberrant Caucasian stock," as held by prominent ethnologists, but represent an earlier Primitive Malayan wave of migration. They show a close relationship physically, and especially in language, to the eight so-called "Christian" peoples who constitute nine-tenths of the population

(7,600,000) of the islands. These are, in the order of their numerical importance: The Visayan or Bisayan, the Tagalog, the Ilocano, the Bicol or Vicol, the Pangasinan, the Pampangan, the Cagayan, and the Zambalan. Of these, the Tagalogs, who dwell in the provinces about Manila, are decidedly the most prominent politically.

The Moros (cf. Moors of Spain), that is, the Mohammedans of the Sulu and other southern islands, are closely related to the Christian peoples ethnically, but are less in sympathy with European civilization. They stand seventh in population among Philippine peoples. The Igorots of the north stand next numerically. They are the best-known representatives of the Primitive Malayan stock, still head-hunters and non-Christian for the most part, but settled agriculturists. Another well-known ethnical division is the dwarf Negro stock known as "Negrito," numbering now only 24,000. This is a disappearing remnant of one of the earliest and lowest races of mankind and can be traced throughout Malaysia as far east as the somewhat similar Paupans of New Guinea and as far west as the Andaman Islanders, in the Bay of Bengal. There are many mestizos, especially of Tagalog-Chinese and of Tagalog-Spanish ancestry. The Chinese form an important element of the urban population, especially in Manila.

The United States immigration and Chinese-exclusion laws are applied to aliens entering the Philippines. Although Filipinos are not legally citizens of the United States, they are not counted as immigrants upon coming to this country. Chinese, however, coming from the Philippines to the United States are subject to the usual restrictions. Modern Filipinos are not known as an emigrating people. Few come to the United States except as protégés of the Government.

FINNIC, FINNO-HUNGARIAN, FINNO-UGRIC, UGRO-FINNIC, UGRIAN. The language of the Finns, using this word in the wider sense to include the Magyars and, sometimes, the Bulgarians. (See *Finnish*, *Ural-Altaic*, and *Ugro-Finnic*.)

FINNISH. Best defined for the purposes of this work from a linguistic point of view in a narrow sense as the race or people of Finno-Tataric stock which now constitutes the chief population of Finland and embraces also the related peoples of northwestern Russia, exclusive of the Lapps (see). This group may be also called the "Finns Proper" or "Western Finns," and includes the Esths, Livs, Vots, Veps, Tavastians, and Karelians, together with the Ijores and Chudes, subbranches of the last named. The Karelians extend nearly to the center of Russia and are called by some "Eastern Finns." It would appear more significant to reserve this latter name to designate the Ugro-Finnic peoples living in Eastern Russia and in Asia. Although speaking languages similar to the Western Finns or Suomi, they are widely different from the latter in blood, and to a great extent in civilization. The Western and Eastern Finns are more unlike than the North and South Italians, who are, for a similar reason, counted separately by the Bureau of Immigration.

Finnish immigration has been larger in recent years than that of most other races having so small a population. It is practically confined to the Western Finns or Finns proper. These are Caucasian rather than Mongolian in appearance, while the Eastern or Volga Finns, who are not known to come as yet to America, show distinctly their Asiatic origin. They are divided from the Finns proper by a broad band of Great Russians which extends through Central Russia from north to south. The Lapps and Samoyeds, another very different stock, may be called the "Northern Finns."

The term "Finn" or "Finnic" is equivalent to "Ugro-Finnic" (see) when employed in a still wider sense to include all thus far mentioned and in addition the Magyars and possibly the Bulgarians (see). The former are linguistically Ugro-Finnic; the latter were so originally. The word "Finnic" is even used at times to designate the entire Finno-Tataric division of the Sibiric branch of the Mongolian race. It then includes the Turks (see). Even the Japanese, Manchus, and Kalmuks belong to coordinate stocks. (See *Ural-Altaic* for the relations of all Mongolian languages.)

Finally the term Finns is used in a fourth sense, narrowest of all, to designate only the Finns of Finland; that is, little more than the Tavastians, considering the Esths and Livs, for instance, as distinct races. It is evidently necessary to analyze further this complex subject.

The Eastern Finns number about 2,000,000; the Northern Finns, or Lapps and Samoyeds, only 17,000; the Western Finns, or Finns proper, nearly 4,000,000. Of the last named, 2,350,000 live in Finland. Certain districts in the western part of Finland are occupied almost entirely by the blondest of Teutons, Swedes, who number not less than 350,000. The total population of the country is about 2,850,000. Until 1809 Finland was a part of Sweden, and before the dawn of history the Finns and Swedes were no doubt intermingling. This will account in part for the prevailing blondness and European cast of countenance amongst the Finns, which has led the Bureau of Immigration to put them into the "Teutonic division" of races. But the entire Ugro-Finnic stock seems to have been, in origin, lighter in color than most other Mongolians, perhaps as a result of their northern residence. Formerly they were taken out of the Mongolian grand division by certain ethnologists and put into a separate division of "allophylian whites." Whatever their original stock, the Finns of Finland are to-day the most truly European of any race possessing a Mongolic speech, and in some respects their institutions are abreast of any in Europe.

Other branches of the Ugro-Finnic stock are classified as below in the census of the Russian Empire for 1897. Since this census does not cover Finland, the first item in the table is taken from the census of Finland for 1900. (See article *Russian* for additional statistics.)

Finnic population of the Russian Empire, 1897.

Branches.	In Europe.	In Asia.	Total.	Branches.	In Europe.	In Asia.	Total.
Total	5,782,127	88,850	5,870,977	Eastern Finns—Con.			
Western Finns	3,739,947	6,513	3,746,460	Mordvinian	989,959	33,882	1,023,841
In Finland[a]	2,352,990	....	2,352,990	Votyak	420,673	297	420,970
Finnish	141,184	1,884	143,068	Permyak	103,347	1,344	104,691
Karelian	208,083	18	208,101	Zyrian	144,369	9,249	153,618
Esth	998,096	4,606	1,002,702	Vogul	2,850	4,801	7,651
Ijore	13,774	....	13,774	Ostyak	....	19,663	19,663
Chude	25,820	5	25,825	Northern Finns	6,656	11,988	18,644
Eastern Finns	2,035,524	70,349	2,105,873	Lapp	1,812	....	1,812
Cheremiss	374,326	1,113	375,439	Samoyed	3,940	11,931	15,871
				Magyar	904	57	961

[a] Census of Finland for 1900. Subdivisions of Finns in Finland not given.

WESTERN FINNS.

Only brief additional data may be given concerning the above-mentioned and other divisions of the Ugro-Finns. Chude is an old name once applied to all Finns by the Russians. The census limits the name to those locally called "Chotscher" or "Kaivan," who speak a Karelian dialect. They live in one of the two Karelian provinces, Olonetz; that is, northeast of St. Petersburg. The Veps are northern Chudes; the Vots, southern Chudes. The largest Karelian population is found in Tver province, southeast of St. Petersburg. The Karelians are the easternmost branch of the Finns proper, and show perhaps more trace of an Asiatic origin. They are mainly agriculturists. The Ijores, on the contrary, are found mainly in the city of St. Petersburg. They are descendants of the Ingers, but no longer a pure Tavastian stock, and therefore not good types of the Western Finns. Yet they apparently constitute the group called "Finns" in the Russian census, as the latter live mostly in St. Petersburg.

The Finns of Finland are mainly Tavastians, or Hemes, and Savolaks. The Kwaenes extend farther north and are in a transitional stage between the more cultured Finns toward the south and the Lapps on the north. The Esths and Livs do not differ much from the Finns of Finland in stock. They live south of the Gulf of Finland and along the Baltic, forming about 90 per cent of the population of Esthonia and 40 per cent of that of Livonia. The extinct Krevs formerly lived near these in Courland, in Esthonia, and especially in Livonia. The agglutinative language of the Finns is modified by the radically different Aryan speech of the Letts and Lithuanians (see), who adjoin them on the south. In the province of Pskof they speak a dialect called the "Verros." Other names given to certain Baltic or Western Finns are the Lopari, the Evremeiseti, the Savakoti, and the Izhora (Ijores) or Ingers. In religion nearly all the Western Finns are Lutherans.

EASTERN FINNS.

Most of the Eastern Finns live in the middle Volga region of Eastern Russia. Those farthest west are the Cheremisses, in Viatka and Kazan provinces. Not long ago they were nomadic. Though nominally Orthodox, their religion is corrupted with Tatar Mohammedanism and even Mongolian Shamanism. The Chuvashes, adjoining the Cheremisses on the north and the Kazan Tatars on the east, have some of the characteristics of both. Many of them speak Türki, the Tatar tongue. They are thought by some to be a branch of the Mordvinians, but are counted in the Russian census as Tatars (see).

The Mordvinians form the largest division of the Eastern Finns, numbering over 1,000,000. They are most numerous farther down the Volga basin, in the provinces of Samara, Simbirsk, Penza, and Saratov, reaching to within one province of the Caspian Sea. They are also widely scattered through the Great Russian and Tatar populations of other provinces, and are often Russified in language and customs. The Erzu and Mokcha are two dialects of the Mordvinian.

The Votyaks, Permyaks, and Zyrians are the northernmost of the Eastern Finns in Europe. The last named extend to the Samoyed country on the Arctic. Most of the Voguls and all the Ostyaks, who are nomads, live in Siberia. These two peoples, small in number, may be called the Ugric division of the Ugro-Finnic stock (see). They are nearly as Asiatic and primitive in their manner of life as are the stunted Samoyeds and Lapps of the frozen ocean. Finally, the Bessermans are a small group of Mohammedans distinguishable only by their religion from the Votyaks, among whom they live, but related to the Voguls.

Finnish emigrants to the United States are all, so far as known, Western or true Finns. Immigration has been rapid in recent years. In the thirteen years from 1893 to 1905 Finland lost 128,600 by emigration. Nearly all of these came to America—in 1905, all but 37. In the twelve years 1899–1910, 151,774 Finnish immigrants were admitted to the United States, the race ranking fourteenth in that regard among all races or peoples. The rate per 1,000 of the population of Western Finns arriving per year (4 in 1907) is only half that of the Italians, Irish, or Norwegians, and less than one-fourth that of the Hebrews or Slovaks. During the twelve years mentioned, 109,229 of the Finnish immigrants admitted were destined to four States as follows: Michigan, 40,915; Massachusetts, 25,153; Minnesota, 22,799; New York, 20,362. It will be seen that about 27 per cent of the Finns went to Michigan and 15 per cent to Minnesota, which States received, respectively, only 2.4 and 1.9 per cent of all immigrants during the period.

FINNO-TATARIC or **FINNO-TURKIC PEOPLES.** A term sometimes used to embrace the Finnic and Tataric (see) groups of the Siberic stock of the Mongolian race. To be defined as that group of Mongolian races speaking the Ural-Altaic languages (see).

FLEMISH. (See *Dutch and Flemish.*)

FLORENTINE. Counted in immigration statistics as South Italian. (See *Italian.*)

FRANKISH or **FRANCONIAN.** (See *German* and *Dutch and Flemish.*)

FRENCH. The principal race or people of France; the northern branch of the Romance-speaking peoples, including, besides the French of France, the French Belgians, the French Swiss, the French of Alsace-Lorraine (now a part of Germany), and the French Canadians of the New World. As thus defined the French constitute about 93 per cent of the population of France, nearly one-half that of Belgium, about one-fourth that of Switzerland, and nearly one-third that of Canada. According to the census of 1900 there were 395,000 Canadian-born French persons in the United States, and 436,000 native-born persons one or both of whose parents were Canadian-born French. The French is not a well-defined race ethnologically, being a mixture of the three chief prehistoric races of Europe, the broad-headed "Alpine" or "Celtic" element predominating. Linguistically French belongs to the Romance or Italic group of the Aryan family. The French are put into the "Keltic division" by the Bureau of Immigration, while they are usually classified with the Romanic peoples.

The **French Belgians** are found mainly in the southeastern provinces of Belgium. (See article *Dutch and Flemish.*) They speak a dialect called the "Walloon." They are supposed to be descended from the Belgae of Cæsar, are tall and long-faced, and resemble the French of Normandy. The **French Swiss** constitute the greater part of the inhabitants of the western cantons of Switzerland. They belong to the broad-headed Alpine race, are brunette, and much shorter in stature than the French Belgians. **French Canadian** (see) is an expression used to designate the inhabitants of Canada, especially those of the province of Quebec, who are descendants of the French. They speak a dialect which possesses many peculiarities developed on Canadian soil. Their blood has been more or less mixed with that of the English-speaking Canadians and has had some infusion of the Indian, though to a much less degree than is generally supposed.

The term "French language" may be used in a broad or generic sense to

French.

include not only the modern literary French, but all the dialects of Old French still in use, as the Walloon, the Provençal, and the Catalan. In a narrower or restricted sense it means the "langue d'oil," which is now the literary as well as the general and official language of France. Old French had two distinct and equally important dialects—the "langue d'oil," spoken north of the Loire and eastward to Berne, Switzerland, and the "langue d'oc," in the south. The former is now spoken by about 22,500,000 persons in France. It is one of the two official languages of Belgium, Switzerland, and Canada. It is the diplomatic language of many countries. Owing to its clearness and precision it is the language par excellence of science and criticism. One of its dialects, the Walloon, is still used familiarly by about 3,000,000 persons living in Belgium and the northeastern part of France. This is especially characterized by a large number of Celtic and German elements. Though it once had a literature of its own, it is now assuming the character of a patois.

The Provençal, often called the "langue d'oc," is the native language of the southern half of France. With the closely related dialects, such as the Gascon, Limousin, Auvergnat, and Savoisin, it is spoken by over 12,500,000 persons in southern France and by several hundred thousand in Switzerland and Italy. The Catalan dialect, spoken on both sides of the Catalonian border, occupies a place between Provençal and Castilian. (See *Spanish.*)

Physically the French are not a homogeneous race. There has been much blending of racial elements even within historic times. At the present time France presents three distinct ethnic types, whose persistence depends in part on their geographical location and in part on more recent intrusions. France appears to have been once occupied quite generally by a broad-headed, rather brunette ("Alpine") race which still characterizes the central part of the country, especially among the Auvergnats, and is found in considerable numbers in Brittany among the Bretons (see). It is estimated by Brinton that this Alpine element forms fully three-fifths of the French race. A tall, long-headed, Teutonic type predominates in the northeastern part of France, especially in Normandy. Many of the inhabitants of this region are blond. In fact, it is said that northern France is more Teutonic than is southern Germany. (See *German.*) In the most southern part of France, especially along the Mediterranean coast, the inhabitants are of the long-headed brunette or "Mediterranean" type. These three types are fairly well amalgamated in the great cities of France into what is generally recognized as the typical Frenchman. His ethnic position is that of an intermediate between the northern and the southern races. The Basques (see) of southwestern France seem to be a peculiar modification of the Alpine race of central France.

France is thus seen to present great diversities in language and physique. It is the only place on the Continent where a Celtic tongue is spoken—the Breton. With Spain, it is the habitat of the Basques, who speak a non-Aryan tongue.

France has a population of 38,500,000. French, using the term in the broad sense, is spoken throughout France, except in four small districts—the western part of Brittany, occupied by the Bretons (1,350,000); a Flemish section (230,000) on the Belgian border; the extreme southwestern corner, occupied by Basques (150,000), and a district occcupied by Italians (330,000) on the Italian border. Outside of France French populations are found in Belgium (nearly 3,000,000), in Germany (200,000), in Switzerland (730,000), and in the northwestern part of Italy (80,000). The total French population of Europe is, therefore, about 39,000,000. It is estimated that 4,000,000 more are found in Canada, the United States, and the Antilles. According to the United States census of 1900 there were in this country 104,197 persons born in France, and 395,066 French persons who were born in Canada.

The Breton immigrants from western France and the Basque immigrants from the southwestern part are counted for convenience as French in immigration statistics. During the twelve years 1899–1910, the total French immigration to the United States from all sources was 115,783, the race ranking eighteenth in point of numbers during that period. Even the immigration of Finns or Roumanians exceeded the immigration from France in 1907. The rate of immigration from this country is low, about 2 per 10,000 of its population. This rate is surpassed by that of all important immigrant races or peoples, excepting the Great Russians, by whom it is equaled. The chief destinations of French immigrants in 1909 were Massachusetts (4,383), New York (4,215), New Hampshire (2,377), and Rhode Island (1,559).

FRENCH CANADIAN. That section of the French race or people which lives in Canada. According to the Canadian census of 1901 there were 1,649,371 persons of French race or origin in the Dominion, and of these 1,322,115 lived in the province of Quebec, where they constitute a large majority of the population. (See *French* for general description.) It need only be further said here that the French language as spoken in Canada has become considerably modified during the two hundred years or more of its exile. There is also some slight physical change going on in the race, although it is not widely intermingled with Indian blood, as some misinformed persons think. The French Canadians have been sending a large contingent to the States for a long period, although, as explained in the article on French, a record of this immigration is not available. French Canadians form an important part of the population in many New England towns. In 1884 Catholic statistics showed 326,000 to be living in New England. According to the census of 1890 there were 302,496 Canadian-born French persons in the United States and in 1900 the number had increased to 395,066. (See *Canadian.*)

FRISIAN. A name given to a Low German people living in Friesland, Holland, and in the adjacent islands. (See *Dutch* and *German.*)

FRIULAN or **FURLAN.** A Rhæto-Romansh (see) people living northeast of the Italians.

G.

GAELIC. (See *Celtic*, *Irish*, and *Scotch.*)

GAGAOUS. A name given by Bulgarians to the mongrel people of the coast of the Black Sea. (See *Bulgarian.*)

GALICIAN. Has two meanings: (1) Generally any native of Galicia, a province in Austria, north of Hungary, and therefore of any race or people found there, but generally Ruthenian (see); (2) a native of Galicia in northwestern Spain or of northern Portugal. The latter speak a Portuguese dialect and are also called "Gallegos." (See *Spanish* and *Portuguese.*)

GALLEGO. Same as the **Galician** (see) of northern Portugal. (Also see *Spanish.*)

GASCON. A native of Gascony, the southwestern part of France. (See *French.*)

GEG. A name applied to the northern Albanians (see) as distinguished from the southern Albanians or Tosks.

GENOVESE. Counted in immigration statistics as South Italian. (See *Italian.*)

GEORGIAN. In a broad sense the Kartvelian or Southern Division of the Caucasus peoples (see), including the Georgians proper, the Mingrelians, the Imeretians, and the Svanetians. All these groups speak non-Aryan languages more or less distantly related. They belong to the Caucasian race, although there is some admixture with Mongolian elements. They number about 1,150,000.

The Georgians proper or Grusians are the best known of these peoples. They live in Transcaucasia and are renowned for their physical beauty. They are tall, broad-headed, and have black hair. Their women, like those of the Circassians (see), are prized as slaves and members of harems in Turkey and Egypt. Georgians do not appear by name in immigration statistics, and if they come at all are counted among "Other peoples."

GERMAN (incorrectly **Dutch**). The race or people whose mother tongue is the German language in the narrower sense of the word; that is, excluding the Dutch, Flemish, English, and Scandinavian divisions of the Germanic or Teutonic group of languages, but including the German dialects found in all other countries, as in Austria and Switzerland; the race which uses the modern literary German. Although this is the definition that tacitly underlies all emigration and immigration statistics and censuses of races as taken in various countries, the "race" so defined is a somewhat arbitrary or artificial division of mankind. Like many of the so-called "races" of Europe, it is not a unity from a physical point of view. Nor will it even stand the linguistic test adopted in this dictionary. (See Introductory and *English.*) For, if we make the mother tongue the test, the Dutch and the Flemish are as much German as are other Frankish or Saxon populations. Merely the historical or political accident that Holland and Belgium have established by law another literary standard than that of Germany leads to their being considered non-German in race.

Some German scholars have no doubt been influenced by pan-Teutonism—that is, the ideal for a common bond of sympathy, if not of political unity, among all Teutonic peoples—to overstate the linguistic unity of the Germans with the Dutch, the English, and the Scandinavians. It is the same tendency which is found in much more exaggerated form among the panslavists farther east. English and the Scandinavian languages are often classified as divisions of the Low German. It needs but a moment's reflection to realize that though English may have been Low German in origin, it is now, especially in its vocabulary, more like French or other Romance tongues than like German. The ease with which an Englishman learns the former proves this. The physical anthropologist recognizes a still greater difference in type, and therefore in origin, between the broad-headed and brunette southern Germans, "Alpine" in race, and the typical English or especially the Scandinavians, who are the extreme of the opposite type, long-headed and pure blonds. Some confusion may arise from the fact that certain ethnical terms are used in opposite senses in the English and the German languages. It has elsewhere been explained that the English word "Dutch" (see) is never properly applied to a German, although the latter calls himself by practically the same name, *Deutsch.* Again, English philologists generally employ the word "Teutonic," which comes from the latter word, *Teutsch*, in the broadest sense of all, to include the "German," while German philologists reverse the terminology and make "Germanic" (*Germanish*) include the *Deutsch*.

The Austrians and the Swiss Germans can not be considered non-German in race by the test above applied to the Dutch. Although they may speak dialects very different from the modern literary German, they make the latter the legal language and really belong, themselves, to the High German division of dialects, from which the literary German takes its rise. In other words, the Austrian dialects are nearer the true German than are the North Saxon (Low German) dialects. On linguistic maps the Austrian and the Bavarian groups of dialects are one in name and color. The difference in political affiliation and otherwise does not justify us in speaking of an "Austrian" race, distinct from the German, any more than we can speak of a "Swiss" race (see these). The Swiss Germans are one, linguistically, with the neighboring population in Germany, the Alemanni (Suabian). Their case is, therefore, the same as that of the Austrian, so far as language is concerned. Their case is stronger statistically, for they constitute two-thirds of the population of Switzerland, while the German Austrians number but little over one-third of the population of Austria, not including Hungary. But in the popular mind, as well as scientifically, the word Swiss may mean a Frenchman or an Italian as well as a German. The term "Austrian" may also properly apply to the 25 per cent of Czechs (Bohemians, etc.) or to the 35 per cent of other Slavs found in Austria.

Among the Austrian dialects are the Tyrolese, the Styrian, and the Carinthian. The Zips are certain Germans of northern Hungary. In eastern Hungary, in Transylvania, is a large population of Saxons. Other names applied to Germans on the ethnographical map of Austria are the Walser, the Alemanen, the Pinzgauer, the Pongauer, the Lungauer, and the Gottscheer. The Frisians, a Low German stock, live in northern Holland.

The many other dialects of the German language need no discussion, for the people speaking them are all admittedly German in race. They are confined mainly to Germany, that is, they are German in nationality as well as in race, with the exception of minor segments which have spread over into Bohemia or neighboring countries. Of course, all who speak these dialects call themselves German in race. Of such are the Saxons, already mentioned, the Franconians or modern Franks, the Hessians, the Suabians, the Thuringians, the Westphalians, the Limburgers, and the Luxemburgers. Other Germans bear names of purely political divisions, as the Hanoverians and the Pomeranians. The names of others are sometimes used in two senses. Thus the Prussian, as a term of nationality, is wider than the ethnical term Prussian, which applied to a people of non-German origin, related to the Lettish, in eastern Prussia. The Alsatian is properly a German dialect, as is the Tyrolese, yet Alsace, the province, has also a large French population, as Tyrol has of Ladins (Rhæto-Romansh), and other Latins (Italians). Finally, the Silesians are those who gave their name to the two provinces called Silesia—the one on the Prussian side, the other on the Austrian side of the border. These, the Prussians, and all other divisions of the Germans living in the eastern part of Germany and in German Austria, are intermingled with non-German peoples to a degree that does not obtain in western Germany and on the southern border of the race, adjoining Italy. In the northeast the Poles and, to some extent, the Letts are pressing far over the German line, while the Germans, on the other hand, have scattered settlements far into Russian and Austrian territory.

Properly speaking, there is no German race from the point of view of physical characteristics. It is true that this name, or, better, the name "Teutonic," has been given to the so-called "Nordic" type, one of the three great races of Europe as described by physical anthropologists. But only a part of the people living in northern Germany, especially in the provinces nearest Denmark, are pure representatives of this extreme type, blond, with light hair and blue eyes, tall, and very long-headed. The type is far better represented by the Scandinavians. The German stock in Germany itself includes the most opposite extremes in type from the Nordic, just described, to the so-called "Alpine" race of Bavaria and Switzerland. Among these are some of the broadest-headed men in Europe, as in north Germany are found some of the longest-headed. A cranial index of 87 is found in Tyrol, as contrasted with one of 77 on the Danish border. The Alpine type, further, is brunette and short, although not so dark as the "Mediterranean" type of southern Italy. A unique census of school children by color of hair and eyes was taken some twenty years ago by four countries having a large German population. The results show the region in northwestern Germany already mentioned, and certain districts on the Baltic coast farther east, to be the only parts of Germany in which 50 per cent are pure blond. Farther south from 20 to 40 per cent are pure blond; then from 16 to 20 per cent are pure brunette; and finally, among the Germans of the southern border and of Switzerland and Austria, 20 to 30 per cent are pure brunette. On the average, however, the German population is decidedly of the blond type.

German.

Few of the so-called "races" of Europe include so many dissimilar elements, especially from the point of view of language, as the Germans. The Swiss, the Austrians, and the Mecklenburgers of northern Germany can not understand one another; and were it not for the written language they might be called different races as properly as the Dutch and Flemish. The Germans differ among themselves, as regards language, more than the great Slavic races. As has just been shown, they are also of different races physically. In many other respects they are far from being a homogeneous people. Germany lacks the unifying effect of a national religion, such as that of Russia. While the northern and most of the central portions of Germany are Protestant, the eastern border and the greater part of southern and western Germany are Catholic.

There is no need to speak of peculiarities in customs and the many important elements which determine the place of the German race in modern civilization. The German is too well known in America to necessitate further discussion.

The Germans of Europe number over 72,000,000 as against less than 40,000,000 English, Irish, and Scotch combined. They are larger in numbers than any other European race, if the Great Russian (55,000,000) be considered as separated from the Ruthenian or Little Russian (25,000,000), as is done in this dictionary. The Italian or the French race is only about half as large. The total German-speaking population of the world has been estimated at from 75,000,000 to 85,000,000 (see list following). It is exceeded only by the English-speaking population, which, however, includes nearly as many individuals non-English in race as there are English. The German is one of the most widely distributed of European races. As colonists, and especially as merchants, they are found in nearly every country in the world.

German population of the world.

[From Meyer's Konversations-Lexikon, 1909, Band 21.]

Europe:	
German Empire	55,766,541
Austria	9,170,939
Hungary	2,135,181
Switzerland	2,312,949
Russia	2,000,000
Miscellaneous	834,117
America:	
United States	11,000,000
Canada	309,741
Brazil	400,000
Miscellaneous	88,400
Summary:	
Europe	72,219,727
America	11,798,141
Australia and Oceania	110,035
Africa	61,577
Asia	58,687
Total	84,248,167

Austria has the largest German population of any European country outside of Germany itself, but the German population of America is still greater—in the foregoing estimate nearly 12,000,000. The United States census of 1900 gives the German-born population of the United States at 2,667,000, while the native-born of German-born parents number about 5,000,000 more.

All of "Central Europe," as defined by Partsch to include Holland and Bulgaria, and all between, besides the greater part of Poland and Hungary, is predominantly German (51 per cent). In this territory the most numerous of the other races or peoples reach less than 7 per cent each. These are the Dutch and Flemish, the Serbo-Croatians, the Magyars, the Poles, the Czechs, and the Roumanians. This list, with the addition of the Italians and the French, indicates the ethnical boundaries of the German people. Outside of Germany itself no country is predominantly German by race, excepting Switzerland (69 per cent, or 2,300,000). Cisleithan Austria is 36 per cent German (9,000,000); Hungary, 12 per cent (2,000,000); the little independent principality of Luxemburg is 93 per cent German (220,000). Russia has a large German population, 1,800,000, although this is only 1.5 per cent of the total population of that vast empire. Four-fifths of the Germans of Europe are found in Germany itself.

In Germany 94 per cent of the population is German in race. In the remaining 6 per cent the only race or people largely represented is the Polish. These number about 3,400,000, mainly in Prussia, while the Danes, the Lithuanians, and the Wends, number but little over 100,000 each.

During the period for which immigration statistics are available, 1820–1910, Germany furnished 5,351,746 immigrants to the United States. This is the largest number coming from any single country, although the United Kingdom as a whole furnished 7,766,330. The greatest immigration from Germany occurred in 1882, when 250,630 were admitted. The movement decreased rapidly, however, and at the present time it is a noteworthy fact that more German immigrants come from Austria-Hungary to the United States than from Germany itself—in 1907, 40,497, as against 32,276. In the same year Russia sent us rather more than two-fifths as many Germans as did Germany itself, and the little country Switzerland sent about 3,000 immigrants out of its 2,300,000 German people. The next largest source of German immigration to the United States in that year was British North America, 1,121. The total for the year was 92,936, and for the twelve years 1899–1910, 754,375, which places the German fourth down the list of immigrant races or peoples. The races exceeding the Germans in this regard during the twelve years were the South Italians, 1,911,933; Hebrews,

1,074,442; and Polish, 949,064. Following the Germans in the order named were the Scandinavians, Irish, English, Slovaks, North Italians, and Magyars.

The falling off in German immigration is evident from another comparison. Its rate per 1,000 of the population, only 1.3 in 1907, was the lowest of all the peoples that are now significant in our immigration tide, if we omit the Great Russian, which sends its emigrants elsewhere than to America. Next above the German in rank come the English and the Scotch taken together; then the Bohemian-Moravian group, with a rate of about 2 per 1,000. The German rate of immigration in the year mentioned was only one-fifteenth that of the Hebrews or the Slovaks.

An interesting comparison is furnished by German statistics of emigration for the twenty-seven years previous to 1898. The very period of its highest flood to America, 1881–1883, was also the period of greatest emigration to Australia. But the latter amounted to only 2,100 at the highest; that is, only about one one-hundredth part of the annual emigration to the United States. This emigration to Australia was exceeded in the case of only two other countries aside from the United States—Brazil and Canada. The highest wave of emigration to Brazil came in 1890, namely, 4,000; the highest to British North America in 1893, which reached 6,100. No other country comes near these figures as a destination for German emigration. No other part of the world therefore really competes as yet with the United States for German emigration. Generally speaking, during the period just mentioned, from 1871 to 1897, no other country received more than one-thirtieth part as many German immigrants annually as did the United States.

German immigration stands perhaps next to that of the English-speaking races in the evenness of its distribution in America, although it tends preponderatingly to the Northern States. The States to which the greatest numbers were destined during the twelve-year period 1899–1910 were as follows:

New York	190, 236
Pennsylvania	110, 544
Illinois	73, 408
Ohio	58, 684
New Jersey	45, 923
Wisconsin	33, 523
Missouri	23, 592
North Dakota	23, 521
Michigan	20, 609
California	15, 750
Nebraska	15, 474
Minnesota	13, 865
South Dakota	13, 268
Iowa	12, 413
Kansas	12, 127
Connecticut	11, 333
Massachusetts	10, 720
Maryland	10, 655

GERMAN-SLOVAK. (See *Slovak.*)

GITANO. That is, Egyptian. Same as **Zingaro**, the Spanish name for Gypsy (see).

GOLAD. A clan near Moscow supposed to be of Lithuanian (see) origin.

GOND. A name applied to certain Dravidians of Central India. (See *Hindu.*)

GORAL. Same as **Podhalian.** (See *Polish.*)

GORENCI. A subdivision of the Slovenians (see).

GÖTCHEBE. A wandering group of Osmanli Turks in Asia Minor. (See *Turkish* and *Tataric.*)

GOTTSHEE. A division of Austrian Germans (see).

GREAT POLISH. (See *Polish.*)

GREAT RUSSIAN. Same as **Russian** (see).

GREEK (sometimes **Hellenic**). The modern Greek race or people is that which has descended, with considerable foreign admixture, from the famous race of ancient Greeks, which is one of the oldest branches of the Aryan group (see), and the first to reach a high state of civilization. While the stock has changed much, physically and otherwise, the modern language is more nearly like the ancient Greek than Italian, for instance, is like the ancient Latin. The race is now one of the smaller and comparatively unimportant of Europe, but it has recently developed a high rate of immigration to America.

Are the modern Greeks a different race from the ancient Greeks? Although ethnologists differ upon this question, the answer would appear to be that they are one and the same race when judged by their language, which is the test applied in this dictionary to all European races; but that they differ in part at least when judged by physical characteristics. Von Hellwald calls the ancient race the Hellenic (*Hellenen*) and the later race the modern Greek (*Neugriechen*). The ancient Greeks were of the so-called Mediterranean type, long-headed, and of classic regularity of features. While this type still prevails in Greece the influence of admixture with alien blood has produced a type, indigenous to parts of the country, which differs materially from the ancient Greeks, in that they are broad-headed, broad-faced, and more heavily built, although perhaps no darker than the ancients. Whether the latter were blond or brunette is still a mooted question, with the probability that they were like the "Mediterranean" race of the present day, deeply brunette. Amongst the Greeks of to-day are found two distinct physical types more sharply separated than in most nationalities: One, the ancient, long-headed type of Greece, with a cephalic index of 75; the other, the broad-headed type that comes from the Slavic, Albanian, or Turkish admixture (see these), sometimes with the extremely high index of 88. These, however, must be regarded as extremes, and Ripley says that the cephalic index of the modern Greeks ranges with great constancy about 81. All of the Greeks of Asia Minor are distinctly broad-headed, it is said, like the Turks among whom they live.

To what degree the ancient and the modern races of Greece differ in character and civilization may be still more difficult to determine than their physical types. The most contradictory accounts are given by partisans on this point. It can not be denied at least that the ancient Greeks were leaders in the civilization of their own day, and laid the foundations of modern civilization; while modern Greece is one of the weaker nations of Europe. The ancient Greeks were preeminent in philosophy and science, a position not generally accredited to the modern Greeks as a race, although there is no doubt as to their nimble intelligence. They compete with the Hebrew race as the best traders of the Orient. If there be a great difference between the ancient and the modern civilization of Greece, the question still remains whether this change should be explained as simply the decadence of an ancient race or because of the debasement it has received, as did the civilization of the Roman, through the incursions of barbarian hordes, and, in recent history, through the long oppression of Turkish rule.

It is not generally understood that the language of the modern Greeks is really the language of the ancient Greeks. The difference is only dialectal. The literary language of to-day is but a continuation of the main literary dialect of ancient Greece, the Attic, as modified in passing through the Byzantine. It, or rather the modern vernacular, is sometimes called Romaic, a misleading term, which found its origin in the period of Roman supremacy. To this, day the Greeks living in European Turkey are called *Romnika*. There are several dialects of the modern Greek or Romaic, such as the Mainot, the Phanariot, and the Cypriot, which need no further discussion in this connection. Of late there is a tendency among Greek authors to return more closely to the ancient form of the language. The spoken dialects of Greece vary more widely from it, although the so-called Tsaconic, which is spoken on the eastern side of lower Greece (Peloponnesus or Morea), closely resembles the ancient Dorian. The modern language is much closer to the ancient than any modern descendant of the Latin is to the ancient Latin. Greek is no longer spoken by the Greek colonists of southern Italy, nor even by many of the Greeks of Asia Minor. Crete is practically all Greek, and even southern Macedonia and the coast as far east as Constantinople itself, which has a larger population of Greeks than of Turks. As has been explained in the article "Turkish" (see), the Turks themselves form but a small minority of the population of Turkey.

The Greek race of to-day is intensely proud of its language and its history, and naturally wishes to be considered as genuinely Hellenic. The official title of the country is now the "Kingdom of Hellas," and any citizen, however mixed in race, styles himself a Hellene. The people are wide-awake on political questions, are avid readers of newspapers, and, like the Greek of olden times, eager to learn some new thing. Generally speaking, in customs, superstitions, and folklore, the modern race is a continuation of the ancient. It shows in other respects, as in the clothing now worn, the influence of the mixture of races. As already intimated, the race is commercial rather than agricultural in its instincts, and in that respect differs from the Slavic, by which it is supposed to be modified. In religion it is Orthodox (Greek), which is also the national church of Russia and several other countries of eastern and southeastern Europe. It is from this expansion of the Greek religion that much confusion has arisen in the use of the racial name. Even Ruthenians (see), or Little Russians, in America sometimes call themselves Greeks, apparently in contradistinction from their Slavic neighbors, who are Catholic. Statistics published by Greek partisans are said to exaggerate the number of Greeks found in Turkey by counting as such Bulgarians, Servians, and others who have become Hellenized and are members of the Greek Church.

How many of the inhabitants of Greece itself are really non-Grecian in race is a question difficult to answer. No statistics of the country are taken by race. It is well known, however, that eastern Greece, even in the Peloponnesus, has a large Albanian population, usually estimated at about 200,000. They are so fully Hellenized that but 40,000 now speak the Albanian language. This is perhaps the chief foreign element that is incorporated into the Greek race, although special account must be made also of the Slavic, the Turkish, the Roman, and the Gothic, and even the Roumanian (Kutzo-Vlach, or Tsintsar). The last named is so recent in arrival that it is hardly yet incorporated into the race. It has come in largely since Greece was freed from Turkish rule, in 1830, and still forms large settlements extending from the central part of northern Greece into Macedonia. The Slavic element is the oldest that has profoundly modified the stock of ancient Greece. By the sixth century Greece had been overrun time and again by Slavic tribes to the very southern extremity of the country.

It may not be commonly known that the greater part of the Greeks live outside of Greece. The total population of the country numbers but 2,600,000, much less than half the population of such small countries as Holland and Belgium. Ripley, Chisholm, and others say that the Greek race numbers above 8,000,000, although the more common estimates place it under 4,500,000 in Europe, or something over 5,000,000 in Europe and Asia Minor combined. Chisholm says that the Greeks living outside of Greece are twice as numerous as those in Greece. Ripley says that they form a third of the total population of the Balkan States. The latter number at least 20,000,000. Even the Statesman's Year-Book gives the total number of Greeks as 8,850,000, divided as follows: In Greece, 2,200,000; in European Turkey, 4,000,000; in Asia Minor, 2,000,000; in insular Greece, etc., 650,000. On the other hand, von Hellwald says that of the population of Greece itself only about 1,300,000 are truly Greek in race.

In 1907, 46,283 Greeks were admitted to the United States, the largest number in any single year. Of these 36,404 came from Greece, 7,060 from European Turkey, and 1,353 from Turkey in Asia. In the twelve years 1899–1910, 216,962 Greeks were admitted to the United States, and 79.6 per cent of them came from Greece. The race ranked twelfth in the number of immigrants furnished during that period. Greeks go to the States having the largest cities, the principal destinations during the period mentioned being New York, 70,607, Massachusetts, 34,450, Illinois, 31,014, Pennsylvania, 12,839, and Missouri, 12,673.

Accepting 6,000,000 as a conservative estimate of the population of the race, more than 7 per 1,000 of population came to the United States in the year 1907. The rate of immigration from Greece alone in that year was nearly twice as great, about 14 per 1,000 of the population. This was the highest rate of any country, Norway being second with 10 per 1,000. The Greeks, as a race, came in that year at a more rapid rate than all other immigrant races or peoples with the exception of the Slovaks Hebrews, Croatians and Slovenians, South Italians, Norwegians, Irish, Poles, and Magyars. As shown elsewhere (see *Hebrew* and *Slav*), the Hebrews and the Slovaks in that year stood at the head with about 18 immigrants per 1,000 population.

GRISON. A dialect of the Rhæto-Romansh language. The term is sometimes used in an ethnical sense, but more properly in a political, meaning the inhabitants of the Canton of the Grisons, in the eastern part of Switzerland. This canton has a population of about 108,000, nearly half of whom speak German, over one-third Romansh, and one-sixth Italian (see these). German is now taught everywhere in the schools of the canton. In religion, five-ninths of the Grisons are Roman Catholics and the rest are Protestants.

GRUSIAN. Same as **Georgian** (see).

GUAM, people of. A subject people of the United States belonging to the northern Micronesian stock (see *Micronesian* and *Pacific Islander*); related in language, and to a less degree physically, to the Filipinos (see). Like the latter, they are not counted as immigrants on coming to the United States. They are insignificant in numbers.

GUATEMALAN. (See *Spanish American.*)

GYPSY. A well-known wandering people scattered throughout western Asia, northern Africa, all parts of Europe, and even through parts of the Americas and Australia. As indicated by the language he speaks, which is closely related to Sanscrit, the Gypsy belongs to the Aryan race and is therefore Caucasian. In his own language the Gypsy calls himself "*Rom*," whence comes Romany as a name for the language. Special names are applied to Gypsies in the different countries where they are found. Some of these relate to the supposed origin of this singular people, as Gypsy or Egyptian in the British Isles, Bohémien in France, Gitano (Egyptian) in Spain, and Tatare in Scandinavia. In some countries they are known by a term of contempt, as Heiden (heathen) in Holland, Ḥarami (robbers) in Egypt, and Tinklers in Scotland, but in most parts of Europe a local form of the word Zingani is used to designate them, as Zigeuner in Germany, Cygany in Hungary, and Zingari in Spain.

The Gypsy or Romany language is now considered to belong to the neo-Hindu group, on a level with Hindi and Marathi, but is full of foreign elements borrowed from the various peoples met by the Gypsies in their migration westward. Miklosich distinguishes thirteen Gypsy dialects in Europe: the Greek or Turkish, Roumanian, Hungarian, Moravo-Bohemian, German, Polo-Lithuanian, Russian, Scandinavian, Finnish, Anglo-Scottish, Italian, Basque, and Spanish. These dialects become more corrupt as a rule the farther they are removed from Turkey. Gypsies converse with strangers in the language of the vernacular of the people with whom they dwell. They have no alphabet, no written literature, only a few songs.

Physically the Gypsy is a very mixed people, the chief characters of which are too well known to need description here. They are supposed to have had their origin in northern India and to have entered Europe by way of Persia and Armenia in the early part of the fourteenth century. The exact relationship of the European Gypsies to certain tribes of Asia—the Nats and Doms of India, or the Luri and Karachi of Persia—has not been demonstrated by scientists.

Everywhere the Gypsy resents the restraint of a higher social organization. To him laws and statutes are persecutions to be evaded. He has no history, no tradition, no racial religion, nothing but a remarkable instinct of blood relationship which is manifested in a solidarity of race unequaled by even that of the Jews. So universal are his wandering tendencies that Gypsy camp and caravan are familiar to all. In some parts of Roumania, Hungary, and Spain, however, large groups of sedentary Gypsies are found. But wherever found they incline to occupations that admit of a roving life, or at least of life in the open air. The men are musicians, metal workers, horse dealers, and pilferers. The women are fortune tellers and dancers. As musicians Gypsies are famous; as singers in Moscow, as harpists in Wales, and as violinists in Hungary. Liszt attributes to them the creation of national Hungarian music. As gold washers they have performed valuable service for the economic development of Austria-Hungary. In some parts of Spain the butchers are Gypsies. Rarely do they engage in agriculture. Very few are farmers, even in Austria-Hungary, where the majority are sedentary. Many are day laborers. Some are shopkeepers. A few Russian Gypsies have accumulated wealth.

While the wandering Gypsies live in tents, have little or no furniture, are clad in rags and filthy in their habits, most of the sedentary Gypsies live in small houses, rude huts, or caves on the outskirts of suburbs or villages, and enjoy more of the comforts of civilization. It has been questioned whether the Gypsy can be assimilated into a nation. In Prussia there is a colony of Gypsies that live in small, clean houses, work on the railroads, and send their children, most of whom have not been taught the Gypsy tongue, to the public school.

Auerbach says that 52 per cent of the Gypsies of Hungary are ignorant of the Romany tongue. Intermarriage with other peoples is becoming more frequent. Through loss of language, the assumption of a sedentary life, and intermarriage, Gypsies are decreasing in numbers and seem everywhere doomed to extinction by absorption.

The total population of Gypsies in the world is variously estimated at from 700,000 to 850,000, of whom three-fourths are in Europe. There are 200,000 in Roumania, 100,000 each in Hungary and the Balkan Peninsula, 50,000 each in Spain, Russia, and Servia, and 50,000 in Germany and Italy combined. The number in the British Isles is variously estimated at from 5,000 to 20,000. There are thought to be 100,000 in Asia and 25,000 in Africa. Only a few thousand are found in the Americas. They are included among "Other peoples" in immigration statistics. They are supposed to have first come to this country in the beginning of the eighteenth century. Simson says that many were banished from the British Isles to America in colonial times and that many more were sent to serve in the British army during the Revolution. He found a number of settled Gypsies in the Eastern States, and suggests that many of the keepers of small tin shops and peddlers of tin, as well as many of the fortune tellers of the great cities of the United States, are in reality of Gypsy descent.

H.

HADJEMI. A Persian (see).

HAIDUK. (See *Croatian.*)

HAIK. The native name of **Armenians** (see).

HAMITIC. (See *Semitic-Hamitic.*)

HANAK. A subdivision of the Moravians. (See *Bohemian and Moravian.*)

HANOVERIAN. (See *German.*)

HAWAIIAN or SANDWICH ISLANDER. An individual member of the northernmost Polynesian people subject to the United States. (See *Pacific Islander.*) Not counted among immigrants on arriving in the United States.

HAYTIAN. (See *West Indian.*)

HEBREW, JEWISH, or ISRAELITE. The race or people that originally spoke the Hebrew language; primarily of Semitic origin. Scattered throughout Europe, especially in Russia, yet preserving their own individuality to a marked degree. Linguistically, the nearest relatives of the ancient Hebrew are the Syriac (see *Syrian*), Assyrian, and Arabic languages of the Semitic-Hamitic family (see). The latter constitutes one of the four great divisions of the Caucasian race. While the Hebrew is not so nearly a dead language as the related Syrian, Aramaic, or the ancient Assyrian, its use in most Jewish communities is confined mainly to religious exercises. The Jews have adopted the languages of the peoples with whom they have long been associated. More speak Yiddish, called in Europe "Judeo-German," than any other language, since the largest modern population of Jews borders on eastern Germany and has been longest under German influence.

Physically the Hebrew is a mixed race, like all our immigrant races or peoples, although to a less degree than most. This has been fairly well demonstrated by recent studies, notwithstanding the earlier scientific and present popular belief that they are of pure blood. In every country they are found to approach in type the people among whom they have long resided. The two chief divisions of the Jewish people are the Ashkenazim, or northern type, and the Sephardim, or southern. The latter are also called "Spagnuoli," after the country,

Spain, from which they were expelled in 1492. They are now found mainly in the countries southeast of Austria. They consider themselves to be of purer race than the northern Jews and in some countries refuse to intermarry or worship with the latter. Their features are more truly Semitic. The "Jewish nose," and to a less degree other facial characteristics, are found well-nigh everywhere throughout the race, although the form of the head seems to have become quite the reverse of the Semitic type. The social solidarity of the Jews is chiefly a product of religion and tradition. Taking all factors into account, and especially their type of civilization, the Jews of to-day are more truly European than Asiatic or Semitic. The classification of the Bureau of Immigration separates the Hebrews from the Semites and places them in the Slavic grand division of the Aryan family, although, as is explained above, they are not Aryan. Nine-tenths of the Jewish immigrants to the United States come, however, from Slavic territory.

The total Hebrew population of the world is estimated at 11,000,000. Approximately 8,000,000 are in Europe. The geographical distribution of the greater part of this number is shown by the map opposite this page. Only a remnant, less than 100,000, are found in Palestine; perhaps 250,000 in all Asia. About one-half of the Jews live in Western Russia, about 2,000,000 in Austria-Hungary, and 250,000 in Roumania. About one-fourth of the Russian Jews live in Poland. The emigration from these countries during the last generation has been immense and has reached its culmination in the last five years. The primary causes have been a desire for better economic conditions, and the persecutions directed against the Jewish population. These causes have been reinforced by a religious sentiment that has found expression in the Zionist and similar movements and in the millions of wealth and great organized efforts which Baron de Hirsch and other Jewish financiers have devoted to this cause. The project of again acquiring Palestine as a national home not appearing practical to many, they have looked also to South Africa and to the Argentine Republic for large tracts of land suitable for their purposes. The main result, however, has been immigration to the United States.

Jewish immigration now exceeds in number annually that of any other race with the exception of the Italian. It forms a large part of the total immigration from southern and eastern Europe, which now predominates to the same degree that immigration from northern and western Europe formerly did. (See article *Caucasian* for figures.) Jewish immigration in 1907 totaled 149,182, or about 12 per cent of the total immigration to the United States. In 1906 it was more—153,748. In the twelve years 1899–1910, 1,074,-442 Jewish immigrants were admitted to the United States, a number exceeded by only one other race, the South Italian. Of the total number of Jewish immigrants admitted during the period specified 765,531 came from Russia and 180,802 from Austria-Hungary.

The principal destinations of the Hebrews in the United States during the twelve years specified were as follows:

New York	690, 296
Pennsylvania	108, 534
Massachusetts	66, 023
Illinois	50, 931
New Jersey	34, 279
Ohio	20, 531
Maryland	18, 700
Connecticut	16, 254

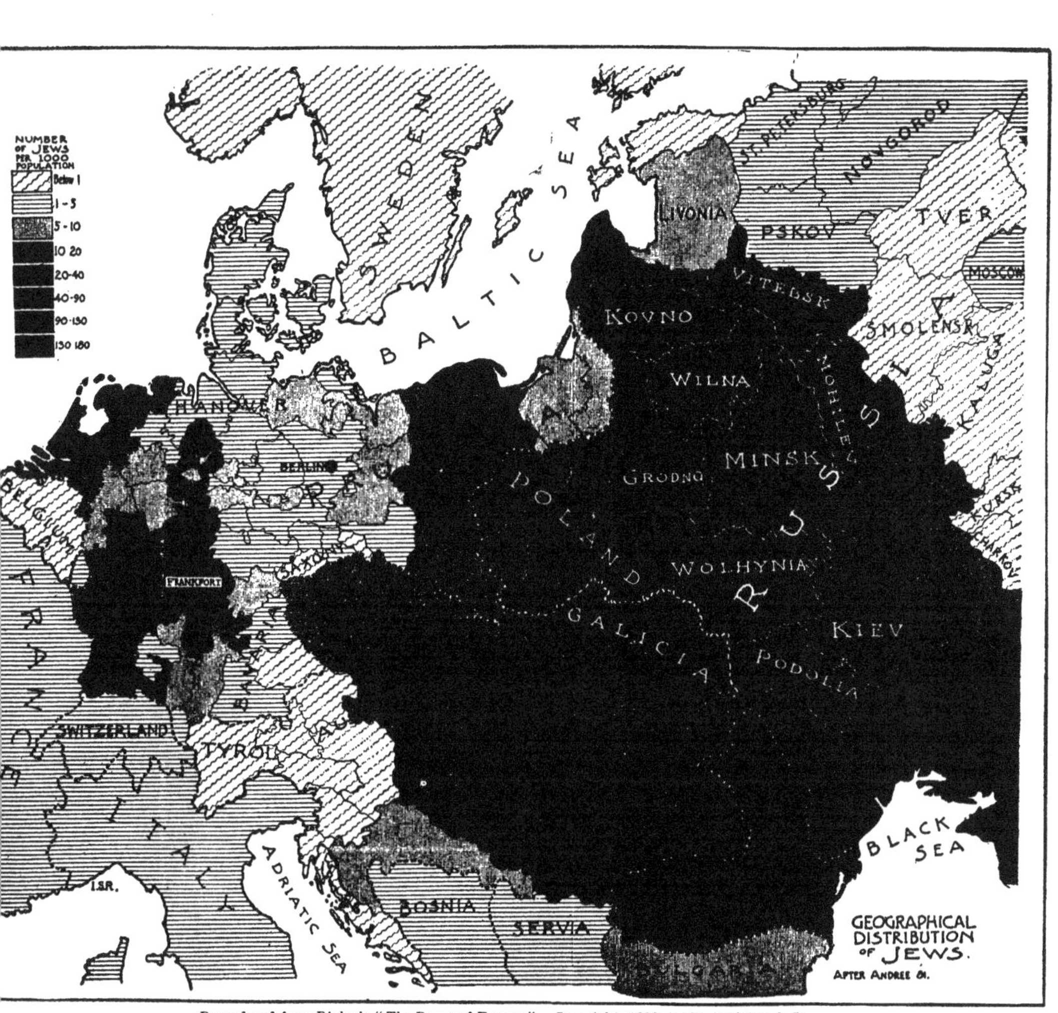

Reproduced from Ripley's "The Races of Europe." Copyright, 1899, by D. Appleton & Co.

60813°—VOL 5—11. (To face page 74.)

Of the 20 races or peoples now contributing the chief tide of immigration to America, the Hebrew and the Slovak stand at the head as regards the rate per cent of population at which they come. In 1907 each of these races sent about 18 immigrants to each 1,000 of its European population. The Croatian-Slovenian group came next with 13 per 1,000; then the South Italians, the Norwegians, the Irish, and certain peoples of eastern and southeastern Europe with from 6 to 9 per 1,000. Future Hebrew immigration, however, could not long compete numerically with that from Italy, because there are less than 8,000,000 Hebrews left in Europe as against 35,000,000 Italians.

Among other factors which would continue a high rate of immigration from the two leading immigrant peoples, the Italian and the Hebrew, is the large number of each already in the United States, many of them of recent arrival and therefore doubly interested in inducing their relatives to follow.

As is well known, Jewish immigrants settle almost entirely in the cities. New York City has the largest Jewish population of any city in the world, now estimated by some at about 1,000,000, or nearly one-fourth of the total population. About 50,000 more are added annually. Among large cities, Warsaw and Odessa have a still larger ratio of Jewish population, namely, one-third. In London, on the contrary, only one-fiftieth of the population is Hebrew. The Jewish population of the entire United States is less than 2,000,000. Jewish estimates place Pennsylvania next to New York with a Hebrew population of 150,000; Illinois next, with 110,000; and Massachusetts next, with 90,000.

HELLENIC. (See *Greek.*)

HEMES or **HEMELAISET.** Same as **Tavastian.** (See *Finnish.*)

HERVAT, HORVATH, HRVAT, KHORBAT, CARPATH, KHROVAT, CROAT, or **CROATIAN.** Different forms of an old Slavic word meaning highlands, mountains (cf. *Carpathians*); hence not strictly an ethnical term, although some immigrants insist that Horvath, and not Croatian (see), is the proper name of their people. *Horvatok* is the name given Croatians on the Magyar ethnographical map.

HERZEGÓVINIAN. A political division of the Serbo-Croatians. (See *Croatian.*)

HESSIAN. (See *German.*)

HIGH GERMAN, HIGH LETTIC, etc. Dialects or divisions of these languages (which see).

HIGHLANDER (SCOTCH). (See *Celtic* and *Scotch.*)

HINDU. In the broadest sense, any native of India; so defined for convenience in this dictionary. In the more ordinary religious sense this word applies only to the two-thirds of the population who are "Hinduized"—that is, who profess Hinduism and have a certain social organization based upon Brahmanism. Ethnologically often defined in a still different sense as signifying the three-fourths of the population in northern India who are of Aryan stock (see) whether professing Hinduism or Mohammedanism.

In immigration questions, where the immense population of India is beginning to arouse some concern, all natives of India are indiscriminately known as "Hindus." Perhaps a few, as the Sikhs, are known by name because of their prominence amongst the native troops. But it is not generally realized how great a number of races and tribes there are in India, many of them extremely low in civilization and approaching the Negro in physical characteristics. Such are some of the Dravidas and Mundas, who occupy all of southern India. In greatest contrast with these are the Aryan Hindus of the north, more closely related in language, if not in physical appearance, to our northern Europeans than are the Turks, Magyars, and various peoples of eastern Russia.

Hindi and Hindustani, the most widely spread modern languages or group of dialects of India, are variously defined. Thus, while Hindustani is generally understood in Europe to be the polite speech of all India, and especially of Hindustan, the name is limited by some philologists to certain subdivisions of the Hindi. Urdu is the form of the language which uses the Persian letters. Other forms use letters of Hindu origin. Hindi, in the wider sense of the term, is spoken by 97,000,000 of people, mainly of northern India.

The population of India is one of the densest on the globe, reaching even in agricultural districts 650 to the square mile. Including the 10,500,000 inhabitants of Burma, it amounts to nearly 300,000,000 souls, or one-fifth of the population of the world. The darker non-Aryans and Mongolians alone of India nearly equal the population of the United States. There are 147 peoples or tribes speaking different languages, of which the principal ones are represented as follows in the Census of 1901:

Population of India.

Language.	Number speaking.	Principal location.
All languages	294,400,000	
Indo-European	221,200,000	NORTHERN INDIA.
Hindi and Bihari	97,000,000	Central part of northern India.
Bengali	44,600,000	Bengal.
Marathi	18,000,000	Western and central India.
Panjabi	17,000,000	Northwestern India.
Rajasthani	11,000,000	Western and central India.
Gujarati	10,000,000	Western India.
Oriya	9,700,000	Eastern India.
Jatki or Lahnda	3,300,000	Northwestern India.
Sindhi	3,000,000	Western India.
Pahari	3,000,000	Northern border of India.
Assamese	1,350,000	Eastern India.
Pashto	1,200,000	Western border of India.
Kashmiri	1,000,000	Northwestern border of India.
Bhil	750,000	Central and western India.
Others	300,000	
Dravido-Munda	59,700,000	SOUTHERN INDIA.
Telugu	20,700,000	Eastern part of southern India.
Tamil	16,500,000	Southern India and Ceylon.
Kanarese	10,400,000	Western part of southern India.
Malayalam	6,000,000	Southern extremity of southern India.
Santali	1,800,000	Bengal.
Gond	1,130,000	Central India.
Kol	950,000	Bengal.
Others	2,220,000	
Indo-Chinese	11,700,000	Burma.
Miscellaneous	1,800,000	

As to religion, Hinduism predominates everywhere except in the northwest, where it shades off into the universal Mohammedanism of the countries farther west. The latter religion is found to some extent in all other parts of India as well, especially in the northeast. Christianity is nowhere strong except among the darker and more backward tribes of the extreme south. Buddhism is confined mainly to the Mongolian population of Burma. There are 8,500,000 who are still animists; that is, who worship the spirits of trees, of rocks, and of most common objects about them. Emigration from India is still small. (See *East Indian* for Hindu immigration and other details.

HOLLANDER or **HOLLAND DUTCH.** (See *Dutch.*)

HONDURAN. (See *Spanish American.*)

HORAK. (See *Bohemian and Moravian.*)

HORVATH, HERVAT, HORVATOK, HRVAT. (See *Hervat* and *Croatian.*)

HRANICAR. (See *Croatian.*)

HUGUENOT FRENCH. A name applied to the French Protestants of the sixteenth and seventeenth centuries. (See *French.*)

HUN. A people that overran eastern Europe in the middle ages, supposedly of Tataric (see) origin. The modern Magyars or "Hungarians" are wrongly called "Huns" in America. (See *Magyar.*)

HUNGARIAN or **HUNKY.** (See *Magyar.*)

HUZUL or **GUZUL.** A very broad-headed people of Bukowina, who speak a Ruthenian dialect (see).

I.

IBERIC or **IBERIAN.** (1) Iberian is a name sometimes given in a narrow sense to the Basques (see) since the latter were thought to be identical with the ancient Iberians who gave their name to the Iberian Peninsula, Spain and Portugal. (2) Iberic or Ibero-Insular is a term sometimes used in a wider sense to indicate the "Mediterranean" race, one of the three or four great races of Europe from a physical point of view. Some make it include the ancient Picts of Britain. As used by the Bureau of Immigration, the "Iberic division" comprises the Spanish and Portuguese, South Italians, Greeks, and Syrians (see these).

IBERO-INSULAR race. (See *Iberic* and *Caucasian.*)

ICELANDIC. (See *Scandinavian.*)

IGOROT. (See *Filipino.*)

IJORE, ISHORE, or **INGER.** A division of the Western Finns. (See *Finnish.*)

ILLYRIAN. Used in two senses: (1) For the old Albanian (see) language and race; (2) less properly for the Southern Slavs. (See *Croatian.*)

ILOCANO. (See *Filipino.*)

INDIAN, AMERINDIAN, AMERICAN, or **RED** race. That great division of mankind which is native to America. To avoid confusion arising from the popular use of the word "American" to indicate the imported Caucasian stock, Brinton calls the natives "Amerinds," a contraction of the term "American Indians." This race includes all the aborigines of North, Central, and South America, with the possible exception of the Eskimos. Although an interesting subject to American ethnologists, but little space can be given it in a discussion of immigration; for, as will presently be seen, it cuts no figure in immigration statistics.

As to ethnical relationships, the Indian stands closer to the Mongolian, physically, than to any other grand division. In language, it is of different type from all. But although undoubtedly of Asiatic origin, at least for the most part, the Indian race has lived so long in American environments that it is now as much different from the Mongolian as the latter is from the Caucasian race. Hence a tendency, especially in America, to hold that the Indian constitutes a distinct race. Other recent classifications, however, regard the American as merely a branch of the Mongolian race. Still more will agree that at least the Eskimo is Mongolian in type and assert that he resembles certain natives of northeastern Asia more than he does the American Indian. There is no doubt that there has been migration into America by way of Bering Strait.

Brinton claims that the peopling of America took place while there was still land connection with Europe. Keane, in like manner, argues that the Eskimo and some of the southernmost tribes, such as the Fuegians, who have, like the Eskimo, relatively long heads, may have come from the primitive long-headed stock of Europe. But little reliance can be placed upon craniometrical resemblances, however, compared with linguistic relationships in classifying American tribes. As a matter of fact, the entire race, excepting the Eskimos, is remarkably homogeneous from a physical point of view. It is unnecessary here to discuss linguistic classifications.

The American is the smallest grand division of mankind, numbering, with half-breeds, at most 23,000,000, or half the population of the next largest race, the Malay. Of these, only 266,000 live in the United States. Indians do not appear by name in the statistics of the Bureau of Immigration, and the few who may come presumably are counted among "Other peoples." Since the term "Spanish Americans," under the statistical rules of the bureau, excludes Indians, presumably no Indians are counted in that division of the Spanish race in America called "Mexicans," nor among immigrants from the West Indies and Cuba who are not Negroes (see these). It is evident also that if there be any Indians among the 20,000 immigrants who came from Canada in 1907, they were found among the 36 "Other peoples." The "Other peoples" from all other American countries numbered only 41. As has been said in the article on Cubans, the Indians of that island are practically extinct. The figures of all American countries make it appear probable therefore that not 100 Indians a year are enrolled amongst our immigrants—probably less than the number that remove annually from the United States. The American race, therefore, like the Malay race, is of no practical importance in this study. Even the small Negro immigration of 5,000 per year, standing thirtieth in number down the list, has far more significance.

INDIAN, EAST. (See *East Indian.*)

INDO-BRITON and **INDO-ENGLISH.** A person of British or English descent born in India.

INDO-CELTIC or **INDO-KELTIC,** and **INDO-CLASSIC.** Same as **Aryan** (see).

INDO-CHINESE. A group of people constituting, with the Chinese and the Tibetan groups, the so-called "Sinitic" branch of the Mongolian race. (See these and *East Indian.*) It is confined to the southeastern peninsula of Asia, known as Farther India, and includes not only the Annamese (see), Cochin-Chinese, Tonkinese, and the Cambodians of French Indo-China, but the Burmese (see) of British India and the independent Siamese. The population exceeds 35,000,000. There has as yet been shown little tendency to emigrate. If any came to the United States, they would be classed as East Indian.

INDO-EUROPEAN or **INDO-GERMANIC.** Same as **Aryan** (see).

INDO-IRANIC. The group of Indo-European languages found in Asia and comprising the Indic of India and the Iranic of Persia. (See these.)

INDONESIAN. A name applied by some ethnologists to Polynesians (see) and certain Philippine tribes. (See *Malay.*)

INDO-TEUTONIC. Same as **Aryan** (see).

INGER. Same as **Ijore.** (See *Finnish*).

IRANIAN TURK. A Turk living in Iran, as Persia is sometimes called, but not of the "Iranic" (Aryan) race. (See *Turkish.*)

IRANIC. The Aryan languages (see) of "Iran," the native name of Persia; including the Afghan, Beluchi, Kurdic, and, according to some, Armenic and Ossetian; that is, all the Indo-European languages of Asia with the exception of those of India (see these).

IRISH. The principal race or people of Ireland; the race which originally spoke Irish, one of the Celtic group of Aryan tongues. The term Irish is generally understood in a wider sense to include also the Scotch-Irish and even the English who have settled in Ireland, with their descendants abroad; but this is a definition of nationality rather than of race. This dictionary considers those to be of the Irish race whose ancestral language was Irish even though English has been the medium of intercourse for generations.

No other race or people of its size has emigrated so extensively to this country. Like the English, the Irish come to the United States speaking our own language and imbued with sympathy for our ideals and our democratic institutions.

The difficulty in determining whether a given immigrant from Ireland is Irish or English, or even Scotch, has already been referred to in the article "English." The common understanding in America that the Irish race includes all of the Irish nationality—that is, all who live in Ireland—is probably not far wrong if we except Ulster province, since the majority of the remaining population are descended from those who spoke Irish. This language is a branch of the Gaelic division of the Celtic group of the Aryan or Indo-European family (see these). It is fast going out of use as a medium of communication. It is said that not 5,000 persons throughout all Ireland are able to read a book in Irish; that not a single Irish newspaper is published; that no church services are conducted in the language, and that it is not taught in the elementary schools. Irish was spoken in 1851 by 1,500,000 persons; that is, by 23 per cent of the population. In 1901 only 640,000 persons, or 14 per cent of the population of Ireland could converse in it—a loss of over one-half in absolute numbers in fifty years. Only 4 in 1,000 are ignorant of English. Irish is now but little used except in the most western part of Ireland.

The Irish type is known to all Americans—tall, long-headed, with dark-blue or gray eyes, and hair more often dark than light. This type predominates throughout the greater part of Ireland. Beddoe considers the Irish of to-day to be at least one-third English or Scotch in blood, Teutonic ("Nordic") in type rather than "Celtic" (see), notwithstanding the opinion long prevalent among ethnologists.

From what has been said of the language and physique of the Irish, it will be seen that it is difficult to determine the population of the race. Reclus and Hanna have pointed out, however, that in Ireland the statistics of religious confession "bear a close affinity to those of the various racial elements of which the population is composed:" that the Roman Catholics represent approximately the Irish element; the Presbyterians, the Scotch or so-called Scotch-Irish; the Episcopalians, the English or Anglo-Irish. In 1901 the Roman Catholics numbered 3,308,661—that is, 74 per cent of the population; and there were 443,276 Presbyterians and 581,089 Episcopalians. On the basis of the number of persons in England and Scotland who were born in Ireland, Ravenstein has estimated the number of Irish in these countries to be 2,000,000. If Ravenstein and Hanna be right, the Irish population of the United Kingdom is in the neighborhood of 5,000,000. It is generally given as less—that is, the number of the Celts in Europe is given as only about 3,000,000 by Brachelli and Hickmann. But they apparently count those only who speak Celtic languages. Longstaff estimates that 22 per cent of the population of Canada, or nearly 1,000,000, are Irish.

THE SCOTCH-IRISH.

The term "Scotch-Irish" does not necessarily indicate, as many Americans suppose, a mixed Scotch and Irish descent, although in many individual cases it could be properly so used. It is an appellation given to the American descendants of the Lowland Scotch, Presbyterians in religion, who emigrated in the early part of the seventeenth century to Ulster province in northern Ireland, and thousands of whom emigrated to America during the following century. At first they called themselves Scotch. They speak an English dialect with a peculiar accent closely akin to that of the northern part of England. Physically they are a mixed race descended from the ancient Britons with later Teutonic additions, especially of Scandinavian, Danish, and Anglian origin. It is claimed by some that difference in religion, strong racial prejudice, and the policy of the Government in land allotments, have all tended to keep the Lowland Scotch of Ulster and the Irish apart. There is a difference of opinion as to the proportion of intermarriages that take place; some say very few. Yet to the average American, an Irishman and a Scotch-Irishman as found in the United States look very much alike. The latter have contributed some of the greatest statesmen of American history.

The Irish were the first people to come to the United States in large numbers as immigrants. During the thirty years 1821 to 1850, Ireland contributed more than two-fifths of all immigrants, and more than one-third during the next ten years. They came most rapidly during the decades of 1841 to 1860. Since then they have fallen off both in absolute numbers and in relative proportion, dropping to the third place in rank—that is, below the German and the English, from 1861 to 1890. The total number of European immigrants admitted to the United States during the period 1820 to 1910 is given as 25,421,929, and of these 4,212,169 are credited to Ireland. The actual number coming from Ireland during that period was considerably larger, for during certain years when immigration from that country was particularly heavy a great part of all immigrants from the United Kingdom were recorded simply as coming from Great Britain, the particular country not being specified. Since the rapid influx of immigrants from southeastern Europe (see articles *Slav* and *Caucasian*), the Irish have fallen (1907) to the twelfth place down the list of immigrant races. The total number coming to the United States for the year was 38,706, of whom 37,660 came from the United Kingdom. During the twelve years 1899–1910, a total of 439,724 Irish immigrants were admitted to the United States, placing the race sixth in point of numbers for the period. Their rate of movement, however, is still high, being, in 1907, 8 per 1,000 of the population of Ireland. This rate is not equaled by any other race from northwestern Europe except the Norwegian, but it was exceeded by some from eastern Europe, for example, by the Hebrew and the Slovak, with 18 each per 1,000 of population, and the Croatian-Slovenian group with 13. It was about equaled by the Polish, but was slightly larger than the Magyar.

The population of Ireland, about 4,500,000, is but little more than one-half what it was sixty years ago. It is too small, when compared with the great populations of the newer immigrating races, to ever again hold first rank numerically for any series of years. As against Ireland's population of 4,500,000, the Great Russians number 57,000,000, the Little Russians 25,000,000, the Poles 17,000,000, and the Italians 35,000,000. The census of 1901 for Ireland shows that there were 433,526 emigrants for the decade of 1891–1900, over 89 per cent of whom were destined to the United States, 4 per cent to England and Wales, 2.4 per cent to Scotland, 2 per cent to Australia, and 1.5 per cent to Canada.

The Irish are shown by the Census of 1900 to hold second place among the foreign-born in the United States. There are, in fact, more Irish of the first and second generations alone in the United States than in Ireland—1,618,567 who were born in Ireland and 3,220,110 native-born of foreign-born parents.

Irish immigrants go mainly to the New England and Middle Atlantic States, although they are fairly well distributed throughout the entire United States. During the twelve years 1899–1910, their principal destinations in the United States were as follows:

New York	159,080
Massachusetts	91,565
Pennsylvania	57,435
New Jersey	24,377
Illinois	22,342
Connecticut	16,368
California	9,867
Rhode Island	9,210

ISRAELITE. (See *Hebrew.*)

ISTRIAN. A geographical, not a racial name, and not used by the Bureau of Immigration; any native or inhabitant of Istria, a crownland of Austria on the Adriatic coast. The Istrians are for the most part Slavs or Italians. The population of Istria is 336,000, of whom 43 per cent are Serbo-Croatians, 40 per cent Italians, 15 per cent Slovenians, and only 2 per cent Germans (see these). The Istrians almost to a man are Roman Catholic in religion.

ITALIAN. The race or people of Italy. The Bureau of Immigration divides this race into two groups, North Italian and South Italian. These two groups differ from each other materially in language, physique, and character, as well as in geographical distribution. The former may be defined as including those Italians who are natives of the basin of the Po (compartimenti of Piedmont, Lombardy, Venetia, and Emelia) and of the Italian districts of France, of Switzerland, and of Tyrol (Austria), and their descendants. All of the people of the peninsula proper and of the islands of Sicily and Sardinia are South Italian. Even Genoa is South Italian.

Linguistically, Italian is one of the grand divisions of the Romance group of languages descended from the Latin stock of the Aryan family. It has many dialects, the separation and preservation of which is favored by the geographical configuration of Italy. Hovelacque divides these dialects into three groups, the upper, the central, and the lower. The first includes the Genoese, Piedmontese, Venetian, Emilian, and Lombard dialects; the central group includes the Tuscan, Roman, and Corsican, and the lower group includes the Neapolitan, Calabrian, Sicilian, and Sardinian. These dialects diverge much more from each other than do the dialects of English or Spanish. In fact, it is said that it is difficult for a Neapolitan or a Sardinian to make himself understood by the natives of the valley of the Po. Perhaps in no other country do the educated classes cling more tenaciously to the familiar use of the local dialects in preference to the national literary form of the language. The latter is the Florentine dialect of Tuscany as embalmed in literature by Dante, Petrarch, and Bocaccio in the fourteenth century. A number of the other dialects, however, have quite a considerable literature, especially the Venetian, Lombard, Neapolitan, and Sicilian. The last named is remarkably rich in poetry.

All the upper group of dialects as defined by Hovelacque, except the Genoese, are North Italian. They contain many Gallic or Celtic elements and show affinities for the Provençal and the Rhæto-Romansh (Ladin and Friulan) languages, which bound them on all sides except the south. The Genoese and the dialects of the central and lower groups are used by South Italians.

Physically the Italians are anything but a homogeneous race. The Apennine chain of mountains forms a geographical line which corresponds to the boundary between two distinct ethnic groups. The region north of this line, the basin of the Po, is inhabited by a very broad-headed ("Alpine") and tallish race, the North Italian. The inhabitants of the eastern and western halves of this basin show slight variations due to some Teutonic admixture in Lombardy and to an infusion of Slavic blood in Venetia. All of Italy south of the Apennines and all of the adjacent islands are occupied by a long-headed, dark, "Mediterranean" race of short stature. This is the South Italian, supposed to be descended from the ancient Ligurians of Italy and closely related to the Iberians of Spain and the Berbers of northern Africa. Indeed, the foremost Italian ethnologist, Sergi, traces their origin to the Hamitic stock (see *Semitic-Hamitic*) of North Africa. It must be remembered that the Hamites are not Negritic or true African, although there may be some traces of an infusion of African blood in this stock in certain communities of Sicily and Sardinia, as well as in northern Africa. The Bureau of Immigration places the North Italian in the "Keltic" division and the South Italian in the "Iberic." Comparatively little admixture has taken place between these two ethnic groups, although many North Italians have found their way around the eastern end of the mountain chain into middle Italy. Therefore, the line of demarcation between the Emilians and the Tuscans is much less sharp than it is between the Piedmontese and the Genoese.

An Italian sociologist, Niceforo, has pointed out that these two ethnic groups differ as radically in psychic characters as they do in physical. He describes the South Italian as excitable, impulsive, highly imaginative, impracticable; as an individualist having little adaptability to highly organized society. The North Italian, on the other hand, is pictured as cool, deliberate, patient, practical, and as capable of great progress in the political and social organization of modern civilization. Both North and South Italians are devoted to their families, are benevolent, religious, artistic, and industrious. Nearly all are Catholic in religion. Most of the Italian immigration to the United States is recruited from the farming and the laboring classes of Italy. In America, however, they have not attained distinguished success as farmers, although as fruit and wine growers, especially in California, they rank among the foremost.

Bosco, the Italian statistician, admits that Italy still holds first place for the number of crimes committed against the person, although these have greatly diminished since the betterment of educational facilities and the large outflow of emigrants. After Italy in this respect come Austria, France, and, considerably farther down the list, Ireland, Germany, England, and Scotland. Niceforo shows from Italian statistics that all crimes, and especially violent crimes, are several times more numerous among the South than the North Italians. Gambling is common. The lottery is a national institution conducted to fill the state coffers. Brigandage is now quite extinct, except perhaps in some parts of the island of Sicily. The secret organizations of the Mafia (see *Sicilian*) and Comorra, institutions of great influence among the people, which take the law into their own hands and which are responsible for much of the crime, flourish throughout southern Italy. The chief difficulty in dealing with the crimes of Italians seems to be their determination not to testify in court against an enemy, but to insist on settling their wrongs after the manner of the vendetta. (See *Corsican.*)

It is significant that Italy is one of the most illiterate countries of Europe. In 1901, 48.5 per cent of the entire population 6 years of age and over could not read or write. In that year in Calabria, the most southern compartimento of the peninsula, the illiterate amounted to 78.7 per cent of the population 6 years old or over. The smallest degree of illiteracy is found in the valley of the Po among the North Italians. The Lombards and the Piedmontese are the best educated of all Italians. Conditions, however, have been gradually improving since the Government made education free and compulsory between the ages of 6 and 9 years in communes where only lower elementary schools are maintained, and 6 to 12 years where there are schools of a higher grade.

The poverty of the lower classes is extreme. They live in miserable habitations and subsist upon poor food, principally badly cured maize. Even in Venice one-fourth of the population are said to be regular recipients of official charity.

The geographical boundaries of the Italian race are wider than those of Italy. Considerable numbers are found in the adjacent countries of France, Switzerland, and Austria. The provinces of Tyrol and Istria, in Austria, are one-third Italian. Large numbers of them are found in the New World. Italy itself is nearly all Italian. It has a population of 34,000,000, and contains only small islets of other races—some 80,000 French in the western part of northern Italy, 30,000 Slavs in northeastern Italy, about 30,000 Greeks in southern Italy, some 90,000 Albanians in southern Italy and in Sicily, and 10,000 Catalans (Spanish) in Sardinia. There are a few Germans in the Italian Alps; perhaps fewer than 10,000. Nearly two-fifths of the population of Italy is found in the valley of the Po; that is, in less than one-third the length of Italy. Roughly divided by compartimenti, the population of this district, which is occupied by North Italians, is about 14,000,000. This includes the Friulans of northeastern Italy, who, although they speak a Latin language distinct from Italian, are hardly distinguishable from the North Italians in race. Their number has been variously estimated at from 50,000 to 450,000. The population of the South Italian districts is about 19,750,000, of whom 125,000 belong to other races. Most of the Italians of France, Switzerland, and Austria are North Italian in race. Those of Corsica, an island belonging to France, are South Italian.

Distribution of Italians.

[Estimated for 1901.]

In Europe:	
Italy	33, 200, 000
France	350, 000
Switzerland	200, 000
Austria	650, 000
Corsica	300, 000
Other Europe	300, 000
Total	35, 000, 000

Elsewhere: [a]

Brazil	1, 000, 000
Argentine Republic	620, 000
Other parts of South America	140, 000
United States	1, 200, 000
Africa	60, 000
Total	3, 020, 000
Total for the world (in round numbers)	38, 000, 000

More than half a million Italians have emigrated in certain years since 1900 to different parts of the world. About one-half of this emigration is to other European countries and is temporary in character, being composed mostly of men. From 1899 to 1910, inclusive, 2,284,601 Italian immigrants were admitted to the United States and a large number also emigrated from Italy to South American countries. A large part of those who come to the United States return to their former homes. The net gain, however, especially in New York and other States of the East, is large. The South Italian immigrants numbered more than 240,000 in 1907—that is, more than half as many again as the next highest immigrant race. The North Italians send only about one-fifth as many.

The immense capacity of the Italian race to populate other parts of the earth is shown by the fact that they outnumber the Spanish race in Spanish Argentina and the Portuguese race in Brazil, a "Portuguese" country. (See *Spanish American.*) Italian immigration to the United States is perhaps of more significance in the study of immigration than any other at the present time, not only because it is far larger each year than that of any other race, nor merely because it stands high in the rate per 1,000 of the population now coming to the United States. More significant still is the fact that this race has a larger

[a] Estimates, mainly from Franceschini.

population than any of the dozen other races ranking highest in the rate of immigration. In other words, out of its 35,000,000 population and the high birth rate that characterizes the race, it can continue to lead in immigration when the other races now contributing largely to the immigrant tide, the Hebrews (population 8,000,000), the Slovaks (2,250,000), and the Croatian-Slovenian group (3,600,000), are depleted, as, in fact, Ireland is to-day.

It is not generally realized that during the decade 1891–1900 Italy was the leading source of American immigration. In the early eighties—that is, nearly thirty years ago—Italy had already begun to gain upon the northern European countries in this regard. Yet it was not until about 1890 that the United States forged ahead of South American countries as a destination for Italian immigrants. During the preceding decade or longer Brazil received more Italians than did the Argentine Republic, although the latter is wrongly supposed to have the largest Italian population in South America. In 1907 the United States received 294,000 out of 415,000 Italian emigrants to transatlantic countries. The total emigration to European countries for that year, mostly temporary, was 288,774. Much of the Italian immigration to the United States has thus far assumed a temporary character. Mosso estimates that the average time spent by Italians in the United States is eight years.

The heaviest transatlantic emigration from Italy is chiefly from districts south of Rome inhabited by South Italians. They come especially from Sicily and Calabria, the least productive and most poorly developed portions of the country. Very few emigrate from Sardinia (see). The compartimento of Liguria, the home of the Genoese, also South Italian in race, contributes more emigrants than any other province in northern Italy. The total American immigration from certain compartimenti has reached phenomenal proportions, being several times the natural increase of the population, with the result that some agricultural districts are already partly depopulated.

Compared with other immigrant races as to absolute number of arrivals, the South Italian heads the list with 1,911,933 in the twelve years 1899–1910. Next comes the Hebrew with 1,074,442; then the Polish with 949,064, followed by the German with 754,375 and the Scandinavian with 586,306. The North Italians occupy the ninth place down the list in the same period with 372,668, next after the English and Slovaks, but above the Magyars, Croatians and Slovenians, and Greeks. In rate of transatlantic movement the North and the South Italians present quite a contrast; for example, the emigration from Calabria was eleven times as great as that from Venetia in 1905. In 1907 the rate of movement of North Italians to the United States was about 3 per 1,000 of their population in Italy, while that of the South Italians was about 12 per 1,000. The rate of movement of the North Italians was about the same as that of the Swedes and the Finns. It was three times that of the Germans, but only half that of the Ruthenians from Austria-Hungary. The rate of movement of the South Italians, on the other hand, is exceeded by only the Croatian-Slovenian group, which sent us 13 per 1,000 of its population in 1907, and by the Hebrews and the Slovaks with 18 each per 1,000 of their populations in the same year.

Italian immigrants come to the United States chiefly from the following countries in addition to Italy: British North America (3,800 in 1907), Austria-Hungary (1,500), the United Kingdom (600), South America (600), and Switzerland (200). Those coming from Switzerland and Austria-Hungary are generally of the North Italian race.

In the twelve years 1899–1910, the principal destinations in the United States of the two Italian groups were as follows:

North Italian.

New York	94, 458
Pennsylvania	59, 627
California	50, 156
Illinois	33, 525
Massachusetts	22, 062
Connecticut	13, 391
Michigan	13, 355
New Jersey	12, 013
Colorado	9, 254

South Italian.

New York	898, 655
Pennsylvania	369, 573
Massachusetts	132, 820
New Jersey	106, 667
Illinois	77, 724
Connecticut	64, 530
Ohio	53, 012
Louisiana	31, 394
Rhode Island	30, 182
West Virginia	23, 865
Michigan	15, 570
California	15, 018

ITALIC group. (See *Aryan.*)

IZHORA. Same as **Ijore**. A division of the Western Finns. (See *Finnish.*)

J.

JAMAICAN. (See *West Indian.*)

JAPANESE. The people of Japan. With the exception of the "Arctic group" the Japanese and Koreans form the easternmost group of the great Sibiric branch, which, with the Sinitic branch (Chinese, etc.), constitutes the Mongolian race (see these terms). As was said in the article on Chinese, the Japanese and Koreans stand much nearer than the Chinese, especially in language, to the Finns,

Lapps, Magyars, and Turks of Europe, who are the westernmost descendants of the Mongolian race. The languages of all these peoples belong to the agglutinative family, while Chinese is monosyllabic.

Although many people may mistake a Japanese face for Chinese, the Mongolian traits are much less pronounced. The skin is much less yellow, the eyes less oblique. The hair, however, is true Mongolian, black and round in section, and the nose is small. These physical differences no doubt indicate that the Japanese are of mixed origin. In the south there is probably a later Malay admixture. In some respects their early culture resembles that of the Philippines of to-day. Then there is an undoubted white strain in Japan. The Ainos, the earliest inhabitants of Japan, are one of the most truly Caucasian-like people in appearance in eastern Asia. They have dwindled away to less than 20,000 under the pressure of the Mongolian invasion from the mainland, but they have left their impress upon the Japanese race. The "fine" type of the aristocracy, the Japanese ideal, as distinct from the "coarse" type recognized by students of the Japanese of to-day, is perhaps due to the Aino.

The social characteristics and importance of the Japanese people are well known from recent history. It is generally well understood that Christianity makes very slow progress. Shintoism, a mixture of nature and ancestor worship, and Buddhism are the prevailing religions. The Japanese now number about 48,000,000. Only about 150,000 live outside of Japan. Since the Russian-Japanese war there are probably 40,000 or 50,000 Japanese resident in Korea. Some 10,000 are found in British lands. From 1899 to 1910, inclusive, 148,729 Japanese were admitted to the United States. Under the so-called passport provision of the United States immigration law of 1907, and by agreement with Japan, Japanese laborers are now excluded from the country. During the twelve-year period referred to 77,777 Japanese immigrants were destined to Hawaii, 32,273 to California, 25,912 to Washington, and 4,485 to Oregon.

JAT. A tribe or caste of India. (See *Hindu.*)

JAVAN or **JAVANESE.** Any native of Java. (See *Malay* and *East Indian.*) They do not emigrate to the United States.

JEWISH. (See *Hebrew.*)

JMOUD, JEMAITIC, SAMOGITIAN, JMUDZ, or **LOW LITHUANIAN.** A division of the Lithuanians (see) living for the most part in the province of Kovno, bordering on Germany and formerly called Samogitia. They number about 450,000.

K.

KAFIR. A name applied to two very different peoples: (1) the Caucasian people of Kafiristan, in Afghanistan, who speak an Indo-European language (see *Aryan*); (2) a Negro or Bantu tribe of South Africa.

KAIVAN. A division of Western Finns who speak a Karelian dialect. (See *Finnish.*)

KALDANI. A name applied to the Ayssores (see), meaning Chaldeans (see).

KALMUK or **CALMUCK.** A race or people belonging to the Mongolic group now living mainly in southeastern Russia. Much smaller in numbers than the Tatars, their neighbors, to whom they are not related in language so closely as to the Mongols of northern China. In appearance and culture also they are more Asiatic than the Tatars (see). They still follow a nomadic life with their herds on the steppes of Russia somewhat as they did in their old home in central Asia around Lake Balkash and at the foot of the Altais. They serve with the Cossack cavalry, mainly in the capacity of herdsmen. In religion they are Buddhists.

They number only 200,000, being found mainly in the province of Astrakhan and midway between the Caspian and the Black seas. The tribe most nearly related to them is the Buriat, far east in Siberia. None are known to come to the United States.

KANAKA. A familiar term for a Hawaiian (see). Often loosely applied to any Polynesian sailor (see).

KANARESE. A branch of the Dravidian race (see) living in the western part of southern India. Their language, the Kanarese, is spoken by over 10,000,000 persons.

KARACHI. A wandering tribe of Persia. (See *Gypsy.*)

KARAIT. A small Tataric people (see) of the Crimea, in southern Russia, now of the Hebrew (see) faith.

KARA-KALPAKS, that is, "black" Kalpaks. A Tataric people (see) of Asiatic Russia.

KARA-KIRGHIZ, that is, "black" Kirghiz (see) of Asiatic Russia.

KARAPAPAKH. A small Tataric people (see) of southeastern Russia.

KARATCHAI. A small Tataric people (see) of the Caucasus in Russia.

KAREL, KARELIAN, or **KARIALAISET.** The easternmost section of the Finns proper. (See *Finnish.*)

KARTVELIAN. A name applied to the Georgian group (see), or Southern Division of the Caucasus peoples (see).

KASHMIRI or **CASHMIRIAN.** A small division of the Indo-Aryan stock living in the valley of the Kashmir on the northwestern border of India. Their language, the Kashmiri, is spoken by about 1,000,000 persons. (See *Hindu.*)

KASHOUBISH or **KASSUBI.** A subdivision of the Poles (see).

KASI-KUMYK. (*See Caucasus peoples.*)

KAZAK. (See *Cossack* and *Kirghiz.*)

KAZAN TATAR. A Tatar (see) living in Kazan province, eastern Russia.

KELTIC. Same as **Celtic** (see).

KERESHEN. Christianized Tatars (see) of Kazan, in eastern Russia.

KHMER. A Cambojan people. Supposed to be of mixed Mongolian and Caucasian race. (See these and *East Indian.*)

KHORUTAN. Same as **Carinthian;** a division of the Slovenians (see).

KHORVAT, KHROBAT, KHROVAT, KHROVATH, or **HERVAT.** Same as **Croatian** (see).

KIPCHAK. A small division of the Turkic branch of the Ural-Altaic stock (see).

KIRGHIZ. Two related Tataric tribes are known as Kirghiz: the Kara-Kirghiz ("black" Kirghiz) or Buruts, of Central Asia (see *Tataric*), and the Kirghiz-Kazaks, better known as the Cossacks (see), who live farther east, mainly in Central Asia.

KIZIL-BASHI. Turks of Asia Minor. (See *Tataric.*)

KOL. A small division of the Munda (Kolarian) group of the Dravidian peoples (see), living north of the Dravidians proper in Central and Eastern India. (See *Hindu.*)

KOPANICZAR. A division of the Walachs. (See *Bohemian* and *Slovak.*)

KOREAN. The people of the Korean Peninsula. They and the Japanese (see) form a distinct physical group, and are linguistically more nearly related to European Mongolians than they are to the neighboring Chinese (see). Under the new leadership of the Japanese they may be expected to make rapid progress. They number about 10,000,000. From 1899 to 1910,

7,790 Koreans came to the United States, but at the present time Korean immigrants are practically excluded from the country.

KRAINER. A native of the province of Carniola (Krain), Austria. Nearly all the inhabitants (95 per cent) are Slovenians (see).

KRAKUS or **CRACOVINIAN.** Same as **Bielochrovat.** (See *Polish.*)

KROAT. Same as **Croatian** (see).

KUMYK. A small Tataric (see) people on the Russian side of the Caspian.

KUNDUR. A branch of the Nogai Tatars. (See *Tataric.*)

KUPRIKE. A subdivision of the Poles (see).

KURD. The largest western section of Indo-Iranic stock, excepting the neighboring Armenians, of whom the Kurds are the notorious and inveterate enemies and persecutors. The Kurdish language is closely related to the Persian, and through that to the Armenian and the Aryan tongues of Europe, rather than to the surrounding Arabian and Turkish. Physically, the Kurds are a mixed people, showing especially Arab (Semitic) and Turkish (Mongolian) elements through their long social and religious contact with these peoples. They are almost uniformly Mohammedans. A few on the Persian border are of the ancient Nestorian sect—Christians. They have pressed northward from Kurdistan into Armenia, and about 100,000 are settled in Russian Transcaucasia. In all, they probably exceed 3,000,000, or somewhat less in number than the Armenians. Nearly one-half of them live in Turkey. They are not known as emigrants to America.

KUTZO-VLACH. Same as **Tsintsar.** A name given by Macedonians to an important division of Roumanians (see) living in the central part of northern Greece. Their native name is Aromuni; that is, Romans. (See *Bulgarian.*)

KUYEV. A subdivision of the Poles (see).

KWAEN, QUAEN, or **KAINALAISET.** The branch of Western Finns (see *Finnish*) living farthest north in Finland and Sweden, and therefore adjoining the Lapps. A few are found even amongst the Norwegians, from whom they are distinguished physically by their darker color. In manner of life they are in a transitional stage between the nomadic Lapps and the cultured Finns.

KYMRIC or **CYMRIC.** (See *Celtic.*)

L.

LADIN. A mountain people of Tyrol and the north Italian border who speak a modern Latin tongue, the Ladin, distinct from the Italian. They are a subdivision of the Rhæto-Romansh group (see).

LAPOTNIKI. Same as **Bugan** (see). A name applied to Ruthenians (see) living on the Bug.

LAPPISH (called by themselves **Samelat**). The westernmost Siberic (Mongolian) race or people, from which Lapland takes its name. This region, of indefinite boundaries, extending across northern Norway and Sweden and into northwestern Russia, is inhabited by the two most opposite racial stocks of Europe—on the one hand the dark, dwarfish, round-headed, and comparatively uncivilized Lapps, of Asiatic origin; on the other, the blond Scandinavians, the tallest, the longest-headed, and perhaps the purest representatives of the so-called "European" race (Lapouge). The languages spoken by these two races are as different as their physical types. That of the Lapps is agglutinative, like that of the Finns and Mongols; that of the Swedes or of the Norwegians is a cross between English and German, that is, inflected and belonging to the

Indo-European (see *Aryan*) family of languages.

Although the subject is interesting to the ethnologist, no great amount of space need be given to the Lapps. They are but a remnant numerically and so different in habits of civilization from ourselves that but few members of the race find their way to America. Their total population in the three kingdoms is only 30,000. In Scandinavia where they are most numerous, they do not number one-half of 1 per cent of the population. Lapland itself has far more Scandinavians, Russians, and Finns than Lapps living in it.

Many Lapps, of course, are of mixed blood, taller and more fair than those of the ancient type. In fact, the race bids fair to disappear by amalgamation. But it is a curious mistake of well-informed persons to think that the Lapps are Norwegians, or even fair. Their nearest relatives in appearance and manner of life, if not in language, are the Samoyeds (see) of northeastern Russia and of Siberia. Although Lapland falls largely within the Arctic Circle, the climate is milder than that of the Siberian coast farther east. Perhaps it is because their hard conditions of life resemble somewhat those of the Eskimos that there is a slight physical resemblance between the two races. In head form alone is there a marked difference. While the Eskimo is long-headed, the Lapp is the broadest-headed of the broad-headed Mongolians and "Alpine" peoples of Europe.

It remains only to be said that the Lapps are nominally Christians, but for the most part very superstitious and ignorant; and that throughout much of Lapland they still lead a nomadic life from the necessity of following their herds of reindeer over vast stretches of desolate mountain, tundra, and swamp. The few that have come to America are lost sight of in the statistics of the Bureau of Immigration. They are a part of the "Other peoples."

LATVI. Same as **Letts** (see).

LAZ. A branch of the Georgians. (See *Caucasus peoples.*)

LEK. Has two uses: **(1)** A name formerly applied to Poles (see), and (2) same as Waterpolak. The latter are considered by some to be Moravians. (See *Bohemian and Moravian.*)

LEMKE. A division of Little Russians, so called because of their peculiar pronunciation. (See *Ruthenian.*)

LESGHIAN. The principal people of Daghestan, in Transcaucasia, or their language; a branch of the Eastern Division of the Caucasus peoples (see).

LETT, LETTISH, or **LATVI.** The northernmost division of the Letto-Lithuanian or Lettic stock. The Letts speak a language related to Lithuanian about as Italian stands to Latin. It is divided into the Low Lettish or Tahmian spoken in Northwestern Courland; the High Lettish toward the east, and the Middle Lettish, which is the literary form. The Letts live for the most part in the southern Baltic provinces of Russia. They are counted as Lithuanians in the statistics of the Bureau of Immigration. (See *Lithuanian* for details concerning them.)

LETTIC, LETTO-LITHUANIAN, LITHUANIAN-LETTISH, or **BALTIC.** The name given to that group of Aryan languages which is made up of the Lettish, the Lithuanian, the Jmoud, and the Old Prussian. (See these, and especially *Lithuanian.*) "Lettic" is sometimes used in the sense of Lettish only.

LETTO-SLAVIC, WENDIC, or **BALTO-SLAVIC.** The closely related Lettic and Slavic (see) groups of languages are sometimes put together under these names.

LIBERIAN. A native of Liberia, Africa. A political, not an ethnical, term. (See *Negro.*)

LITHUANIAN, LITVA, or **LETUVI-NINKAI.** The Aryan race of western Russia, which gave its name to the former principality of Lithuania, and which, with the related Letts, Jmouds, and Old Prussians, forms a distinct subdivision linguistically of the Aryan stock. This subdivision is variously called the Lettic, Baltic, Letto-Lithuanian, or, less properly, the Lithuanian group, using the last given name in the widest sense, and it is sometimes combined with the Slavic (see) under the designation "Letto-Slavic." For convenience Letts and Jmouds are counted as Lithuanians and are put into the "Slavic division" by the Bureau of Immigration. They will be considered together in this article. The Lithuanians are one of the three or four peoples now most active in immigration from Russia.

There is a marked opposition between the conclusions of the philologists and those of the physical anthropologists as to the relationship of the Lithuanians to the Slavs. While the former consider them to be the most closely related to the Slavs of all non-Slavic peoples, the anthropologists, as typified by Ripley, place them at nearly the opposite extreme from the Slavs in European ethnology. The latter are put in the brunette, broad-headed, and wide-faced "Alpine" or "Celto-Slavic" race, while the Lithuanians, and especially the more typical Letts, are said to be "pure blond" and to "approximate quite closely to our Anglo-Saxon model;" that is, to approach the extreme of the long-headed type, and therefore to belong to the "Nordic," or at least to the "Sub-Nordic" race. No doubt both are right. To-day they stand as close linguistically to their eastern neighbors, the Russians, as they do physically to their western neighbors, the Swedes. What they were originally is the question. Is their language or their physical type the last acquired? That it is not the language might be argued from the fact that the Lithuanian is older than perhaps any other Aryan tongue of Europe.

Leaving the ethnical center of the race in Courland, on the Baltic, it is found that it shades off in every direction into the types of the surrounding peoples. Toward the southwest, in Prussia, it has almost disappeared in the German, as the Old Prussian, formerly spoken by the Lithuanians in that region, has entirely disappeared—a dialect, by the way, which must not be thought from its name to be Teutonic: it is purely Letto-Slavic. On the southeastern border it is difficult to draw the line, except in language, between the White Russians and the Lithuanians. On the north, in the province of Livonia, there is clearly an approximation to the Finnish type through intermarriage with the Livs and Esths.

The Lithuanians are interesting historically. Although surrounded by aggressive races, they long retained their own independence, thanks to their impenetrable swamps and forests. But they retained also their pagan beliefs, traces of which may be found even in the peasantry of to-day. Not till the fourteenth century were they Christianized. Through their political union with Poland, the Lithuanians proper and the Jmouds became Catholic, and are to-day the northernmost people of that faith on the Continent. The Letts are divided among the Lutheran, the Catholic, and the Russian or Orthodox churches. The greater number (750,000), who adjoin the Protestant Finnish population on the north and were united politically with it, are Lutherans; toward the east 50,000 affiliate with the great mass of the Russian population in the Greek church; while farther south, in Vitebsk province, which formerly belonged, like the Lithuanian provinces, to Catholic Poland, the Letts are mainly Catholic.

There are several divisions of the Lettic or Letto-Lithuanian group of languages. In the first place, Lithuanian is about as different from Lettish as Latin is from Italian. Then there are subdivisions. The Jmoud, Zmudz, Jemaitic, Samogitian, or Low Lithuanian is a dialect of the Lithuanian. The Lettish has three dialects, one of them called the Tahmian. Another people, considered by some to be Lithuanian, is the black-haired Yatvyags, farther south, who are probably a mixture of White Russians and Mazurs (Poles). These perhaps have been included in the count of Lithuanians in Suwalki and other Polish provinces by the Russian census. (See table.)

The Lithuanian is a small race numerically, only about 1 per cent of the total population of Europe, or 3½ per cent of the population of Russia. It does not exceed 4,000,000 in numbers, and is therefore only one-fourth the size of the Polish race, one-half that of the Hebrew, or one-fifteenth that of the Great Russian, and is about equal to that of the Ruthenians of Austria-Hungary, or of the Bulgarians. The Prussian census shows but little over 100,000 Lithuanians in that country. In the six Lithuanian provinces listed below, the total population is over 7,000,000. More than one-half therefore of the population is of outside peoples, mostly White Russian, Polish, Hebrew, and, along the Baltic, German. That the Letts come from quite different provinces from the Lithuanians proper is evident from the following figures taken from the Russian census of 1897:

Lithuanian and Lettish population of Russia.

Provinces.	Letts.	Jmouds.	Lithuanians.	Total.
Northern:				
Livonia	563,829	100	6,594	570,523
Courland	505,994	1,517	16,531	524,042
Vitebsk	264,032	67	2,335	266,434
Central:				
Kovno	35,188	444,921	574,853	1,054,962
Southern:				
Vilna	471	157	279,720	280,348
Suwalki	74	54	304,548	304,676
Elsewhere	66,349	1,206	25,929	93,484
Total	1,435,937	448,022	1,210,510	3,094,469

In other words, the Letts are found mainly in the northern provinces of this region, the Jmouds in the center, and the Lithuanians, although more scattered, occupy the central and southern provinces. In Suwalki, a province of what is to-day called Poland, the Lithuanians number one-half of the population. In Kovno, adjoining it on the north, they constitute one-third, and the Jmouds, or Low Lithuanians, another third of the population.

While the Lithuanians are small in numbers, they have been among the more active races in immigration to America. In 1907 they stood tenth in rank as to the rate of immigration, 6 per 1,000 of population. In this respect they were surpassed by several Slavic peoples, the Poles, the Slovaks, and the Croatian-Slovenian group. The Ruthenians from Austria-Hungary came in about the same ratio, but the rate of Hebrew or Slovak immigration in that year was three times greater. During the twelve years ending June 30, 1910, Lithuanian immigration to the United States was 175,258, or more than twice as great as the immigration of Russians proper, although the population of the latter race is fifteen times larger. As to the absolute number of immigrants, Lithuanians stood thirteenth in rank during the period last mentioned. While Polish immigrants were more than five times as numerous in the twelve years referred to, their rate of immigration was only a little larger, or 4.6 per 1,000, as compared with 3.6 per 1,000 for Lithuanians. The number of Hebrew immigrants was more than six times that of Lithuanians. Nearly three-fourths of the Lithuanians go to the same States to which most Poles and other typical Slavic peoples go, namely, Pennsylvania, Illinois, New York, and Massachusetts.

LITTLE RUSSIAN, MALO-RUSSIAN, or **RUSSNIAK.** Same as **Ruthenian** (see).

LITVA. Same as **Lithuanian** (see).

LIV or **LIVONIAN.** A division of the Western Finns living in Livonia. (See *Finnish.*)

LOPARI. A division of the Western Finns. (See *Finnish.*)

LOTHARINGIAN. (See *German.*)

LOW GERMAN, LOW LETTIC, LOW LITHUANIAN, etc. Dialects or divisions of these respective languages (which see).

LOWLAND SCOTCH. (See *English* and *Scotch.*)

LUBLINIAN. A subdivision of the Poles (see).

LUNGAUER. A name applied to certain Germans (see) of Austria.

LURI. A wandering tribe of Persia. (See *Gypsy.*)

LUSATIAN. Same as **Wend** (see this and *Slav*).

LUXEMBURGER. (See *German.*)

M.

MACEDONIAN. (See *Bulgarian.*)

MAGYAR (pron. Mä-jår), **Hungarian, Hun,** or **Hunyak** in popular language. The race, of Finno-Tatar origin, that invaded Hungary about the ninth century and is now dominant there. Often called "Hungarian," although this is more properly a political than an ethnological term and may be applied also to that half of the population of Hungary which is not Magyar. "Huns" and "Hunkies" are names still more incorrectly applied to this race and to Slavs indiscriminately in some parts of America. The Huns, properly speaking, were a horde that overran parts of Europe in the middle ages and are supposed to be more closely represented by the modern Kalmuks or Turks than by the Magyars. The "Hunagars" and "Mogers" pushed later over the Asiatic border and absorbed the earlier Mongol and other elements of what is now Hungary. They became Christianized in the eleventh century, the earliest of all the Finno-Tataric tribes of Europe. Thus it is that the Magyars, together with the Finns, are the foremost branches of the Mongolian race, as measured by western civilization.

As has been said elsewhere (see *Finnish* and *Ural-Altaic*), the Magyars are related linguistically to the Turks and Japanese (see), all these belonging to the great Sibiric stock possessing agglutinative speech. But physically the Magyars and the Finns of to-day are not Mongolian as much as Caucasian. Because of mixture with Caucasian peoples, they have deviated more widely from the ancient type than have the Turks. While these latter are becoming southern European in type, the Magyars are often blonds, yet not so generally as are the Finns. In short, while the Magyars have imposed their speech and rule upon

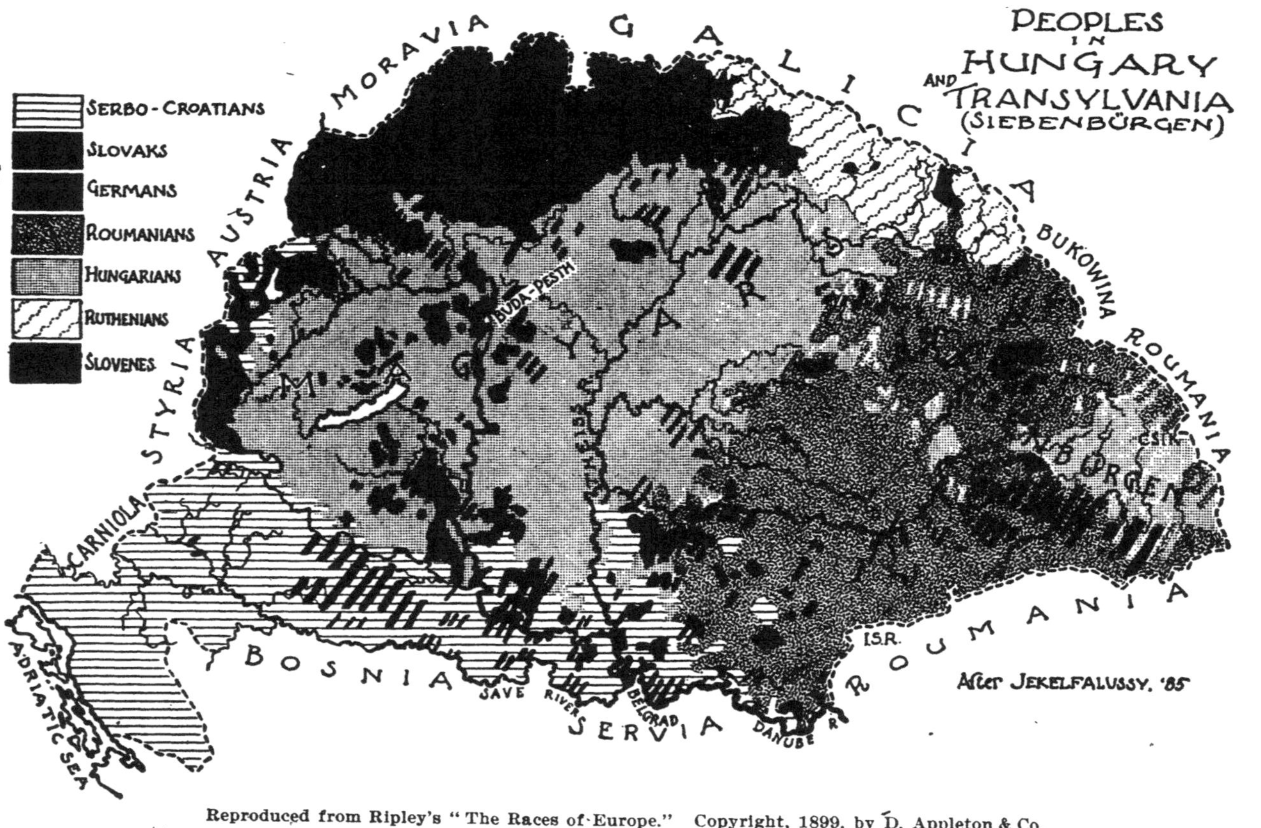

34

Reproduced from Ripley's "The Races of Europe." Copyright, 1899, by D. Appleton & Co.

Hungary, they have taken on the physical characters and the civilization of the subject peoples. Ripley says that they are "perhaps one-eighth Finnic and seven-eighths Alpine" or "Celto-Slavic." They are not counted in the same great divisions with European races by the Bureau of Immigration but find a place with Turks and Armenians among "All others."

The Magyars form a compact population with but minor subdivisions, such as the Szeklers, of Transylvania. The race is confined to Hungary. Standing like an island in the Caucasian population that surrounds them, they steadily increase in numbers and spread their language among the people whom they rule. While they constitute only half the population of Hungary, Magyar is the language of three-fourths of the schools. The other principal peoples of Hungary proper—that is, exclusive of Croatia and Slovenia—are the Roumanians, Germans, and Slovaks, who constitute, respectively, 17, 12, and 12 per cent of the population. In the entire kingdom there were in 1900 about 8,500,000 Magyars. More than half of these are Catholic and one-fourth are "Evangelical." Magyar is also the language of 600,000 Jews. The geographical distribution of the various races in Hungary is shown on the map on page 93.

From 1899 to 1910, inclusive, 338,151 Magyar immigrants were admitted to the United States. This number was exceeded by only nine other races or peoples during the period, and was far ahead of any other people that is Mongolian in origin, the Finnish race, with 151,774 immigrants during the same twelve years, ranking next in this comparison. As regards their rate of immigration to the United States, Magyars in 1907 stood eighth in rank, that is, 7 per 1,000 of population, but still in the lead of most Slavic peoples. The Magyars thus form an important element in the southeastern European immigration to the United States. Only two Slavic peoples, the Polish and Slovak, exceeded the Magyar in absolute numbers of immigrants in the twelve years considered, although the Croatian and Slovenian peoples, also from Hungarian territory, are not far behind them. Like most eastern Europeans the Magyars go to industrial States. During the twelve years considered, 106,641 were destined to Pennsylvania, 64,201 to New York, 55,433 to Ohio, and 51,119 to New Jersey.

MAGYAR-SLOVAK. (See *Slovak.*)

MAHRATTA or **MARATHI.** A mixed Hindu people (see) living in western and central India, between the Dravidians and the Hindus proper. Their language, an Aryan tongue called "Marathi," is spoken by about 18,000,000 persons.

MALAY, MALAYSIAN, or **BROWN race.** One of the five grand divisions of mankind as commonly classified since the time of Blumenbach, but the most disputable one in the view of recent ethnologists. Many consider it to be a branch of the Mongolian race (see), but such admit, at least, that it is the most divergent great branch of the latter. Little attention need be given to the debates amongst scientists concerning it, as it is a race of little consequence in immigration studies. It is the smallest grand division of mankind, numerically, with the exception of the American, having an estimated population of 35,000,000. Practically no Malays come as immigrants to the United States. The few Filipinos (see) that come are not counted as immigrants.

For the purposes of this classification the Malay race may be defined as that grand division of mankind which is distinguished by its brown color and which is native to the Malay Archipelago and Peninsula and the Island of

Madagascar, with perhaps a few related remnants of tribes in Indo-China. The Malay Archipelago includes the Philippines, but not New Guinea on the east. Within this archipelago there is no other native race, with the exception of the small groups of pigmy Negroes called Negritos (see), distantly related to the Papuan of New Guinea, if not to the Australian—unless we consider also that the "Indonesian" element in the interior of the northern islands is Caucasian rather than "Proto-Malayan."

All the languages spoken by the Malay race belong to the great Malayo-Polynesian family of languages, which are found everywhere amongst Polynesians (see); that is, as far east as the waters of South America and northward to include the Hawaiian Islands. The term Malay is also applied in a narrower sense to that part of the Malay race called the "true Malay" or "*Orang Malaya*," that is, the section speaking the standard Malay tongue and which lived originally in and about the Malay Peninsula. Other divisions of the Malay race are then called "Malayan."

While linguistically the Malays are radically distinct from the Mongolians, physically they approach them more nearly than any other great race. The lighter brown color found in some sections approaches the yellow of the Chinese, and the slanting eye or "Mongol fold" of the upper lid is frequently found where no intermixture can be assumed. The appearance of the face and head is also somewhat similar in these races. In temperament and native civilization, however, the Malay is quite distinct. He has primitive, cruel instincts more like those of the American Indian. He has nowhere accepted the Mongolian type of civilization so much as the Caucasian type. The Filipinos are far in advance of any other Malay people in the latter respect, although the earlier Malayan civilization was most highly developed in Java. Buddhism has here been replaced by Mohammedanism, which has extended even into the southern Philippines. (See *East Indian*, *Pacific Islander*, and *Polynesian.*)

MALAYALAM. A branch of the Dravidian people (see) living on the western coast of the most southern portion of India. Their language, the Malayalam, of no relation to Malay, is spoken by over 6,000,000 persons.

MALAY-POLYNESIAN. The family of languages spoken throughout most of the Pacific. (See *Malay*, *Polynesian*, and *Pacific Islander.*)

MALLIESOR. (See *Albanian.*)

MALO-RUSSIAN. Same as **Little Russian.** (See *Ruthenian.*)

MALTESE. A native of the Mediterranean island of Malta, a British colony; generally of Italian or Arabian stock (see these). Arabic is the prevailing language. Ninety per cent of the 200,000 inhabitants are Catholic.

MANCHU. The race or people from which Manchuria takes its name. The leading member of the Tungusic division of the Ural-Altaic or Sibiric division of the Mongolians (see these), and therefore more closely related to the Japanese, Mongols, and Tats in language than to the Chinese. Yet they are not readily distinguished physically from the latter, especially since Chinese blood by intermixture now predominates in Manchuria. China has for two hundred years been ruled by a Manchurian dynasty. (See *Chinese* for immigration, etc.)

MANILAMAN. An old term applied to sailors hailing from Manila, Philippine Islands. (See *Filipino.*)

MANSUR. A branch of the Nogai Tatars (see).

MANX. The native race or people of the Isle of Man. Linguistically the Manx is a corrupt dialect of the Gaelic branch of the Celtic (see) group of the Aryan or Indo-European languages. It is closely allied to Irish and Scotch, but is unimportant. Manx is now spoken by fewer than 5,000 persons; that is, by less than one-tenth of the population of the Isle of Man. Fewer than 100 speak Manx only. It is found only in the northwestern parishes and in a few places along the western coast of the island. It will undoubtedly soon become extinct, as did Cornish, another Celtic dialect, in the last century, since nearly all the inhabitants now converse in English. Manxmen do not appear in immigration statistics. They are probably classed as English.

MARONITE. (See *Syrian.*)

MASUR or **MAZUR.** One of the four dialectal divisions of the Poles (see). Their language is called Mazurian or Masovian and is considered by some to be but a corrupt form of the Great Polish. It is mainly spoken in east Prussia and about Warsaw.

MECKLENBURGER. (See *German.*)

MEDITERRANEAN race. (See *Caucasian* and *Celtic.*)

MELANESIAN. A Negroid people; the central division of the Pacific Islanders (see).

MENNONITE. Not an ethnical term. The name of a religious sect found in the Netherlands, in Russia, and in other parts of Europe.

MESTCHERJAK. A small Tatar people (see) in eastern Russia.

MESTIZO. The issue of a white person by an Indian. (See *Negro.*) A Spanish word originally meaning of mixed blood.

MEXICAN. Any native of Mexico who is neither of Negro nor of Indian descent. Defined thus for immigration purposes, because Negroes and American Indians (see) are listed separately regardless of nativity (cf. *Cuban* and *Spanish American*). The Mexican population, unlike that of Cuba, is mainly of Indian or mixed origin and is therefore largely excluded from this definition. While 70 per cent of the inhabitants of Cuba are white, less than 20 per cent of the people of Mexico are of pure white blood. About 40 per cent (5,000,000) are of pure Indian blood, to whom must be added 43 per cent of mixed blood. The total population is over 13,000,000. Mexico is Spanish as to official language, as to the greater part of its white population, and as to type of civilization, although the last named is perhaps influenced by the United States more than is true of any other Latin-American republic.

For many years there has been a considerable immigration from Mexico to the border States and Territories, but previous to 1908 statistics relative to the overland movement were not recorded by the Bureau of Immigration. In that year, 5,682 persons listed as "Mexicans" were admitted to the United States; in 1909 there were 15,591, and in 1910, 17,760. The great majority of these were destined to Texas. A few immigrants of other races or peoples, including German, Spanish, English, and Syrian, are annually admitted from Mexico. The above figures do not include so-called "nonimmigrant aliens."

MICRONESIAN. A mixed Malayo-Polynesian central group of the Pacific Islanders (see).

MINGRELIAN. A subdivision of the Kartvelian or Georgian group (see) or Southern Division of the Caucasus peoples (see).

MIRDITE. (See *Albanian.*)

MOESIAN. A subdivision of the Bulgarians (see).

MOKCHA. A subdivision of the Mordvinians (see *Finnish*) living in eastern Russia.

MOLDAVIAN. A geographical division of the Roumanians (see) residing in the former principality of Moldavia, which now forms the northern part of Roumania. Not a racial name.

MOLDO-WALLACHIAN. A name applied to the Roumanians (see). The former principalities of Moldavia, Wallachia, and Eastern Roumelia now constitute Roumania.

MONGOL or **MONGOLIC.** The subdivision of the Sibiric branch of the Mongolian race or grand division of mankind from which the latter has taken its name. They are interesting historically, in that at different times they have ruled India and still rule, through the Manchu dynasty, China. In the thirteenth century, headed by the descendants of Genghis Khan, they penetrated into Europe as far as Germany. Their only representatives now in Europe are the Kalmuks (see) of southeastern Russia, a decadent stock.

The term "Mongolic," and even "Mongol," is sometimes used in a wider sense to mean the entire Mongolian race (see). The Bureau of Immigration uses "Mongolic" in a still wider sense to include also the East Indians, Pacific Islanders, and Filipinos (see all these).

The Mongols or natives of Mongolia are comparatively unimportant in immigration and international questions, being small in number and located in the interior of Asia, back of China proper. Estimates of their population rate them at only from 2,000,000 to 5,000,000 in numbers, while of Chinese (see) there are perhaps 300,000,000. The Mongols are not so closely related linguistically to the Chinese as they are to the Japanese and even to the Finns, Turks, and Magyars. The Mongols proper extend at present westward over waste regions as far as the Turko-Tataric populations of Russian central Asia. As they extend on the east nearly to Peking, a few may have found their way to the United States as "Chinese" immigrants, from whom they are not easily distinguishable.

MONGOLIAN, MONGOL, MONGOLIC, MONGOLOID, ASIATIC, or **YELLOW** race. That grand division of mankind which is typically, as to color, yellowish, and as to origin, culture, and present habitat, Asiatic. An important subject in immigration. The Mongolian and the Caucasian (see) are the two largest "races" or divisions of mankind, the latter being somewhat the larger because it includes the greater part of the population of India. The term "Asiatic" may be used in a geographical sense to include India. In this sense the Asiatics are far greater in number than either the Mongolians or the Europeans.

Just as the Caucasian race extends into southwestern and southern Asia, so the Mongolian race extends far into Europe, embracing not only the Lapps of Scandinavia, the Finns, Cossacks, and many other peoples of Russia, and the Turks of southern Europe, but even the Magyars of Hungary, the most advanced of all the Europeans of Mongolian origin. The main western branches of the Mongolians, although Europeanized in blood as well as in culture, still possess a Turanian speech.

The Mongolians have also extended from time immemorial over the Arctic coast of North America, if we accept the view most generally held as to the origin of the Eskimos. Indeed, many ethnologists so define "Mongolian" as to include the entire American and Malay races. Huxley's term "Mongoloid" includes not only these, but also the Polynesians and "Indonesians," who are considered by some to represent an ancient Caucasian element in the Pacific. Huxley therefore finds no race but the Mongoloid on or near the Pacific Ocean, with the exception of a "Negroid" element in Malaysia. The word "Mongolian" is sometimes used in a more restricted sense as equivalent to "Mongol" (see), the name of a small group of Japanese-like people living northwest of China proper in Mongolia. The term "Mongolic grand division" is used by the Bureau of Immigration in the widest sense of all, to include the Malays, as well as the Chinese, Japanese, and Koreans.

All of northern, central, and eastern Asia was originally occupied exclusively by the Mongolian race, if we exclude from this grand division the doubtful Eskimos near Bering Sea and the Ainos of northern Japan and the Malays and Negritos of the Malay Peninsula.

Brinton divides the Mongolian race into two great branches, the Sinitic and the Sibiric. The former is the more populous, and is confined to Asia, being subdivided into the Chinese, Indo-Chinese, and Tibetan groups (see these). The Sibiric branch includes all the invaders into Europe above mentioned, who are therefore more closely related linguistically to the Japanese than to the Chinese. This branch includes, besides the Japanese, Arctic, and Tungusic groups, the Finnic, Tataric, and Mongolic. It is the three last-named groups that are represented in Europe; the Finnic by the Finns, Lapps, Esths, Livs, Mordvinians, and others of Russia, and the Magyars of Hungary; the Tataric group by the Kirghiz-Kazaks, Turkomans, and kindred tribes in Russia, and the Osmanlis, or Turks of Turkey; and the Mongolic group by the Kalmuks of eastern Russia. (See articles on the above and summary under *Ural-Altaic.*)

Southwestern Asia is practically occupied by Caucasians, with the exception of the Turkish race in Anatolia (Asia Minor). West of the Hindus come their Aryan kinsmen, the Afghans, Beluchis, Persians, Armenians, and Kurds, many of whom are Mohammedan; then come the Semites, including the Jews, Arabs, and Syrians.

Among the many other definitions of "Mongolian race," which vary from those given above, it is most important to notice those illustrated in the usage of Keane and Linnæus. These authors consider Blumenbach's Malay race (see) to be only a branch of the Mongolian, while they do not put the American Indian (see) into that category, as does Huxley. Furthermore, Keane, following Quatrefages in having no Malay race into which he can place the "Indonesians" and Polynesians of the Pacific, considers these to be an aberrant Caucasian stock.

Friedrich Müller, the German ethnologist, considers the American and Malay races to be distinct from the Mongolian, but separates from the latter a "Hyperborean" race, which includes the Eskimo and certain Siberian tribes. Far more reprehensible was the tendency, once widespread, to find "Lappic" skulls and vestiges of "Turanian" speech everywhere in Europe. Fragments of the latter speech were even detected in America. The word "Turanian" finally became discredited and was generally replaced by "Ural-Altaic" (see). It is sufficient at this point to say that this term denotes the agglutinative speech of the Sibiric branch of Mongolians, the latter including, as just said, the Magyars and others in Europe. The Sinitic branch, typified by the Chinese, possesses a monosyllabic speech. Both of these types of speech differ widely from the inflected tongues of western Europe and southwestern Asia. In this particular the Malays resemble the Sibiric branch.

Passing to physical characteristics, but little need be said. The Chinese type is well known. Close observation will show that the peculiarity of the "Mongolian eye" does not consist in its being set obliquely, but in having a fold of the upper lid at the inner angle of the eye, which covers the caruncle. The latter is exposed in the Caucasian eye and generally amongst the modified Mongolians of Europe. This fold is found also amongst Malays. Finally, the short, or brachycephalic, type of head is more characteristic of the Mongolian and Malay races than of any other. The eastern Eskimos, however, like most American Indians and Negroes, have long heads. The short-headed type of Europeans found in central Europe is traced by some to an Asiatic origin. If this view be correct, the type goes back to prehistoric times. It may be safely said that no considerable invasion of the Mongolian race into Europe can be proven except those of the Christian era, as above indicated.

The population of the Mongolian race will be best discussed in articles pertaining to its most important divisions, such as the Chinese. As already indicated, it rivals the Caucasian race in numbers, sometimes being estimated as larger, but generally as about 200,000,000 less. A safe estimate of the total Mongolian population is about 600,000,000. The population of Asia, however, is nearly 900,000,000. It will be remembered that nearly 300,000,000 of these are Caucasians, living mainly in India. While the density of the great populations of India and China is unparalleled in any equal area, it is only the Chinese that have shown a great tendency to emigrate. (See *Chinese.*) Of the 1,100,000 immigrants that arrived in 1906, barely 16,000 were from eastern Asia—that is, not 2 per cent. Of these, 14,000 were from Japan and 1,500 from China. The result is here seen of the exclusion laws of the United States directed against Chinese laborers.

MONGOLO-TATARIC or **MONGOLO-TURKIC.** Same as **Ural-Altaic** (see).

MONTENEGRIN. A political division of the Serbo-Croatians. (See *Croatian.*)

MOOR. A historical rather than an ethnographical term applied to very different peoples of northwestern Africa. In Roman history it is applied to inhabitants of Mauretania (Morocco and Algeria), who were in part Phœnician colonists. In Spanish history the "Moors" and "Moriscos" were mainly Berbers rather than, as commonly supposed, Arabs. To-day the word is wrongly applied to the Riffs of Morocco and to the town dwellers of Algeria and Tunis. The latter call themselves generally "Arabs," although often in part of Berber blood. The Moors, in a stricter ethnological sense, are the mixed Trarza and other tribes on the western coast, from Morocco to the Senegal, mainly of nomadic habits. They are of mixed Berber, Arab, and often Negro blood. Many speak Arabic. (See *Semitic-Hamitic.*)

MORAVCICI. A branch of the Hanaks, who form a subdivision of the Moravians (see).

MORAVIAN. (See *Bohemian and Moravian.*)

MORAVIAN-SLOVAK. (See *Slovak.*)

MORDVINIAN. The largest division of the Eastern Finns. (See *Finnish.*)

MORISCO. A Moor (see) of Spain.

MORLAK. A branch of the Servians living in northern Dalmatia and adjacent territory. (See *Croatian.*)

MORO. (See *Filipino.*)

MOROCCAN. Any native of Morocco. About two-thirds of the 8,000,000 population are Berbers (see), occupying four-fifths of the land. The remaining one-third are mainly Arabs (see), who predominate in the cities.

MULATTO. Any person of mixed white and Negro blood. Classed as a Negro (see) in immigration statistics.

MUNDA. A name applied to certain tribes of Bengal. (See *Dravidian.*)

MUSCOVITE. Same as **Russian** (see).

N.

NAT. A wandering tribe of India. (See *Gypsy.*)

NAZAIRI, NUSARIEH, or **NAZARINI.** (See *Syrian.*)

NEAPOLITAN. (See *Italian.*)

NEGRILLO. (See *Negro.*)

NEGRITO. A Philippine tribe. (See *Malay, East Indian,* and *Filipino.*)

NEGRO, NEGROID, AFRICAN, BLACK, ETHIOPIAN, or **AUSTAFRICAN.** That grand division of mankind distinguished by its black color and, generally speaking, by its woolly hair. While the black, like the white and yellow races, is accepted by practically all ethnologists as a primary division of mankind, there is the greatest difference of opinion as to what should be included in it. Some would put the Hottentots and Bushmen of South Africa into a separate grand division. Still more would set apart the "Oceanic Negroes"—that is, the Negritos of Malaysia and the Papuans of New Guinea, and especially the Australians. Some call these doubtful branches "Negroid," a name applied by Huxley to all Negroes excepting the Australians.

In a simple classification for immigration purposes it is preferable to include all the above under the term "Negroes." They are alike in inhabiting hot countries and in belonging to the lowest division of mankind from an evolutionary standpoint. While the Australians do not have the kinky hair of the African Negroes, they are still lower in civilization. Only the Negrillos or dwarf Negroes of Africa and the Negritos of Malaysia equal them in this respect. The definition must exclude, however, the dark, almost black, Veddahs and Dravidian tribes of India, and especially the dark Hamites and Semites of northern and northeastern Africa. (See these.) The two latter groups belong to the Caucasian stocks of southwestern Asia, linguistically, as well as, to a certain extent, in temperament, civilization, and regularity of features. They inhabit nearly one-third of Africa, including Abyssinia. The so-called "Ethiopic" language and old form of Christianity are found in the latter country, and not in the misnamed "Ethiopian" race.

The only Negroes to whom practically all ethnologists are willing to apply the term are those inhabiting the central and western third of Africa, excluding even the Bantus, who occupy practically all Africa south of the Equator. The Bantus, well typified by the Zulu subdivision, are lighter in color than the true Negroes, never sooty black, but of a reddish-brown. From the Negroes proper of the Sudan have descended most American Negroes.

To some extent the northern Negro stock has become intermixed with the African Caucasian, already mentioned, especially about the Upper Nile, in Abyssinia, and in Gallaland and Somaliland farther east. Brinton's term for the Negro race, "Austafrican," is justified perhaps on Keane's theory that the Australians and Africans represent the earliest offshoots of the precursors of man who inhabited the continent now submerged in the Indian Ocean. In line with this theory is the claim that the Veddahs and Dravidians of India are still more divergent branches toward the north which have become more affected by Caucasian or, perhaps, Mongolian elements.

Excluding these 50,000,000 or more dark inhabitants of India, the Negro race numbers perhaps 150,000,000, or about one-quarter the population of the Mongolian race. The total number of Negroes in the Americas is estimated at 20,000,000. Brazil alone numbers in her population between 6,000,000 and 7,000,000 Negroes and mulattoes, not much less than the colored population of the United States.

There is a bewildering confusion in the terms used to indicate the different mixtures of white and dark races in America. Thus, all natives of Cuba, whether colored or white, are called "creoles," as this word is loosely used in the United States; but creole, as more strictly defined, applies only to those who are native-born but of pure European descent. This is the use of the word in Mexico. In Brazil and Peru, on the contrary, it is applied to those possessing colored blood in some proportion, in Brazil to Negroes of pure descent, in Peru to the issue of whites and mestizos. "Mestizo" is the Spanish word applied to half-breeds (white and Indian).

Immigration statistics count as Negro, or "African (black)" "aliens whose appearance indicates an admixture of Negro blood," "whether coming from Cuba or other islands of the West Indies, North or South America, Europe, or Africa." Only American-born immigrants of pure European blood are counted as Cuban, Spanish American, Mexican, and West Indian (see). All these "natives of the Western Hemisphere," together with American Indians and Negroes, are included with the Magyar, Turkish, and Armenian races in the term "All others," the sixth grand division of immigrant races as classified by the Bureau of Immigration.

The immigration statistics of the race are of no significance so far as Africa is concerned, for only 15 are recorded as having come from that continent in 1907. About nine-tenths of all Negro immigration in that year came from the West Indies, where the mulatto population alone, it is said, is three-fifths of the entire population. It may therefore be assumed that we get but few Negro immigrants of pure blood. Perhaps such come in largest numbers from Portuguese territory, including the Azores and the Cape Verde Islands, off the coast of Africa, which, next to the West Indies, send the largest number of Negro immigrants. This number, however, is of little consequence—341 in 1907. During the twelve years 1899–1910, 33,630 Negro immigrants were admitted to the United States, most of whom were from the West Indies. They ranked twenty-ninth among immigrant races during that period, among the races which they surpassed in point of numbers being the Armenian, Chinese, Welsh, and Turkish. The chief destinations in the United States of Negro immigrants during the twelve years specified were: Florida, 13,112; New York, 10,126, and Massachusetts, 5,361.

NESTORIAN. An ecclesiastical, not an ethnographical, term applying to an early Christian sect in Asia not subject to Rome, which has to-day but small importance. (See *Kurd* and *Assyrian.*)

NETHERLANDER and **NETHERLANDISH.** (See *Dutch and Flemish.*)

NEWFOUNDLANDER. Like Canadian (see), a term of nationality, not of race.

NEW ZEALANDER. Any inhabitant of New Zealand. Counted as English, Scotch, etc., in immigration statistics. The aborigines, called Maoris, are Polynesians (see).

NICARAGUAN. (See *Spanish American.*)

NISTROVINIAN. A mixed stock of Little Russian and Roumanian blood. (See *Ruthenian.*)

NOGAI TATAR. A small Tataric people (see) living in the Caucasus near the Caspian and formerly in the Crimea, in southern Russia.

NORDIC race. (See *Aryan* and *Caucasian.*)

NORSE. (See *Scandinavian.*)

NORTH AMERICAN. All immigrants born in North America are classified in immigration statistics according to the European or other stock from which they sprang (see each race).

NORTH EUROPEAN race. (See *Caucasian.*)

NORTH ITALIAN. (See *Italian.*)

NORUZ. A branch of the Nogai Tatars. (See *Tataric.*)

NORWEGIAN. (See *Scandinavian.*)

O.

OCCIDENTAL or **WESTERN** race. (See Introductory, table.)

OCEANIC CAUCASIAN, OCEANIC MONGOLIAN, OCEANIC NEGRO. Branches of these races found on the islands of the Pacific Ocean, according to some writers.

OPOVAN. A subdivision of the Moravians. (See *Bohemian and Moravian.*)

ORIENTAL or **EASTERN** race. (See *Caucasian* and *Slav.*)

OSMANLI. The name by which European Turks call themselves. (See *Turkish* and *Tataric.*)

OSSET or **OS.** An Aryan people living in Caucasia. (See *Caucasus peoples.*)

OSTYAK. A Finnish people (see) of Siberia.

OTTOMAN. (See *Turkish.*)

P.

PACIFIC ISLANDER. A native of those Pacific Islands which lie between the Philippines, the Celebes, and Australia on the west and America on the east. The Hawaiian Islands on the north are included. A loose geographical rather than an ethnographical term. It is defined in a narrower sense by Brinton to comprise only the Polynesians and Micronesians, excluding the Melanesians on the west. It is more convenient, however, for the present purpose to include in the term all islanders toward the west, with the exception of the Malaysians, who are called East Indians (see). The term then corresponds to Oceania as generally defined. But this latter term also is made by some to include Malaysia.

De Quatrefages has said that all the types of mankind, white, black, and yellow, are found in Oceania. It is possible at least to find types that resemble these. Malaysia has the yellow race as represented in its offshoot, the brown Malay. The Malayo-Polynesian speech, if not Malay blood, is found throughout the easternmost islands as well. The eastern Polynesians, called by some "Indonesians" or "Oceanic Caucasians," have, on the other hand, strong Caucasian features which are regular and light in color, and they are often tall. The Hawaiians and Samoans are good examples. Finally, the Melanesians, the people of New Guinea and the islands immediately east of it, are almost as black as Negroes, and have frizzled, though long, hair. Only the last-named people possess languages that are not Malayo-Polynesian—that is, that are not related to Philippine tongues. Micronesia shows a mixture of these three racial types. All Pacific Islanders are put by the Bureau of Immigration into the "Mongolic grand division."

Pacific Islanders are the smallest in number of all the "races" that come to the United States as immigrants, only 357 having been admitted during the twelve years ending June 30, 1910. Their entire population is only 1,500,000, not counting the 40,000,000 "East Indians" of Malaysia. Hawaiians, like Filipinos (see), are not counted as immigrants on coming to the States.

PAMPANGAN. (See *Filipino.*)

PANAMAN. A geographical term. Immigrants from the Canal Zone are treated like citizens of Panama or any other foreign country and counted as immigrants, different from citizens of other American possessions. Most are, therefore, counted as Spanish American or as Negro (see these).

PANGASINAN. (See *Filipino.*)

PANJABI. Same as **Punjabi.** (See *Hindu.*)

PAPUAN. (See *Pacific Islander* and *Malay.*)

PARAGUAYAN. (See *Spanish American.*)

PARSI. A small Persian people (see), now largely settled in India.

PERMYAK. A division of the Eastern Finns. (See *Finnish.*)

PERSIAN. The Persian race or people is quite different from the Persian nationality. The latter includes several very different peoples, as will presently be seen. Linguistically, the Persian is the chief race of Persia speaking an Iranic language, that is, one of the Aryan tongues most nearly related to the Hindi (see these). Physically, the race is of mixed Caucasian stock. It is almost entirely composed of Tajiks. The small section known as "Parsis" or, incorrectly, "Fire worshipers," have for the most part emigrated to India. The Armenians are so closely related to the Persians linguistically as to be put with them by some into the Iranic branch. The Kurds, the Beluchis, and the Afghans also belong to the latter.

Of the 9,500,000 estimated population of Persia about two-thirds are true Persian or "Tajik." The other third is also Caucasian for the most part, including Kurds (400,000), Armenians (150,000), and other Iranians (820,000), and the non-Aryan Arabs (350,000). There are 550,000 Turks and 300,000 Mongols in the Empire. The only Christians are the Armenians and a small group of 25,000 "Chaldeans," "Assyrians," or "Nestorians," really eastern Syrians (see these terms), about Lake Urmia, on the northwestern border.

In intellect, if not in civilization, the Persian is perhaps more nearly a European than is the pure Turk. He is more alert and accessible to innovation. Yet he is rather brilliant and poetical than solid in temperament. Like the Hindu he is more eager to secure the semblance than the substance of modern civilization.

Immigration from Persia is a negligible quantity. It is included in the 171 "Other peoples" from "Other Asia" in the immigration report of 1907.

PERUVIAN. (See *Spanish American.*)

PHILIPPINE ISLANDER. (See *Filipino.*)

PINSGAUER. A subdivision of Germans (see) living in Austria.

PODHALIAN. A Slavic population of about 40,000 speaking Polish (see), but having a physical resemblance to the neighboring Slovaks.

PODHORAK. A subdivision of the Moravians (see).

PODLACHIAN. A name applied to mixed Poles living west of the Polesians in Grodno province, West Russia. (See *Polish.*)

PODOLIAN. A geographical term applied to the Poles (see) living in Podolia in southwestern Russia.

POIK. An Istrian division of the Slovenians (see).

POKUTI. A mixed stock of Little Russian and Roumanian (see) blood.

POLAK. Same as **Podlachian.** (See *Polish.*)

POLESIAN. A mixed Polish (see) population in West Russia.

POLIECHUK. A division of the White Russians much mixed with Little Russian. They live on the border of Little Russia and near Poland. (See *Russian.*)

POLISH (formerly called **Lech**; often incorrectly called **Polack** in the United States). The West Slavic race (see) which gave its name to the former Kingdom of Poland, now divided among Russia, Austria, and Germany. Of high interest in an immigration study, for the Poles have risen to the third place in point of numbers coming to the United States, being exceeded only by the South Italians and Hebrews.

The Poles stand physically and socially, as they do geographically, between the Russian peoples of eastern Europe and the Teutonic peoples of western Europe. They are neither the one nor the other. In language they are Slavs. In religion they reject the Russian church and adhere for the most part to the Catholic. Politically and socially they look upon Russia as their enemy, but this is mainly a historical distinction. It must be said that their civilization has lacked some of the stable qualities shown by nations farther west. Finally, in their physical inheritance, they resemble the "Eastern" or Slavic race more than that of northwestern Europe, although probably modified by racial intermixture from the earliest times.

In more technical language, the Poles verge toward the "Northern" race of Europe, although still more closely related to the Eastern race, especially those speaking the Mazurian dialect. Deniker puts them in a race quite apart from both these and names them after their chief river, the "Vistulan." He finds them to be somewhat shorter than the Lithuanians and White Russians of the Eastern race, and not quite so broad-headed. While darker than the Lithuanians, the Poles are lighter than the average Russian. In other words, they show more of the Teutonic and little or none of the Asiatic element of eastern Europe. In temperament they are more high-strung than are the most of their neighbors. In this respect they resemble the Hungarians farther south.

The Poles are surrounded on the east by the White Russians and Little Russians or Ruthenians; on the south by the Slovaks and Moravians, both of them with languages more closely related to the Polish than is Russian; and on the west and north by the Germans, with the exception of the non-Slavic Lithuanians, who touch their territory on the northeast (see articles on these races). The Poles are now divided among Russia, Austria, and Germany. Once their proud kingdom extended from the Baltic to the Black Sea and rivaled Russia. At one time or another it included the territory of the Lithuanians, the Livs, the White Russians, the Slovaks, most of the Little Russians, the Moravians, and even the Bohemians and the Germans westward to the vicinity of Berlin. In 1795 came the final partition. Six-sevenths of Poland proper now belongs to Russia, and only one-seventh of this fraction is called Poland today. In this small territory now reside nearly two-thirds of the Poles. The rest of the estimated population of 17,000,000 or more are divided as indicated below:

Number and distribution of Poles.

Countries.	Number and census year.	Mainly in provinces of—
Russia	7,931,307 (1897)	Poland (6,621,497), White Russia (424,236), Little Russia (388,582), Lithuania (308,444).
Austria	4,259,152 (1900)	Galicia (3,988,702).
Germany	[a] 3,394,134 (1900)	Posen (1,162,539), Silesia (1,141,473), West Prussia (546,322).
Elsewhere in Europe	[b] 1,000,000 (1900)	
America	[b] 1,000,000 (1900)	

[a] Including 148,000 Mazurs, mainly in East Prussia, and 101,000 Kashoubs, mainly in West Prussia.
[b] Estimated.

The Polish language has four dialects—the Great Polish, the Mazurian, the Kashoubish, and the Silesian. The Great Poles live west of Warsaw province. The Mazurian or Masovian is said in Poland to be but a corrupt form of the Great Polish. It is spoken mainly in East Prussia and about Warsaw. The Kashoubs, who call themselves "Kaszebi," live still farther northwest on the Baltic. Those in West Prussia are Catholics; those farther west, in Pomerania, are Protestants. The Silesian dialect is spoken in the German and Austrian provinces of that name. The names Podhalians, Porals, and Gorals (that is, "mountain dwellers") apply more properly to the Poles living north of the Tatra Mountains, between Moravia and the main range of the Carpathians. This population approaches the Slovaks in physical type, as it does geographically. It is said to be in part of German blood, like the neighboring Gluchoniemcy, or "Deaf Germans," who also speak Polish.

Other names applying to subdivisions of the Poles are the Bielochrovats (the same as the Krakuses or Cracovinians), the Kuyevs, the Kuprikes, the Lublinians, and the Sandomirians. Podolian is apparently a geographical term applying to the Poles of Podolia, in southwestern Russia; and Polesian is the name of the mixed Polish population living farthest toward the east, in West Russia. Finally, the name Polak, or Podlachian, applies only to the mixed Poles living just west of the Polesians, in Grodno province. The Polabs are extinct. They were not Poles, but Wends (see); that is, of a related linguistic stock.

Of the population of Russian Poland only about two-thirds are Poles—that is, 6,621,497. Next comes the very large Hebrew population of 1,267,000, numbering nearly as many as the four other principal peoples of that country combined, namely, the Germans, the Lithuanians, the Ruthenians, and the Great Russians. While the last named are rapidly increasing in Poland, the Poles themselves are gaining ground in Germany. The unusually large Jewish population of Poland is its most remarkable feature and had its origin in the early hospitality shown by the Polish Government to this race. Warsaw was the chief Jewish city of the world until New York recently succeeded to that distinction.

It is significant to the student of immigration that the Jews and the Poles reside mainly in the same region. Excepting the Italian, these are the races now coming in greatest numbers to America. They are therefore largely representatives of the same type of civilization as well as the same expulsive causes. About 1885 the Russian Government prohibited all emigration except that of Poles and Jews. The Polish people may be supposed to be a more permanent factor than the Hebrew in future immigration, for although its rate of immigration per 1,000 of population is only one-half that of the Hebrew, that is, 9 as compared with the Hebrew 18 per 1,000, the number of Poles in Europe is twice that of the Hebrews. The Polish is the largest race in Russia next to the Russian itself, although it forms only 7 per cent of the population.

During the twelve years 1899–1910, 949,064 Polish immigrants were admitted to the United States. Of these 471,378 came from Russia and 432,809 from Austria-Hungary. In 1907 their rate of immigration was 8.1 to 1,000 of the population. The Polish is the most significant Slavic race now coming to America when one considers both the size of its population and the rate of its immigration. Of the Slavs only the Slovaks and the Croatian-Slovenian group excel it in the rate per 1,000 coming. To sum up: While the Polish stands behind only the South

Italian and the Hebrew races in the number of immigrants, it has twice as large a population as the Hebrew to draw upon and stands but seventh in the rate per 1,000 of population annually coming to the United States. It has, however, only half the population of Italy. Up to 1904 German immigration exceeded that of the Poles. The latter belong to the new tide from Russia and the southeast that has in recent years replaced the steady stream of immigration from northwestern Europe.

In the twelve-year period considered, Polish immigrants went chiefly to the States favored by other Slavs: Pennsylvania, 254,281; New York, 205,430; Illinois, 122,741; New Jersey, 83,297, and Massachusetts, 82,079.

POLISH-SLOVAK. (See *Slovak.*)

POLYNESIAN. The Caucasian-like or eastern portion of the Pacific Islanders (see).

POMAK. A name given to the Mohammedan Bulgarians (see).

POMERANIAN. (See *German.*)

PONGAUER. A local name applied to Germans (see) in certain parts of Austria.

PORAL. Same as **Podhalian.** (See *Polish.*)

PORTO RICAN. Any citizen of Porto Rico regardless of race. Not counted as an immigrant on arrival in the United States. (See *Spanish American, Cuban,* and *Negro.*)

PORTUGUESE. The people of Portugal, including their descendants in America who are not of mixed Indian or Negro blood. (Cf. *Spanish American* and *Mexican.*) They are put into the "Iberic division" by the Bureau of Immigration, together with the Spanish (see), to whom they are closely related in language. The language belongs to the Italic group of Aryan tongues. The primitive Iberians and Basques of Portugal early received a Keltic admixture. Later Arab and Hebrew blood is found largely present in central Portugal, and even Negro blood in the south, resulting from the introduction of many thousands of slaves. The people of northern Portugal, from which emigration chiefly proceeds, resemble those of Spanish Galicia or the Basques. The Portuguese are physically undersized, averaging 5 feet 4 inches in the south and 5 feet 5 inches in the north.

The population of the mother country is only 5,000,000. The emigration of the last fifty years to Brazil, to which important nation the Portuguese have given their language, was nearly 500,000. This number was doubled, however, by the Italian emigration to Brazil. During the ten years ending in 1900 Portuguese emigration was 27,323. During the twelve years ending June 30, 1910, 72,897 Portuguese were admitted to the United States. A large part of this movement originated in the Azores. During the period referred to, the Portuguese ranked twenty-fourth in point of numbers among immigrant races or peoples. The principal destinations of Portuguese immigrants during the twelve years were as follows: Massachusetts, 45,466; California, 10,537; Rhode Island, 7,040; New York, 4,196, and Hawaii, 3,470.

PROVENÇAL. The chief southern dialect spoken by the French people (see).

PRUSSIAN. (See *German.*)

PUNJABI or **PANJABI.** A native of Punjab, a northwestern province of British India. Three-fourths of the people speak an Aryan tongue, Panjabi, and over one-half profess Mohammedanism. (See *Hindu.*)

Q.

QUAEN. (See *Kwaen.*)

R.

RAGUSAN. A native of the old city of Ragusa; usually of the Serbo-Croatian race. (See *Croatian.*)

RAJPUT. The name of a ruling "tribal caste" of India; not a race. (See *Hindu.*) They number about 10,000,000.

RED race. (See *Indian.*)

RED RUSSIAN. (See *Ruthenian.*)

RHÆTO-ROMANSH, including **Romansh, Ladin,** and **Friulan.** A group name given to certain races or peoples living in the region of the central Alps of Switzerland, Austria, and Italy who speak an Italic tongue and are, therefore, Caucasian. Although small in population, these peoples form one of the great divisions of the Romance group of the Aryan family of languages. They are thought by some to be the modern representatives of the ancient Rhætians of the Roman Empire who once occupied the entire region of the central Alps. They are now broken up into small groups and established in the canton of the Grisons, Switzerland; in parts of Tyrol, Austria; and in Italy north of the Adriatic.

This Rhæto-Romansh group may be subdivided into three parts, both linguistically and geographically—the Romansh proper, the Ladin (a name sometimes given to the entire group), and the Friulan. These languages are now recognized to be a thoroughly independent neo-Latin group on a level with Italian, Spanish, French, Provençal, and Roumanian. Romansh proper, sometimes called Grison, resembles the dialects of the "langue d'oc" of southern France, but it contains a number of German elements. It is the language of about 40,000 Grisons (see) living in the valleys of the Rhine and the Inn in eastern Switzerland. Romansh is surrounded by German on three sides and by Italian on the fourth, the south.

Ladin, as the name indicates, is to-day more closely related to the ancient Latin than is Italian. It resembles the dialects of northern Italy and is spoken by about 90,000 Tyrolese (see), who are bounded on the north by Germans and on the other sides by Italians. It is separated from the Romansh proper by a strip of territory occupied by Germans and Italians.

Friulan is the name applied to that group of the Rhæto-Romansh peoples living in the old province of Friuli, the most northeastern part of Italy. They extend over the border line as far as Göritz in Austria and number, according to Hovelacque, about 400,000 persons. Reclus, however, says that the number in Italy still speaking the Friulan dialect does not exceed 50,000. They are bounded on the north by Germans, on the east by Slovenians, on the south by the Adriatic Sea, and on the west by North Italians.

Physically the Rhæto-Romansh are a mixed people, but preponderantly of the broad-headed, brunette "Alpine" type. Those in the west, like the Lombards of Italy, show some Teutonic admixture, while those in the Friulan district, like the Venetians, show an infusion of Slavic blood. In religion they are for the most part Catholic, especially those of Italy and Austria. Their literature consists chiefly in periodicals and numerous religious works. They are being pressed upon from all sides and their speech is being gradually replaced by German and Italian. Rudler and Chisholm consider them a doomed race.

They are not listed separately in immigration statistics, but those from Italy and Switzerland are probably counted as North Italian. (See *Italian.*)

RIFF. A division of the Libyan group of Hamites living in Morocco. (See *Semitic-Hamitic.*)

ROMANY. Same as **Gypsy** (see).

ROMAIC. Same as modern **Greek** (see).

ROMANSH. (See *Rhæto-Romansh.*)

ROUMANIAN, DACO-ROUMANIAN, VLACH, or **MOLDO-WALLACHIAN,** including the **Moldavians** and **Macedo-Vlachs (Aromuni, Tsintsars,** or **Kutzo-Vlachs)** of northern Greece. The native race or people of Roumania; linguistically the easternmost division of the Romance (Italic) branch of the Aryan family tree; physically a mixed race, of Slavic or "Eastern" type in the west, but in the eastern part showing the influence of the old Roman colonies from which it has received its name and language. The Roumanians are the largest race numerically of southeastern Europe (not including the Russian), but have sent a very small stream of immigration to America as yet.

Like the Bulgarians south of them, the Roumanians are an exceptional people in being linguistically of one race and physically of another, at least for the most part. As in Bulgaria, also, it was apparently but a small body of invaders who gave their name to the Slavs who were found in occupation of this region. But while the Bulgarians, of Mongol origin, lost their language, exchanging it for a Slavic tongue, the Roman soldiers who settled on the Danube gave their speech to modern Roumania. The people are proud to call themselves "Romani," but their civilization and history are part and parcel of those of the Balkan Peninsula. They are of the Balkan States, if not strictly in them. Some geographers place them in that group topographically, as well as politically. But strictly speaking, it would appear more logical to consider them as outside the peninsula, because they are north of the Danube. Like the Balkan States proper, Roumania was until a generation ago a part of Turkey. The race was, in fact, but little known until recently. It has even been supposed that their language belonged to the Slavic group, because it was written, like most of the latter, in the Cyrillic characters. This, with the fact that the greater majority of the people are Slavic in appearance and civilization, is, no doubt, what has led the Bureau of Immigration to place them, as it did the Hebrews, in the "Slavic division." (See *Slav* and *Caucasian.*) As an immigrant type, they may well be placed there; but in conformity with the principles of classification elsewhere explained (see Introductory), this dictionary, like all foreign censuses taken by race, places them in the Italic or Romance group. (See *Aryan.*)

Since the Roumanians have adopted the Roman alphabet, which they did recently, the language looks far more familiar to one acquainted with Romance or Latin languages. The chief peculiarity that strikes the eye is the annexation of the article to the end of the noun. This is but rarely found among the Aryan tongues. From the fact that it is found in the neighboring languages to the southwest, the Bulgarian and the Albanian, it would appear to be a survival of an ancient language common to all these, perhaps Dacian. The language has indeed undergone profound internal changes, although in some respects it reminds one forcibly of the ancient Latin. Two-fifths of the vocabulary, however, is now Slavic, borrowed, of course, from the tongue of the predominant element in the population. While only one-fifth of the words can be traced to the Latin, they are the words in most common use, the most significant fact in determining the earliest form of the language.

Since community of ideas and, ultimately, the type of social institutions and of the civilization itself, are profoundly dependent upon a community of speech, we should expect the Roumanians to be more in sympathy with the Latin races and civilization than with the Slavic. This will no doubt be more fully the case when the people are more widely educated. Already their leaders are found frequenting the universities of Paris and Rome. The progress of the country has of course been retarded, as that of all the Balkan States, by the generally unsettled condition of affairs in this region. Roumanians appear to compare favorably with the races of the Balkans, although some say that they are more backward. They are preeminently agriculturists, like the Slavs in general; but they are prominent also in commerce, even in the capitals of Austria and Hungary. In religion they are mainly Greek. In customs and traditions they show both their Latin and their Slavic origin. In temperament they are more emotional than the Slav, less stolid and heavy than the Bulgarian.

It is concerning the physical anthropology of the Roumanians that there is the greatest difference of opinion. They have not been as yet sufficiently studied on the field. There would seem to be little doubt, however, that in Roumania, as in Bulgaria, which adjoins it on the south, there are two distinct types. While that of the east, reminds one of the Italian or "Mediterranean" type, long-headed, dark, and slender in build, that far in the west, in Hungary, is typically Slavic or "Hungarian"—that is, broad of face and head, shorter, and lighter in complexion. Partisanship is bound to appear in this question as everywhere in Balkan ethnography. There are those who unduly emphasize the Roman element in the origin and present type of the Roumanians. Slavic writers, on the other hand, have been inclined to belittle this element. The medium position would seem more reasonable in recognizing both constituents of the race. It is improbable that the 240,000 Roman colonists who settled on the opposite bank of the Danube under Trajan could have peopled the territory now occupied by 10,000,000 Roumanians, half of which extends outside of Roumania itself into Hungary and Russia, especially since it seems to be the fact that these colonists withdrew to Macedonia in the third century and did not cross the Danube into Roumania until the thirteenth. It is, therefore, the theory of some writers that the Pindus is the real center of dispersion of the Roumanians. It is in this region, in the central part of northern Greece, that resides an important division of the race, the Kutzo-Vlachs or Tsintsars. These are sharper in feature, although they, too, have deviated from the Roman type through admixture with Albanians and Greeks (see these). Even in the valleys of the Carpathians, the northern Vlachs or Roumanians are often dark and short and quite Roman in type of face. But the average cephalic index of the entire race is nearer that of the Slavic. They are not only broad-headed, but of medium height, as are the Northern and Eastern Slavs, much shorter than the Serbo-Croatian or Albanian type along the Adriatic.

A word of explanation may be given to the many names borne by the Roumanians. They indicate political divisions rather than linguistic. Thus the Moldavians and the Wallachians or Vlachs are found, respectively, in the former principalities of Moldavia, which now constitutes northern Roumania, and Wallachia, or its southern part. Combined they are called Moldo-Wallachians. Vlach is a familiar Slavic word, originally meaning horseman, and sometimes applied to people of entirely different stock, as the so-called "Walachs" of eastern Moravia. (See *Bohemian and Moravian.*) The

Morlaks, a Serbo-Croatian stock living on the Adriatic, were formerly considered by ethnologists to be Vlachs, whose name they appear to retain in another form. The Macedo-Vlachs call themselves Aromuni, that is, Romans, but are called by other Tsintsars or Kutzo-Vlachs.

The Roumanians are the largest both in numbers (10,000,000) and in the extent of territory covered of all the many peoples of the Balkan Peninsula and Austria-Hungary combined, that vast territory which has been called "the whirlpool of Europe." They occupy more space than all the Serbo-Croatian peoples together (see *Croatian*), or than the Greeks, or the Bulgarians, or the Magyars. They are nearly half as large in numbers as the Little Russians who adjoin them on the north, nearly one-third as large as their linguistic kinsmen nearest them on the west, the Italians. The Roumanians occupy nearly one-half of Hungary and number one-third as many as the Magyars themselves. On the ethnographical map, the eastern point of Hungary and of the Carpathian range stands in the very center of Roumanian territory. Here is found the curious islet of eastern Magyars known as Szeklers, entirely surrounded by the expanding Roumanians. The latter number over 1,000,000 also in Russia, mainly in the province of Bessarabia, which was formerly a part of Moldavia. They extend across the Danube only near its mouth on the Black Sea into what is known as the Dobruja. With this exception the Roumanian territory is for the most part separated from the sea by Bulgarians, Little Russians, and a few Tatars. The Little Russians of Russia and Ruthenians of Austria-Hungary (one in race) border the Roumanians on the north; the Bulgarians border them on the south; the Servians on the southwest; and the Magyars, or "Hungarians," on the west.

These peoples, with the others found in the Balkan Peninsula, are the ones that typify the newer flood of immigration to the United States. As shown elsewhere (see *Slav* and *Caucasian*), they, with the Poles and other subject races of western Russia and the Italians, who may be designated as Southeastern Europeans in type, have replaced the Northwestern Europeans as our predominant and typical annual accession. The Roumanians, however, contribute a very small portion of this so-called Slavic flood. In this they resemble the Bulgarians, located also on the eastern side of the Peninsula. They stand almost the lowest of all the Slavs in their immigration rate per 1,000 of population, while the Slovenians and Croatians, on the western side of the Peninsula, together with the Slovaks and the Hebrews, lead all immigrant races in this respect. The Roumanian rate of immigration in 1907 was less than 2 per 1,000 of the population, while the rate of Slovaks and Hebrews was about 18 per 1,000. The Roumanian immigration during the twelve years 1899–1910, was 82,704, placing it twenty-third in rank among immigrant races. The great majority of these, 76,755, came from Austria-Hungary, with comparatively a few from Roumania and Turkey. Their chief destinations during the period were as follows: Ohio, 31,835; Pennsylvania, 22,301; Indiana, 7,479, and New York, 5,582.

Nearly nine-tenths of the population of Roumania is Roumanian in race. Among the rest are to be noted in the following tables the predominance of Gypsies and Jews:

Population of Roumania.

[Reclus, 1893.]

Races:	
Roumanians	4,700,000
Jews	300,000
Gypsies	200,000
Bulgarians	50,000
Armenians	15,000

Races—Continued.	
Russians	16, 000
Turks and Tatars	3, 000
Magyars	1, 500
Foreigners	80, 000
Miscellaneous	434, 500
Total	5, 800, 000

Distribution of Roumanians (1900).

Countries:	
Roumania	[a]5, 500, 000
Hungary	[b]2, 800, 000
Austria	[b]230, 000
Russia	[a]1, 170, 000
Servia	[b]90, 000
Turkey Greece	[a]150, 000
Elsewhere	[a]60, 000
Total (approximate)	10, 000, 000

RUSNAKY. (See *Ruthenian.*)

RUSSIAN, GREAT RUSSIAN, VELIKO-RUSSIAN, MUSCOVITE. (See also *White Russian*, or *Bielo-Russian*, and *Black Russian* following.) This article will discuss, first, the Great Russian race, or the Russian proper; then all other divisions of the Russian (in the wider sense) excepting the Ruthenian or Little Russian, which is given a separate article (see), and, finally, the Russian Empire as a whole, to present a general or statistical view of the hundred and more other peoples and tribes who are Russian in nationality but not in race or language.

Russian may be defined in the wider sense as the largest Slavic group of Aryan peoples. Linguistically it belongs to the Eastern Slavic division and includes the Great Russian, the Little Russian, and the White Russian. Physically it may be placed in the "Eastern" (Caucasian) race, but it is extensively mixed with Finno-Tataric and other elements.

GREAT RUSSIAN.

The Great Russian, or simply "Russian" in the narrower sense of the word, is that division of the Russian group (see above) which is dominant in Russia and which is the largest Slavic race numerically. "Veliko-Russian" means Great Russian. "Muscovite" is a name sometimes applied to the Great Russian people, because they first prominently appear in history as the race of the early "Empire of Moscovy." Moscow was its capital until St. Petersburg was founded by Peter the Great. The people of Moscow are still the purest in stock of the Great Russian population.

The Great Russians, or Russians proper, emigrate to America to a smaller degree in proportion to their population than any other Slavic people. Space need not be taken here to repeat what has been said in the article on the "Slav" (see) as to temperament, character, civilization, language, physical type, and statistics of population and immigration, excepting so far as to point out in what the Russians differ from other Slavs. As is said in the article on the Ruthenian (see), the Great Russian has usurped to himself the name Russian from the so-called Little Russians, as he has succeeded to their dominion. He is perhaps of purer Slavic blood than they, although some claim that the Great Russian is more of a Finn than the Little Russian is of a Tatar. Both have more of this Mongolian element in the race than has the White Russian. The most ancient race of Russia, that of the kurgans or mounds, was undoubtedly more long-headed than the present population. Indeed, according to current tradition, "the founders of the Russian nation were Norsemen." So wrote Nestor, the first historian of the race. At any rate, it is evident that the Asiatic element in the race is of a later intrusion, which continued far into the middle ages. As late as the fourteenth century Moscow was tributary to the Tatar rule which was set up in southern Russia.

The Russian race of to-day is consequently more broad-headed or Asiatic in appearance than the typical peoples of northwestern and southwestern Europe. It belongs mainly to the so-

[a] Estimated. [b] Census.

Russian.

called "Alpine," "Eastern," or "Celto-Slavic" race, which penetrates somewhat westward of Russia into the highland region of Central Europe. As in the case of other Slavs (see), however, other European races, as the "Northern" and the "Cevenole," are found represented among the Russians. It is to the Northern or Teutonic race that the Western Finns belong physically, in spite of their Mongolian origin, and the Great Russians are more modified by the Finnic stock than by any other. They are therefore, especially in the north, more blond in type than are the Slavs farther south. Their neighbors on the west, the Lithuanians, and even the Poles, approach more nearly than they to the Northern type, and thus mediate between them and the western Europeans physically as they do in language and in political sympathies.

In temperament the Great Russians are more practical and persevering than are their racial brothers and competitors, the Ruthenians or Little Russians of southwestern Russia and of Austria. The Great Russians have been said to have approached the Finn in physical type but the Tatar in temperament, the latter not so much through racial admixture as through their struggle with the Tatar hordes of Asia. Their temper and their strength as a people have been developed by struggle. Russia is a buffer state, as the early Slavs were a buffer race between Europe and Asia. Little Russia was permanently weakened by the tribute of her best men, whom she offered up in the strife.

In language the Great and the Little Russians differ less from each other than do the High and the Low Germans. The Little Russian is sometimes said to be only a dialect of the Great Russian, but this may be regarded as a prejudiced statement. Philologists and anthropologists have often been drawn into the strife for supremacy and leadership between rival Russian and Slavic races. Panslavism, or the aspiration for a united Slavic people and state, suffers from this cause. There can be no doubt that the primacy of the Slavs belongs henceforward to the Great Russians, whatever be the sentimental claims of the Little Russians, the Poles, or the Czechs. The supremacy of the Great Russian language and literature must go with the Empire; the power, the wealth, and the political expansion of the latter are the decisive factors. The Russians even force the use of their language into Little Russian and Polish territory.

In the religious world there is the same strife. The autocratic claims of the Russian church have been successfully opposed by the Lutherans of Finland and the Catholics of Poland. Even the Little Russians have succeeded in establishing a church that is partly Russian and nominally Roman. Among the Great Russians themselves a large number are dissenters from the state church. "Raskolnik" is the name applied to the schismatics in general, but there is a great variety of minor sects. Of these sects the Dukhobors are perhaps best known in America. They have emigrated to Canada in considerable numbers and have gained notoriety by making pilgrimages without clothing about the country, and by refusing to use animals, preferring to hitch their womenfolk to the plow. The Dukhobors seem to have originated in central Russia, to have flourished for over a hundred years, and to have received the especial encouragement of Tolstoi.

Aside from the names of religious sects, such as Dukhobors and Mennonites—the latter not confined, by the way, to Russia—there is no such list of subdivisions of the Great Russians needing definition as is found among Little Russians and Poles. The Great Russian territory is a homogeneous whole from St. Petersburg to the Lower Don. Indeed, it extends north to the Arctic, a vast region 500 or 600 miles wide, separating the Finns of Finland from their kinsmen and the Tatars on the Asiatic border; and it extends east to Asia with the exception of the Finnic and the Tataric islets that dot the map of Eastern Russia. (See *Tataric* and *Finnish.*) The greatest expanse of European Russia that is not Great Russian is southwestern Russia, and that is Little Russian. The "Cossacks of the Don" (see) were Great Russian; those of the Dnieper, Little Russian.

The Great Russians number nearly half of the total population of European Russia, excluding from this term Finland, Poland, and Caucasia, as is done in the official census. Over 5,000,000 of them live in Asia. In the entire Empire there are 55,000,000 Great Russians out of a total population of 125,000,000 of all races.

The emigration of Great Russians is peculiar in that it is mainly from Europe to the Russian possessions in Asia, not to America. In the year 1907, 577,000 persons migrated from European Russia to Siberia, and during the fiscal year 1907, 258,943 came from Russia to the United States. The movement to Siberia is partly the result of the building of the great railway to the Pacific, but mainly because southern Siberia has been found to be a pleasant country and capable of supporting millions of population, while the Government encourages and assists the migration of peasants as a means of relieving the relative congestion of population in agrarian Russia. Southern Siberia is a wheat country, resembling the Dakotas and western Canada. In its rapid development it resembles in many respects our own West.

Immigration to the United States from Russia, including Finland, was 1,749,075 in the twelve years ending June 30 1910. Of this number only 77,321 are reported as Russian by race, while the total immigration of this race from all sources was 83,574 during this period. The Great Russians, therefore, stand twenty-second down the list of immigrant races. Of the number admitted during the twelve years considered, 26,477 went to New York, 17,839 to Pennsylvania, 6,294 to Massachusetts, 6,026 to Illinois, and 3,069 to California.

WHITE RUSSIAN AND BLACK RUSSIAN.

"Black Russia" is a historical term that may be disposed of in a brief paragraph. It appears on the fourteenth century map some distance north of the Black Sea, directly east of Kiev and the Dnieper, and southeast of White Russia. At that time it formed part of the important kingdom of Lithuania. It was afterwards embraced in Poland, and is now swallowed up in Little Russia. Ripley applies the term "Black Russian" to quite a different district, that of the Gorals, or "mountaineers," of the Austrian Carpathians, and finds that the name distinguishes the latter, as a very brunette stock, from the neighboring "Red Russians" or reddish blonds. The western Gorals, however, are of Polish speech.

The White Russian is one of the three distinct branches of the Russian language and race, although of far less importance numerically and politically than either of the other two. It is as much a "race" as the Great Russian ("Russian") or the Little Russian (Ruthenian), although usually considered simply as Russian in America. Unlike the term "Black Russia," "White Russia" is still found on the ethnographical map. It is a compact but small district roughly corresponding with what is now called "West Russia," though reaching somewhat nearer Moscow on the east. It is bounded on the northeast and east by Great Russian territory, on the northwest by Lithuanian, on the southwest by Polish, and on the south and southeast by Little Russian. The

White Russians constitute over three-fourths of the population of Mogilef and Minsk provinces and about half of Vitebsk, Vilna, and Grodno. In Kovno and Courland they approach the Baltic.

The White Russians have long been in political subjection, first to Lithuania, then to Poland, and, finally, to the Great Russians, although their lot now appears preferable to that of all the other subject peoples of western Russia. For this reason, among others, we hear little of them as a distinct race. They are said by travelers to be a distinctly weaker stock than the Great Russian, and less prepossessing in appearance. They are usually considered to be of purer Russian stock than either the Great or the Little Russians. Both the latter are far more modified by Mongolian elements, Finnic and Tataric. The White Russians are naturally more influenced by their Lithuanian and Polish neighbors (see) on the west, and these, especially the former, as has been said elsewhere, approach the blond Teutonic type more than the Slavs in appearance. Yet the White Russians are truly Slavs in breadth of head. Their cephalic index is 82, which is but slightly below that of the Little Russians. They are, therefore, of the purest type of the so-called "Eastern" or "Celto-Slavic" race.

But few subdivisions of the White Russian need be mentioned. The Poliechuks (see *Ruthenian*) are a White Russian population much mixed with Little Russian and very broad-headed (cephalic index, 85). They live in Minsk and Volhynia provinces; that is, on the border of Little Russia and near Poland. The Zabludov, a transition dialect standing between the Little and the White Russian, is found in this district.

The White Russians number less than 6,000,000, or but little over one-tenth as many as the Great Russians. They are not counted separately as immigrants.

OTHER RACES OR PEOPLES OF RUSSIA.

The term "Russian" in the last United States census, and until recently in United States immigration statistics, included more persons who were not of the Russian race than those who were. In fact, not 5 per cent of the "Russians" of the Census of 1900 are true Russians, as defined above. They are merely citizens of Russia. Probably over 50 per cent of them are Jews. Certain nationalities are grouped together to constitute the group of "Slavs," and New York is made to appear as their chief residence. On the contrary, they are largely Jews from Slavic countries, of whom it is estimated that 1,000,000 reside in New York City.[a]

It is deemed wise to indicate what a variety of peoples go to make up the Russian nationality and which of them are the chief ones that come to America (see table following). About 100 races are listed in the Russian census of 1897, of which number perhaps 20 are confined almost entirely to Asia. In European Russia itself there are as many Mongolian as Caucasian "races" or languages represented. Of the Caucasians, most of the divisions speak, not Indo-European or Aryan languages, like the Russian, but the peculiar agglutinative tongues of the Caucasus, more different from ours than are the Semitic of Western Asia and the Hamitic of North Africa. The great majority (about 80 per cent) of the population, however, is Slavic, especially Great Russian (nearly 50 per cent), Little Russian (20 per cent), and Polish (7 per cent). Next in numbers come the Jews, Semites (5 per cent); then the Lithuanians, Aryans who resemble Teutons more than Russians physically, if not

[a] The common use of the term "nationality" instead of "race" in public discussions has created an endless amount of confusion in the public mind, if not of absolute misinformation, as indicated above.

in language (3 per cent); then the Finns, Mongolian by language but Caucasian in appearance, especially those who have long intermarried with the Swedes (nearly 3 per cent); and finally the Tatars (also about 3 per cent).

It has been made clear in the articles on the leading races of Russia that our immigration comes almost entirely from those living on the western border, who are in a sense subject races, not from the Great or true Russians. In absolute numbers, of all immigrants to the United States the Hebrews stand second, the Poles third, and the Germans, most of whom come from Russia and Austria, fourth. The Ruthenians stand sixteenth down the list; the smaller populations of Lithuanians and Finns thirteenth and fourteenth, respectively; and the Russians proper, usually lower. As shown in the article on the Slavs, however, all these come at about the same rate per 1,000 of population (4 to 8) except the Germans, the Russians proper, and the Jews. The Jews exceed all other races from Russia in the rate of immigration (185 in 10,000), while the Great Russians come to a less degree (2 in 10,000) than any other people which characterizes recent American immigration.

The following table is taken from the only complete census of the Russian Empire, that of 1897. Finland has a separate census (total population, 2,592,864 in 1900). For most non-Russian races of Russia only the group totals are given. Detailed statistics of these will be found in the articles discussing each race, especially those on the Tatars, the Finns, and the Caucasus peoples. The peoples that are practically confined to Siberia naturally need no discussion in a dictionary of immigrant races. (See article *Ural-Altaic* for linguistic classification.)

Races or peoples of the Russian Empire, exclusive of Finland (1897).

Races or peoples (linguistic).	European Russia with Poland.	Caucasus.	Asia.	Total.
Total	102,845,117	9,289,364	13,505,540	125,640,021
Aryans	89,635,187	4,901,412	5,794,917	100,331,516
Slavs	83,514,884	3,183,870	5,390,979	92,089,733
Russians	75,428,814	3,154,898	5,349,855	83,933,567
Great Russians	48,825,881	1,829,793	5,011,795	55,667,469
Little Russians	20,750,203	1,305,463	324,885	22,380,551
White Russians	5,852,730	19,642	13,175	5,885,547
Poles	7,865,437	25,117	40,753	7,931,307
Other Slavic languages	220,633	3,855	371	224,859
Lithuanians	3,077,436	6,687	10,346	3,094,469
Latins	1,132,858	8,955	1,187	1,143,000
Germans	1,719,462	56,729	14,298	1,790,489
Armenians	49,511	1,118,094	5,491	1,173,096
Other Aryans	141,036	527,077	372,616	1,040,729
Jews	4,982,189	40,498	40,469	5,063,156
Ural-Altayans	8,221,201	1,902,142	7,542,330	17,665,673
Ugro-Finns	3,417,770	7,422	76,955	3,502,147
Turko-Tatars	4,626,454	1,879,908	7,094,889	13,601,251
Samoyeds	3,946	....	11,931	15,877
Tunguzes	1	....	66,269	66,270
Mongols	173,030	14,812	292,286	480,128
Georgians	1,461	1,350,275	799	1,352,535
Other Caucasians	818	1,088,373	2,591	1,091,782
Chinese, Japanese, Koreans	53	15	86,045	86,113
Hyperboreans	....	....	36,996	36,996
Others	4,208	6,649	1,393	12,2[illegible]0

Races or peoples of Finland (1900).

Finns	2, 352, 990
Swedes	349, 733
Russians	5, 939
Germans	1, 925
Lapps	1, 336
Others	639
Total	2, 712, 562

RUSSIAN, BLACK, RED, WHITE, and **GREAT.** (See *Russian;* for *Little Russian* and *Red Russian.* see *Ruthenian.*)

RUSSINE or **RUSSNIAK.** (See *Ruthenian.*)

RUTHENIAN (synonyms, **Little Russian, Malo-Russian, South Russian, Yugo-Russian**; in Austria, **Russniak, Russine, Red Russian, Galician**; in Russia, also **Ukrainian, Cherkasi**; in addition some call themselves simply "**Russian**" (*Rusy*) and sometimes in America, even "**Greek**"). The name Little Russian would seem most available of all this list at present for a clear and scientific definition. The Little Russian "race" or linguistic subdivision is that branch of the Russian, a "Southern Slavonic" (see) division of Aryan tongues, which is found native throughout southwestern Russia and in Galicia (Austria). Physically Little Russians are Caucasian, infrequently modified by a Mongol element. The Little Russians (Ruthenians) furnish more immigrants than any other true Russian stock coming to America.

"Little Russia" is a literal translation of the term "*Malo-Rossiya.*" "South Russian" and, less frequently, "Yugo-Russian,", and even "Cossack" or "Cherkess," are among the many names which have been bestowed upon this people by their more powerful kinsmen of the north, the Muscovites, who have assumed to themselves the name "Russian" (see) and the hegemony of the race. For similar, that is for political, reasons, Austria has found it convenient to name her Little Russian subjects "Ruthenians;" and this word is now commonly, but loosely, applied, even in scientific usage, to all Little Russians, including those of Ukrainia, in Russia. Still the Galicians call themselves "*Rusyny,*" which is sometimes translated "Russine." "Russniak" is a less common equivalent of Ruthenian.

"Red Russian" is a historical term which still designates one of the three dialects of the Little Russian language, the western. It appears that "Ruthenian" comes from the same root, meaning "red." Upon immigrating to America, some refuse to acknowledge that they are Ruthenians, a name fastened upon them as a subject people. In some communities they are known here as "Greeks" when they are of the United "Greek" Church, and thus distinguished from the Roman Catholic Poles and Slovaks of the community. Of course there is not a true Greek among them. Some American districts confer still other names upon them, lumping them together with Magyars (see) and perhaps with all Slavs under the picturesque, but stupid, title "Huns" or "Hunkies." The "Ruthenian (Russniak)" column of our immigration tables apparently includes all Little Russians, although but few are reported as coming from Russia. It is to be understood that all who bear the foregoing names are of one "race." They read one and the same language, which differs both from the White Russian (see) and from the Great or true Russian. The Ruthenian alphabet itself is an earlier form of the Russian.

What has been said in the articles on the Slavs and the Russians (see) applies in general to the Little Russians or Ruthenians so far as concerns their physical qualities, their intellectual and emotional make-up, their civilization, and the notable increase in their immigration. But little need be repeated here except to make clear in what respects they differ from other Slavs.

They are still more broad-headed than the Great Russians. This is taken to indicate a greater Tatar (Mongolian) admixture than is found among the latter, probably as does also the smaller nose, more scanty beard, and somewhat darker complexion. While hardly so muscular as the Great Russians, they are slightly taller. They are perhaps less practical, solid, and persevering than their competitors of the north, and therefore have been less successful as empire builders. But they often show a higher grade of intelligence and taste, and once led the Russias in scientific work. Their literature and their early history warrant them in claiming that they are the true Russian race rather than the northern stock which has usurped the name and the rule—the Great Russians. A large section of them have broken away from the Greek or Russian Church and have united with the Roman Catholic under a particular dispensation which allows them peculiar features of the Greek service and a married clergy. Hence the name "United Greek Church."

Although the Little Russians stand much closer to the Great Russians than do the Polish, Hebrew, Lithuanian, and German elements in Russia's population, nevertheless the use of their language has been discouraged and in a very remote sense they are a subject people in Russia as well as in Austria.

Their ethnical subdivisions and intermixtures are difficult to disentangle, as is the case with other Slavic peoples. The Boikos evidently belong to the Red Russian division of the Ruthenians. They live in the Carpathians of Galicia and Bukowina. The Huzuls or Guzuls, a very broad-headed people of Bukowina speaking a Red Russian dialect, have evidently grafted a Mongolian element upon the Ruthenian stock. This element may have come down from the extinct Uzes or Kumans (Tatars) who early penetrated this region, or it may be of Daco-Roumanian origin. The Huzuls are not friendly to the Boikos, their neighbors. The Touholtses, Ruthenians of Galicia, are very broad-headed like the Huzuls. The Little Russian stock is also found mixed with the Roumanian in the Pokutis and the Nistrovinians; with the Polish in the Belsans; and with the White Russian in the Poliechuks.

As has been explained at length in an article on the Cossacks (see), the Cossacks of the Dnieper have been an important branch of the Little Russians historically. The Zaparogs, named from their geographical position on the river, and the Chernomorishes are divisions of these. Little Russian populations have often received names because of some natural location or social condition. Such are the Stepoviks (of the steppes), the Poliechuks (of the forest), the Werchowinci (of the mountains), the Haiduks (or "robbers"), and the Lemkes (so called because of their pronunciation). The last named, who live in the Beskids, call themselves "*Rusnaky*"—that is, Ruthenians, although they resemble the Slovaks in language and physical type. Finally, there are the self-explanatory geographical terms by which certain Little Russians are known, as the Bukowinians, the Galicians, the Ukrainians, and the Bugans, or dwellers on the Bug. The Bugans are also known as the Lapotniki and are of a distinct type.

It must not be inferred that the majority of the inhabitants of Galicia, Bukowina, and the Ukraine are Little Russians. In Galicia they are surpassed in numbers by the Poles; in Bukowina nearly equaled by the Roumanians. In each of these districts the Germans stand third in population, with 210,000 and 160,000 souls, respectively. In the Ukraine many peoples are represented: the Great Russians, the present masters of Little Russia; the Poles, its former masters; large colonies of Germans, with some Bohemians and more Bulgarians; Tatar communities in the south; Roumanians annexed with their territory on the southwest; and multitudes of Jews, besides Armenians, Greeks, and Gypsies everywhere.

The Little Russians themselves are distributed geographically as shown in the following table:

Number and distribution of Little Russians (Ruthenians).

Country.	Estimated for 1897.	Census.	Chief location.
Total	25,000,000		
Russia	20,750,000	20,750,000 (1897)	
Little Russia	17,006,000	17,006,000 (1897)	Bessarabia.
Central Great Russia	2,180,000	2,180,000 (1897)	White Russia.
Elsewhere	1,564,000	1,564,000 (1897)	Poland.
Austria	3,285,000	3,375,000 (1900)	
Galicia	....	3,074,000 (1900)	
Bukowina	....	298,000 (1900)	
Elsewhere	....	3,000 (1900)	
Hungary	415,000	429,000 (1900)	North Central Hungary.
Elsewhere in Europe	50,000		
United States	500,000		

Roughly speaking, one-half of Russia south of the latitude of Moscow and eastward along the Black Sea as far as the Caucasus, the Kalmuks, and the Cossacks of the lower Don, is Little Russian. The race also covers all of eastern Austria—that is, Galicia and Bukowina—with the exception of a small district about Cracow (Polish), and spreads out far beyond the Carpathians into Hungary. Among the Slavic peoples their total population is second only to that of the Great Russians. During the fiscal years 1899 to 1910, inclusive, 147,375 Little Russians (or Ruthenians as they are designated in immigration statistics) were admitted to the United States and the race ranked sixteenth among all races in this regard. Of these, 144,710, or 98.2 per cent, came from Austria-Hungary, and only 1,034 from Russia, although, as will be noted from the preceding table, there are approximately 20,750,000 Little Russians in Russia and only 3,700,000 in Austria and Hungary. Their large population makes it appear probable that the Little Russians will be more largely represented in the Slavic immigration of the future.

The principal destinations of Ruthenians in the United States during the twelve-year period referred to were: Pennsylvania, 73,449; New York, 31,307; and New Jersey, 16,615.

S.

SAMARITAN. A branch of the Chaldean group of the Semitic stock (see).

SAMELAT. Same as **Lapp** (see).

SAMOAN. A Polynesian inhabiting the Samoan Islands. (See *Pacific Islander.*)

SAMOGITIAN. Same as **Jmoud.** (See *Finnish.*)

SAMOYED. The Ugro-Finnic people living on the Arctic Ocean in northeastern Russia and northwestern Siberia. Of little importance numerically (population about 15,000) or in civilization. They are still more primitive in manner of life and more Mongolian in appearance than are their western relatives, the Lapps. (See above terms; also *Finnish* and *Ural-Altaic.*) While having a similar language to the Europeanized Finns, they are quite the opposite to them in appearance, true Asiatics. None are known to come to America.

SANDOMIRIAN. A subdivision of the Polish (see).

SANDWICH ISLANDER. (See *Hawaiian.*)

SANSKRITIC. A term sometimes applied to all the Aryan languages (see). The Sanskrit is the oldest of these languages.

SANTAL. A small subdivision of the Dravidian race (see) living in Bengal. (See *Hindu.*)

SARD or **SARDINIAN.** A native of the island of Sardinia, a possession of Italy. The language is a dialect of Italian (see) peculiar to the island, called "Sardinian." Physically the Sardinians are one of the most homogeneous groups of Europe. Like their neighbors, the Corsicans, they are supposed to be at bottom Iberic, thus being related to the South Italians and the early inhabitants of Spain, and perhaps to the Berbers of northern Africa. The Sardinian, of all the Italians, is the purest representative of the "Mediterranean" race in head form and color of hair and eyes. He is the most dwarfish in stature of European peoples, the average being several inches shorter than the Teutonic average of northern Europe. The facial features often betray an infusion of African blood.

The Sardinians are illiterate, very backward, have no great industries, and but little foreign trade. In religion nearly all are Catholic.

The population of Sardinia is 850,000, nearly all of whom are South Italians, except 10,000 Catalans (see *Spanish*) in the northern part of the island. The latter form the aristocracy of Sardinia. Comparatively few Sardinians emigrate, and those who come to the United States are probably listed as South Italian.

SARTE. A Tataric (see) tribe of Asia.

SAVOLAK, SAVAKOTI, or **SAVOLAISET.** A division of the Western Finns. (See *Finnish.*)

SAVOYARD. (See *French.*)

SAVRIN. An Istrian division of the Slovenians (see).

SAXON. (See *German.*)

SCANDINAVIAN (sometimes **Norse**), including the **Norwegian, Danish, Swedish,** and **Icelandic** races or peoples. The native, Teutonic, race or races of Scandinavia in the wider sense. The name "Scandinavia" is sometimes applied to the northern peninsula only—that is, to Norway and Sweden—but it is also properly applied to Denmark and Iceland. The Scandinavian is the most familiar in America of the older immigrant types from the Continent of Europe, with the exception of the German; that is, it is the most numerously represented, especially in the North Central States.

The definitions of the subdivisions of the Scandinavian group are self-evident, to wit, the Teutonic races of Norway, Sweden, Denmark, and Iceland, respectively. The term "Norse" is applied only to themselves by the Norwegians, who are called "*Norsk*" in their own language. But it is better justified in international usage as a name of the entire Scandinavian group of languages. The Old Norse, or the early language of Iceland, was the predecessor of all modern Scandinavian languages. It is hardly necessary to remind the reader that the term "Norseman" or "Northman" was applied during the middle ages to the viking rovers of all these countries, who established dynasties in England, Russia, France (Normandy), and Sicily, settled Iceland, and without doubt preceded Columbus to America. Nor is it necessary to remind the student of ethnology that the Scandinavian is considered to be the purest type of one of the three great races of Europe as divided from a physical point of view; that is, of the "Northern" or "Teutonic" race in contradistinction from the "Alpine" and "Mediterranean" races farther south. (See *Caucasian* and *Aryan*.)

If races be divided merely by physical characters, all Scandinavians form a homogeneous race more truly than any of the large populations or races south of them. The English, and especially the French and the German, are much more mixed in physical type. The typical Scandinavians average as the longest-headed and most purely blond, if not the tallest people of Europe. In height they appear to be surpassed only by the Scotch. Both the height and the cephalic index increase as we pass from Denmark to Sweden and from Sweden to Norway. The cephalic index in these countries rises in the order named from 77.8 to 78, then to 78.5; the height from 1.68 meters to 1.70 meters, and then to 1.72 meters. In English measures, the Norwegian average, the last named, is about 5 feet 8 inches, which the Scotch exceeds by one-half inch.

It must be remembered that the small population of Lapps, 30,000, in northern Scandinavia is of entirely different race, the very opposite of the Scandinavian, in fact, both in language and in physical type. As elsewhere explained (see *Lappish*), they still speak a Mongol or Ugro-Finnic tongue—agglutinative in structure, instead of inflected, as is the Aryan family of languages, to which the Scandinavian belongs. Physically the Lapps are very short and indicate in their dark features and extremely broad heads their Asiatic origin. Very little intermixture has taken place with this stock considering the length of time the Scandinavians and Lapps have lived in neighboring districts, unless a broader-headed and darker type of Norwegians found in the extreme southwest indicates an ancient infusion of this sort. Ripley prefers to think it a survival of an early "Alpine" element from Central Europe.

The character of the Norse element in America is well enough known to need no detailed description. They make ideal farmers and are often said to Americanize more rapidly than do the other peoples who have a new language to learn on their arrival. In Norway the rate of illiteracy is the lowest in Europe. In religion the Scandinavians are Protestant almost to a man—over 99 per cent, according to the censuses of these countries.

NORWEGIAN.

The most difficult question that remains for discussion relates to the Norwegian race or people and language. Are the Norwegians to be considered a separate race or people from the Danes? Of course, as a nationality they are different. In fact there exists a separatist feeling among the three Scandinavian nationalities which persists to a degree even in America. But the literary language of Norway and that of Denmark are generally supposed to be one and the same. As has been repeatedly explained (see Introductory, *English*, and *German*), this dictionary adopts the test of race which is followed in all national censuses, namely, that of language; and it was found in the case of the Dutch and the Flemish (see *German*) that only the literary languages, and not a difference in spoken dialects, justified separating them from other "Germans."

A fair answer to the question just raised appears to be that the Norwegian can now be called, technically, a different race or people from the Danish, although this was not true a century ago. Of course, this is only an arbitrary distinction and is one of the most artificial distinctions we are called upon to make among the so-called European "races," as determined by language or by any other standard. Physically, as already shown, the Norwegians and the Danes are, to a remarkable degree, homogeneous. Furthermore, so far as dialectal differences are concerned, there is no more reason for separating them from one another than for dividing the Norwegians themselves into different races.

The fact is that from 1397 to 1814, when Norway regained her independence from Denmark, a modified Danish was not only the literary language of Norway but was generally used in the cities and among the educated classes. Since this date a new literary language, the "Dano-Norwegian," has been rapidly developed at the hands of Norway's greatest litterateurs, including Ibsen. While this language is based upon the Danish formerly in use, it has incorporated 7,000 words from the Norwegian dialects, enough to suffice almost for a language. Indeed, other writers, like Aasen, insist on using only Norwegian dialectal forms. The Norwegian may, therefore, in accordance with the language test, be considered a separate people.

A few facts bearing upon Norway's remarkable emigration may be reserved for the table which appears near the end of this article. In short, Norway has sent a larger per cent of its population to America than any other country excepting Ireland. Considering the smallness of its population, but little over 2,000,000, as compared with the 72,000,000 of Germans and 40,000,000 of English, Scotch, and Irish, it has done its full share in populating America. Although Scandinavian immigration has greatly diminished in its relative rank since 1885, the United States census of 1900 gives 336,985 of the population as of Norwegian birth and 452,896 as children of parents born in Norway. Counting these two generations only, the Norwegian population of the United States is already more than one-third that of Norway.

DANISH AND ICELANDIC.

The two smallest in extent of the Scandinavian peoples may next be considered, those of Denmark and her insular possession, Iceland. They are entirely different from each other in language, and therefore are distinct in race, according to the usual test. While Denmark gave its language in recent times to Norway, as has already been said, Iceland gave the Old Norse in written form to all Scandinavia. During that period of the northern literature, Norway took precedence of Denmark and of Sweden. The Sagas and the Eddas belonged in a sense to her as well as to Iceland and gave to Scandinavia the proud distinction of bequeathing to posterity an older and more famous literature than any of the German tongues farther south.

The population of Iceland is purely Scandinavian, but is so small in numbers, about 80,000, as to be of no importance in immigration. Icelanders do, however, come to the United States and also to Canada. In Denmark itself it is estimated that fully 97 per cent of the population is Danish, notwithstanding the closeness of its relations to Germany. On the other hand, there are at least 140,000 Danes living on the other side of the border in Germany. If one may contrast the three Scandinavian peoples in a slight degree, it might be said that the Norwegian is rather more of a democrat—slow, sturdy, and independent; the Swede, as he has been called, "the Parisian of the North;" and the Dane, the cosmopolite. The royal family of Denmark stands in extraordinary personal relations with those of a number of European powers. Members of the family of the late King Christian are now rulers or consorts of rulers in several of the European countries.

SWEDISH.

The Swedes may be considered to be entirely distinct in race from the Danes and the Norwegians. Their language is so different that it can not be read by the Danes and Norwegians without some study. The Swedes have expanded in Europe more than their sister Scandinavians. For five hundred years Finland was ruled by Sweden. Although this rule ceased a century ago, in 1809, Swedish is still the language of the higher classes of Finns and is used in official and scientific publications of their country. Fully 350,000, or 13 per cent, of the population of Finland is Swedish to-day. The Finns themselves, as found in Finland, show a large admixture of Scandinavian blood, for they are Teutonic in physical type rather than Ugric. (See *Finnish.*) While there is no doubt that they are Asiatic, Mongol, in origin, they are to-day of entirely different type from the Finns of eastern Russia. In America they are often taken to be Scandinavians, but are to be distinguished by their mother tongue, which is absolutely different from any Aryan language, agglutinative rather than inflected in type.

The Scandinavian population of the world is about 13,000,000. Their approximate distribution is shown in the following table:

Scandinavian population and immigration.

Countries.	Number.	Immigration (1907).	
		Number.	Rate per 1,000.
Total population of—			
Denmark (1906)	2,605,000	7,163	2.7
Norway (1905)	2,311,000	22,043	9.5
Sweden (1907)	5,377,000	20,534	3.8
Scandinavians in—			
Finland (Swedes, 1900)	350,000		
Sleswick (Danes)	200,000		
Iceland (1901)	78,000		
United States (estimated)	2,000,000		
Elsewhere (estimated)	79,000		

It is interesting to note that the smallest of the continental Scandinavian peoples in numbers, the Norwegian, doubles or trebles each of the others in its rate of immigration. This rate, 9.5 per 1,000 of the population in 1907, although much lower than it was twenty years ago, was surpassed in the year mentioned only by those of Slovak, Hebrew, Croatian and Slovenian, and South Italian races. The Irish, which had nearly the same rate, resembles it also in the large total immigration it has sent out of a very small population. The Scandinavians, taken together, stood twice as far down the list of immigrant races in their rate of 5 per 1,000 of population. In absolute numbers, Scandinavian immigration is fifth in rank, 586,306 for the twelve years 1899–1910, being exceeded only by that from the much larger populations of the Germans, Italians, and Poles, as also by the

Hebrews. The English, Irish, and Scotch taken separately rank below it.

The Scandinavians differ from the British, naturally, in coming to the United States almost entirely to the neglect of the British colonies. It is probable that more Scandinavian farmers per year now emigrate from our own Northwestern States into Canada than come direct to Canada from Europe. It is possible for the Scandinavian element to increase in future American immigration more than, for instance, the Irish, for there are 11,000,000 Scandinavians in Europe as against only 4,500,000 Irish.

Scandinavian immigrants still go, as they always have gone, to the North Central States to a greater degree than almost any other people, although New York stood first in this regard with 107,775 during the twelve years under consideration. The other principal destinations during that period were: Minnesota, 89,093; Illinois, 75,669; Massachusetts, 43,427; Wisconsin, 36,472; North Dakota, 26,447; Washington, 24,950; Iowa, 23,812; Michigan, 20,977; Pennsylvania, 19,190, and South Dakota, 14,132.

SCLAVE, SCLAVONIAN, and **SLAVE**. Same as **Slav** (see).

SCOTCH (including **Highland Scotch** or **Gaelic**). A term applied (1) in the wider sense to both races of Scotland, the Celts of the north (Highlanders) and the Anglo-Saxons of the south (Lowlanders); (2) in a narrower sense, only to the Celtic race of Scotland, the Highland Scotch. Gaelic is another name for the latter. The word "Scotch," as a linguistic term, means the language spoken by Scotchmen. When unqualified it means the dialect of English spoken by the Lowland Scotch. Highland Scotch is a synonym for Scottish Gaelic, the most northern branch of the Celtic group of Aryan or Indo-European languages (see these). The words "Scotch" and "Scotchmen," used as terms of nationality, include all citizens of Scotland, and therefore other peoples besides the Highland Scotch and the Lowland Scotch. "Scots" is a synonym used in Scotland for Scotchmen generally. In deference to common usage this dictionary must deviate from the linguistic principle of classification elsewhere explained (see Introductory and *English*) and consider Scotch to include both the Highland and the Lowland Scotch. To avoid confusion, however, the term "Highland Scotch" will be generally used for the Celtic linguistic stock of the Highlands and "Lowland Scotch" for the English-speaking population of the Lowlands.

HIGHLAND SCOTCH.

The Highland Scotch language, the modern Erse or Gaelic, is said to be a much more modern language than Irish. These two Celtic tongues are said to differ from one another no more than the English of the Lowland Scotch does from ordinary English. Highland Scotch is meager in its literature and is fast losing ground as a speech. English is rapidly replacing it in commerce, in church services, in the schools, and even in the home. It is only in the most western part of Scotland and in the islands of the Hebrides that Highland Scotch is still spoken by a majority of the population.

There are partisan views as to the origin and racial affinities of the Highland Scotch. Some contend that they are descended from the ancient Caledonian Picts; others that they are the descendants of the so-called "Scots" (Irish) who emigrated to Scotland from northern Ireland about the sixth century and gave their name and language to the new country as did the Angles to England. Perhaps the more reasonable view is that of the physical anthropologists, who say that the

Highland Scotch are a mixed people, a product of Pict, Irish, and Scandinavian. The prevailing type, as among the Irish, is tall, long-headed, and harsh-featured. But there is a greater proportion of blonds, especially of the red-haired and freckle-faced type. Dark eyes, rare among the Irish, are quite common among the Highlanders. Contrary to the time-honored opinion of ethnologists of the linguistic school, physical anthropologists now state that the "Celtic" or "Alpine" (see) physical type, one of the three great physical divisions of the races of Europe, is rarely found in either Scotland or Ireland. Most of the brunette individuals found in these countries are long-headed and are thought to be representatives of the "Southern" or "Mediterranean" rather than of the broad-headed "Alpine" race.

Geographically the Highland Scotch originally occupied the northern islands and all the territory north of the southern firths of Scotland, the firths of Clyde and of Forth; that is, the territory north of the cities of Glasgow and Edinburgh. But as Saxons and Danes pressed upon them from the south and Norwegians from the north they were driven into the Highlands of Scotland. These are generally understood to comprise all the territory northwest of a line drawn diagonally from the Clyde to Aberdeen on the eastern shore. This territory occupies more than half the area of Scotland, but is sparsely settled. And even the entire eastern part of northern Scotland has become Anglicized. Only about 5 per cent of the people of Scotland can now speak Gaelic, and of this small number, about one-half, or 112,000, live in three counties in the heart of the Highlands. Less than 500 persons of the Lowlands speak Gaelic only. Highland Scotch is practically extinct in the northern islands.

LOWLAND SCOTCH AND NORTHERN ISLANDERS.

The people of the Lowlands and of the northern islands bear certain resemblances to each other. Both have been Teutonic in language for centuries. Both have been much modified physically by Scandinavian elements. Both are often classed as "English" (see) in race. The term "Lowland Scotch" is a name given to the people of the Lowlands of Scotland. They speak a dialect of English known to every schoolboy through the ballads of Burns. It is closely related to the Northumberland dialect of the northern part of England, but contains more Celtic and Scandinavian elements.

Physically the Lowland Scotch are very mixed, being descended chiefly from Scandinavians and Saxons, but also from Picts, Celtic-Scots, and Norman French. These various elements do not seem, however, to be as thoroughly amalgamated as in the case of the English. A type largely represented approaches that of the Englishman, long-headed, with light eyes, and with hair varying from light to brown, but taller, heavier, and more muscular. The features are rounder and the cheek bones less prominent than those of the Highland Scotch. This Lowlander is the type sometimes pointed out as the one toward which the American people is evolving. The chief racial elements of the mixture have been much the same in either case. The Norse type also has many representatives. It is tall (the tallest of all Europe, over 5 feet 8 inches), very long-headed, with light eyes and hair flaxen or sand colored. This type is found not only in the Lowlands, but is predominant in the northern islands, the Shetlands, and the Orkneys. It is also found in the Hebrides. So thoroughly did the Norwegians invade these islands that not only were they dominant there for centuries, but their language was in use in the Hebrides from the eighth to the fourteenth century, when it was replaced by Gaelic, and still longer in the northern islands, where it survived until superseded by the English in the eighteenth century.

From what has been said it will be seen that the English-speaking populations of Scotland now occupy the entire lowlands, the Shetland and Orkney islands, and the northeasternmost county of Scotland. They are bounded on the west by the Highland Scotch and on the south by the Northumberland dialect of English. The population of this territory is about 3,850,000, practically all of whom except some 50,000 (Highland Scotch) speak English.

The Scotch, both Highlanders and Lowlanders, are too well known in other respects as American citizens to need further discussion here. Topographical conditions have had much to do in developing their differences. The Highlander, living in the unfertile mountains covered with rocks and heath and barren of mineral wealth, is given to sheep herding and cattle grazing. The Lowlander, having rich fields and mines of coal and iron, is an agriculturist, a miner, and a manufacturer. The population of his district is five times as dense as that of the Highlander.

The population of Scotland in 1901 was 4,472,103. Outside of Scotland, the Scotch, using the term to include both Highlanders and Lowlanders, are found in considerable numbers in Ulster province in Ireland (see *Irish*), in England, in the United States, and in the British colonies. There are 600,000 of the first and second generation only in the United States. Longstaff says that Canada is to a great extent a Scotch country. He estimated that there were (1881) about 700,000 Scotch in Canada. In religion the Scotch are for the most part Protestants. There are about 400,000 Catholics.

During the twelve years 1899–1910, 136,842 Scotch immigrants were admitted to the United States, 20,516 arriving in 1907. This places them seventeenth on the list of immigrant races or peoples. Their rate of movement from Europe in 1907 was 4 per 1,000 of the population of Scotland. This was nearly four times that of the English, but only about half that of the Irish or the Norwegian, whose rate of movement is the greatest of all northwestern European peoples. It was, however, less than one-fourth that of the races having the highest rate of movement, the Hebrew and the Slovak (18 per 1,000 of the population in 1907). The principal destinations of the Scotch during the twelve years considered were: New York, 34,917; Massachusetts, 18,295; Pennsylvania, 16,258; Illinois, 8,000; New Jersey, 7,855, and California, 6,067.

SCOTCH-IRISH. (See *Irish.*)

SELJUK TURK. A peasant class of Asia Minor. (See *Tataric* and *Turkish.*)

SEMITIC-HAMITIC. One of the four chief divisions or stocks of the Caucasian race. The others are the insignificant Basque and Caucasic stocks and the great Aryan division. The Semitic-Hamitic is considerable in extent, covering one-third of Africa; but its population is only 50,000,000 as against 800,000,000 Aryans. They and the Aryans are the only peoples of the world having inflected languages. For this reason they may be grouped together, perhaps with more propriety than because of their physical similarity. Many Hamites would be taken by travelers to be Negroes; yet because of the regularity of their features, and certain other characteristics, they are felt to be Caucasian rather than Negro.

The Semites may be defined as that branch of the Caucasian race indigenous to southwestern Asia, and the Hamites as that branch indigenous to northern Africa; but the Hamites also are supposed to have come originally from the Euphrates region, while one branch of the Semites, the Abyssinians, are found in Africa. While the languages of the Hamites and the Semites are not very closely allied, there can no longer be any doubt that they should be grouped together. The linguistic relations of these peoples will be best seen in the following classification from Brinton. (Some extinct peoples are omitted and others are in italics.)

The Semitic-Hamitic family.

Stocks.	Groups.	Peoples and tribes.
I. Hamitic	1. Libyan	*Guanches*, Berbers, Rifians, Zouaves, Kabyles Tuareks, Tibbus, Ghadumes, Mzabites, *Etruscans*, *Assyrians* (early), *Hittites*.
	2. Egyptian	Copts, Fellaheen.
	3. East African	Gallas, Somalis, Danakils, Bedjas, Bilins, Afars Khamirs.
II. Semitic	1. Arabian	*Himyarites*, Arabs, Bedawin, Ehkilis.
	2. Abyssinian	Amharnis, Tigris, Tigrinas, Gheez, Ethiopians, Harraras.
	3. Chaldean	*Assyrians* (later), *Babylonians*, Israelites, Arameans (Syrians, etc.), Samaritans.

Hovelacque classifies the Semites as follows:

1. Arabic group: Arabic proper and idioms of South Arabia and Abyssinia.

2. Canaanitic group: Hebrew and Phœnician.

3. Arameo-Assyrian group: Aramaic (Chaldee and Syriac) and Assyrian.

The "East African" of the foregoing table is often called the "Ethiopian" group. It extends on the coast below Abyssinia as far south as the game regions visited by the Roosevelt hunting expedition in 1909. These Hamites, and others bordering on the true Negro country, are naturally in large part of mixed blood. This is true also of the Arabs found everywhere in northern Africa and even of those of Arabia. It is due to the Arabs, however, that we sometimes find a distinctly light Berber or other tribe in this region. These are true Caucasians. They are sometimes even blonds. The Hamites are held by Sergi, the Italian anthropologist, to have been the original stock that peopled southern Italy and spread over the northern shore of the Mediterranean.

The Libyan group, said to present the purest type of the stock, extends to the western coast. In Morocco they are known as Riffs and Berbers; in Algeria, as Zouaves and Kabyles; further south, as the Tuaregs and Tibus of the desert and as the Ghadames, the Serkus, and the Mzabites. An extinct Riff tribe, the Guanches, once inhabited the Canary Islands. The Senagas, further south, have given their name to the French colony of Senegal. This lies upon the borderland of the typical Negroes, the Sudanese, whose descendants are found in the United States.

The Semitic-Hamitic family comprises tribes and peoples as different in civilization as they are in color. As has been said elsewhere, the Hebrews (see) are to-day European or Aryan rather than Semitic in residence, in civilization, and even in language and blood. Excepting them and the Christianized Syrians and Abyssinians, practically all are Mohammedans, from the Arabs on the east to the Riffs and Senegas on the west. Many Pagan beliefs survive in places.

As to immigration, the chief race of this linguistic group, the Hebrews, are second only to the Italians in point of numbers coming to our shores. Statistics concerning these, the Syrians, and the Arabs will be found under their respective names in this dictionary. Indeed, if we consider the South Italians, as does Sergi, to be of Hamitic origin, we might rightly say that the dominant type of recent immigration is Western Asiatic (Semitic-Hamitic), where but recently it was Northern European (Aryan); for the South Italians and the Hebrews are now far in the lead amongst immigrants. All the Semitic-Hamitic immigration that remains, aside from that mentioned above, is exceedingly small. It is included in the 49 immigrants of "Other peoples" that came from Africa in 1907 as reported by the Bureau of Immigration. This, it will be remembered, does not include Negro immigration (see).

SENAGA. (See *Semitic-Hamitic.*)

SEPHARDIM. The Spanish-Portuguese Jews as distinguished from the German-Polish Jews, called Ashkenazim. They form only 10 per cent of the Jewish race. (See *Hebrew.*)

SERB, SRP, SORB, or **SERBO-HORVATIAN.** Same as **Croatian** (see).

SERBO-CROATIAN. Same as **Croatian** (see).

SERBO-LUSATIAN or **SORBIAN** (not **Serbo-Horvatian**). Same as **Wend** (see).

SERVIAN or **SERB.** Same as **Croatian** (see). A political and ecclesiastical division of the Serbo-Croatians.

SIAMESE. The principal people of Siam; a division of the Indo-Chinese (see) group of the Sinitic branch of the Mongolian race (see). They form nearly one-third of the total population (5,000,000) of Siam. Their language, official throughout Siam, is, like the Chinese, of the monosyllabic type. Physically they are much mixed through intermarriage with other peoples of Siam, especially the Chinese, of whom there are some 600,000. In religion they are generally Buddhists.

SIBIRIC. That branch of the Mongolian race which comprises the Japanese, Arctic, Tungusic, Finnic, Tataric, and Mongolic groups (see these), and therefore all the Mongolian peoples which have invaded Europe, such as the Finns, Lapps, Magyars, and Osmanlis or Turks (see these).

SICILIAN. Not the name of a race and not used by the Bureau of Immigration. Any native or inhabitant of the island of Sicily. This is inhabited for the most part by South Italians, who speak a dialect peculiar to the island called Sicilian. The population is very mixed physically, being at bottom Ligurian or Iberic, but much modified by the many invading peoples, including even North Africans.

The Sicilians are vivid in imagination, affable, and benevolent, but excitable, superstitious, and revengeful. Prior to 1860, when it became a part of United Italy, the Island of Sicily was a part of the Kingdom of the Two Sicilies. It is now a compartimento of Italy. In 1901 Sicily had a population of 3,529,799, which was greater than that of any other compartimento except Lombardy.

The population of Sicily, excepting about 15,000 Albanians, is Italian. About 50,000 speak the Lombard dialect. The Albanians (see), locally known as "*Greci,*" speak their own language, and observe special religious rites. The Sicilians proper are nearly all Catholic.

The population of the island is being rapidly depleted of its younger blood by voluntary emigration. As many as 100,000 in a single year have emigrated to the Americas. It is not known to what extent they are coming to the United States, as they are listed as "South Italian" in immigration statistics. Immigrants are not listed by provinces.

SIKH. A politico-religious group in northern India. Not the name of a race. (See *Hindu.*)

SILESIAN. A geographical term; a name given to those living in the German and Austrian provinces called Silesia. Also the name applied to both Polish and German dialects spoken in Silesia.

SINDI or **SINDHI.** A branch of the Indo-Aryan stock (see *Hindu*) living in the province of Sind, British India. It has a population of about 3,000,000, most of whom profess Mohammedanism.

SINHALESE (CINGALESE). The principal native people of Ceylon. They live in the central and southern part of the island, and form nearly two-thirds of the entire population of 3,577,000. They speak an Aryan tongue, sometimes called Ceylonese, although they are thought by some to belong physically to the Dravidian (see) stock. The other native peoples of the island are the Tamil and the Veddah, also branches of the Dravidian. The Sinhalese are Buddhists in religion, while the Tamils are adherents of Hinduism.

SINITIC. That branch of the Mongolian race which comprises the Chinese, Indo-Chinese, and Tibetan groups. (See articles on these and on the *Sibiric*, the only other branch of the Mongolian race.) Not to be confused with the word "Semitic," a term referring to certain Caucasian stocks, as Hebrews and Arabs. The word "Sinitic" is derived from the late Latin "Sina," China.

SIRYAN or **SIRYANIAN** (not **Syrian**). Same as **Zyrian** (see).

SKIPETAR. The native name of the Albanians (see).

SLAV (SCLAVE), SLAVIC, or **SLAVONIC**; sometimes wrongly called in the United States "Hun" (see *Magyar*). To be defined as that Aryan "race" or linguistic group which occupies the greater part of Russia and the Balkans. The Russian and the Polish (see) are its leading tongues. (See below and table in Introductory.) The Slavic, the Teutonic, and the Italic or "Latin" are the three great stocks that furnish the most of the population of Europe as well as of our annual flood of immigrants. Of these three, the Slavic and the Italic have been rapidly replacing the Teutonic in American immigration, and the Slavic is perhaps the most significant for the future because of its great population. (See also *Caucasian* and *Aryan* and cf. *Slovenian.*)

Physically, and perhaps temperamentally, the Slavs approach the Asiatic, or particularly the Tatar, more closely than do the peoples of western Europe. In language they are as truly Aryan as ourselves. Of course, languages do not fuse by interbreeding; physical races do. There is some truth in the old saying, "Scratch a Russian and you find a Tartar," especially if he come from southern Russia, where once lived the Mongol conquerors of the Russias. Yet the common conception of the Slav as dreamy and impractical does not seem to fit with the greatness of the new nation which impresses the imagination of the beholder more than any other in Europe. The fact is that we do not know the Slav. Unfortunately the unlikeness of the language to those of western Europe, perhaps even the unfamiliarity of the alphabet used, has delayed the study of what must soon be regarded as one of the great languages and literatures of civilization. Its spread, like that of the Russian Empire, has been more rapid than that of any other in the present century.

If the Slav be still backward in western ideas, appliances, and form of government, it is nevertheless conceivable that the time is not far distant when he will stand in the lead. The race is still young. Its history is shorter than that of any other important people of Europe.

As to the Slavic temperament and character, it will no doubt be safest to generalize what has been said of the Russian by a Russian sociologist, Novicow. Roughly condensing a chapter into a paragraph, the Slav may be said to be inequable or changeable in mood and in effort—now exalted, now depressed, melancholy, and fatalistic. Much goes with this: Fanaticism in religion, carelessness as to the business virtues of punctuality and often honesty, periods of besotted drunkenness among the peasantry, unexpected cruelty and ferocity in a generally placid and kind-hearted individual.

It will conduce to a clearer comprehension of the many-sided Slavic stock if we first analyze it into the numerous "races" which comprise it. The following classification is based upon that of Pypin:

Classification of Slavic tongues.

Division	Group	Subdivision	Dialects
Eastern and Southern Division.	Russian	Great Russian	Moscow. Novgorod. Don Kossack. Siberian.
		White Russian.	
		Little Russian (Ruthenian)	Ukranian. Galician. Carpathian.
	Bulgarian	Old Bulgarian (Church Slavonic). New Bulgarian.	
	Serbo-Croatian	Servian. Croatian. Dalmatian. Syrmian.	
	Slovenian	Carinthian. Styrian.	
Western Division	Bohemian	Tsekh. Moravian. Slovak.	
	Polish	Mazurian. Great Polish. Silesian. Kashubian.	
	Lusatian (Sorb)	Upper Lusatian. Lower Lusatian.	
	Polabish	Polabish (extinct).	

Many variations from this scheme might be cited. We should recall first of all the system adopted for practical reasons by the Bureau of Immigration. In it the Serbo-Croatian group is increased by the Bosnian and the Herzegovinian, which are counted together with the Dalmatian, and by the Montenegrin, which is put with the Bulgarian and the Servian into one column. The Croatians and the Slovenians are counted together. Instead of "Bohemian" as a group name, the Bureau uses "Czech," and in this it has good scientific support. Serbo-Croatian is called by Miklosich "Serbo-Horvatian," which illustrates the identity of Croatian and Horvatian. "Macedonian" is recognized by others as a dialect of Bulgarian. "Wend" (see) is another name for Lusatian.

All these languages are said to be more closely related to one another than are the Teutonic tongues. Difficulties have been made in their mutual study by the use of three different alphabets—the Roman, the Cyrillic, and the Glagolitic. The Cyrillic, which is a modified, or more properly a mutilated, Greek alphabet, is used by the largest population, namely, by the Russians, the Bulgarians, and the Servians, or at least by those Servians who belong to the Greek Church. The

Slav.

alphabet question is mainly a question of religion. The use of the Glagolitic has been encouraged by the Catholic Church in the Catholic parts of Servia, Croatia, and Dalmatia. It is said to be now used only in the liturgical writings of the Dalmatians. While this alphabet is losing ground, the use of the Roman is increasing. The Poles and the Bohemians have always used the latter.

The foregoing classification is of Slavic languages, not of physical races. The Bulgarians belong there only by adoption. They are mainly of a Mongol or "Turanian" stock which borrowed a Slavic tongue. Just the opposite is the case of the Roumanians (see) or "Moldo-Wallachians," who are mainly Slavs by blood but Latinized in speech.

Turning to the physical characteristics of the Slavs, it is found that there is not, properly speaking, a Slavic race. The "Alpine" type predominates; that is, the broad-headed, brunette type, which extends westward from Asia through the uplands of Central Europe. We find this type accentuated as we proceed from north to south in Russia. Deniker, with his more minute classification, says that no fewer than five European races are represented among the Slavs, besides Turkic and Ugric or Mongolian elements. These are the fair, but broad-headed and short, "Eastern" and "Vistulan" races, in Poland and White Russia especially; the dark, very broad-headed, and short "Cevenole" peoples among the Little Russians of the south, the Slovaks, and some Great Russians; and the taller, but still dark and broad-headed, "Adriatic" and "Sub-Adriatic" races amongst the southwestern Slavs or Serbo-Croatians and some Czechs and Ruthenians. In the northwest the Russians have been modified by the blond or Teutonized Finns, in the northeast by the dark Finns, and in the southeast by the Tatars; but all such alike are broad-headed Mongolians in origin. With the exception of these Asiatic remnants and the related Magyars and Turks, and the Greeks, all of Europe east of Germany is filled with Slavs. They occupy more than one-half of the Continent of Europe.

All these peoples of eastern and southern Europe, including the Greeks and the Italians, are the ones that give character to the immigration of to-day, as contrasted with the northern Teutonic and Celtic stocks that characterized it up to the eighties. All are different in temperament and civilization from ourselves and this difference is accentuated as we go south. Statistics have been given in the article *Caucasian* which compare Slavic immigration with that of the Teutonic and Italic races and throw into startling relief its changed character. Of the total immigration to the United States about one-fourth is now Slavic, over one-third comes from eastern Europe, over three-fourths comes from eastern and southern Europe.

It only need be added here that the Slavic race numbers over 125,000,000 as against about 130,000,000 of the Teutonic race (including Great Britain) and 110,000,000 Greco-Latins.

It is interesting to note in the following table that the Western and Southern Slavs and those associated politically with them—the Hebrews, Magyars, Lithuanians, and Finns—are making their descent upon America at a relatively high rate per 1,000 of population. All these emigrating multitudes are subject peoples, unless we except the Magyars, who have fallen at least into economic subjection to their landlords. The Great Russians and the Hebrews, standing at the two extremes politically in Russia, are found also at the two extremes as to rate of immigration to the United States from Europe. In 1907 Hebrews came at the rate of 183 per 10,000 of population, or double that of any other immigrant race from Russia, while the Great Russian came at the low immigration rate of 2 per 10,000 of population. It must be remembered that Great Russian emigration is directed mainly toward Siberia, but other Russians as well are offered unusual inducements to settle in that country. Compared with the regularity of migration among the Slavs, the remaining immigrant peoples of Europe show great dissimilarity in their rate of movement.

Rate of immigration per 1,000 of population among the leading European races or peoples.

Race or people.	Estimated population in Europe.	Immigrants from Europe.	
		Number in 1907.	Rate per 1,000.
Slavs of Eastern Europe:			
Slovak	2,250,000	41,900	18
Croatian and Slovenian	3,600,000	47,300	13
Polish	17,000,000	137,100	8
Ruthenian (Austria-Hungary)	3,900,000	23,900	6
Dalmatian, Bosnian and Herzegovinian	1,573,000	7,300	4
Bulgarian, Servian and Montenegrin	9,000,000	26,900	3
Bohemian and Moravian	6,000,000	13,500	2
Russian (with Little Russians of Russia)	78,000,000	16,600	$\frac{2}{10}$
Other east Europeans closely in touch with the Slavs:			
Hebrew	8,000,000	146,400	18
Magyar	8,500,000	59,700	7
Lithuanian	4,000,000	25,800	6
Finnish (Western)	3,700,000	14,500	4
Contrast all other Europeans exceeding 10,000 immigrants in 1907:			
Norwegian [a]	2,311,000	22,000	9
Italian	35,000,000	288,900	8
Irish [b]	4,500,000	37,700	8
Greek	6,000,000	44,200	7
Swedish [c]	5,727,000	21,900	4
Roumanian	10,000,000	19,000	2
English and Scotch [d]	35,300,000	61,800	2
German	72,200,000	91,100	1
Dutch and Flemish	9,000,000	12,100	1

[a] Scandinavians from Norway.
[b] Population of Ireland.
[c] Scandinavians from Sweden and Russia.
[d] Population of England and Scotland.

Recent immigration from Russia and the Balkans is therefore equaled in rapidity by that of only four other countries: Ireland and Norway in the northwest, Greece and Italy in the southeast. The future possibilities of Irish and Norwegian immigration are small indeed when compared with that of the southern and eastern races. Ireland is already depopulated. She has only about 4,500,000 inhabitants left, and Norway has only half as many. European Russia, on the other hand, has over 100,000,000, twice the population of any other country of Europe, excepting Germany. Italy has 34,000,000 inhabitants, or seven times as many as Ireland. The immigrating Slavs, even if we deduct the 55,000,000 Great Russians, still number over 70,000,000, or nearly as large a population as that of England and France combined.

Slavic immigrants go mainly to the great manufacturing and mining States of Pennsylvania, Illinois, and New York.

SLAVONIAN. Used in two senses: (1) The entire Slav (see) group of races; (2) a native of Slavonia, a province of Hungary (see *Croatian*), being then a term of nationality, not of race.

SLOVAK (called **Totok,** that is, "Slavs," by Hungarian Magyars). The easternmost division of the Czechish-speaking peoples; the "race" occupying practically all of northern Hungary excepting the Ruthenian territory in the northeast; also densely settled in southeastern Moravia. A small population, but of considerable interest to America, since in their rate of immigration they outrun any other race or people, unless it be the Hebrew. "Slovakland" is a political dream and probably an unrealizable one. It has no definite boundaries, as has Bohemia or Moravia. In physical type, also, no dividing line can be drawn between the Slovaks and the Moravians. Even in language it is often claimed that Slovaks speak only a dialect of Bohemian. It is only in their social and political condition that they are sharply distinguished from their Czech brothers on the west. Properly speaking, they are hardly a distinct "race" even in the sense in which the Germans and the Dutch of Holland are different races. They are merely those Moravians who were conquered by Hungary, says Colquhoun.

Much of what has been said in the article *Bohemian and Moravian* (*Czech*) applies here and need not be repeated at length. As there indicated, the eastern Czechs, including the Slovaks, are among the broadest-headed of all the peoples of Europe, not excepting the Asiatic Tatars and Turks. They are of medium stature, some rather low; but they are well built, and, like most Slavs, make excellent farmers. In their own country most are engaged in agriculture and herding.

There is much difference of opinion on the subject of their language. Here, as is often the case, scientific discussions have been influenced by religious and political considerations, it being denied in some quarters that the Slovaks are Bohemians or even Czechs. On the other hand, Protestant leaders, and philologists, even, have claimed that Slovak is merely Old Bohemian and have urged the use of Bohemian as the sole written language. To this day, it is said, the Bible has not been translated into any purely Slovak dialect. The connection of the Slovak Protestants, that is, of one-fourth of the population, with the Moravian and Bohemian Brethren is, therefore, close. On the other hand, Catholic writers have urged the literary development of various dialects spoken by the Slovaks. One fact is clear, that Slovak, as a distinct written language and literature, is not 50 years old. Even to this day where the population is uniformly Slovak, that is, over the western border in Moravia, Slovaks are taught only Bohemian in the schools, and all of the people use it in reading and writing.

In the Slovak counties of Hungary the Magyars have attempted to replace this Slavic tongue, distantly related to our own, with one of Asiatic or Mongol origin, agglutinative, totally different in type, the Magyar. Here, in three-fourths of the elementary schools, Magyar is taught; in one-half of them Magyar alone. One-eighth only of the schools of "Slovakland" are conducted entirely in the Slovak tongue. In the 200 or more higher schools the use of the Slovak tongue, even as a medium of conversation, is still more restricted. Forty per cent of the population of North Hungary are counted as Magyars because they use that language. The Slovaks say that in this way the census misrepresents their actual number.

Among a people so long and so largely deprived of a written language of their own, there is not only an extraordinary degree of illiteracy—50 per cent—but a great divergence of spoken dialects. To an unusual extent these dialects are modified by surrounding languages of the most opposite type. Thus we find in the west, Moravian-Slovak; in the north, Polish-Slovak, sometimes called Sotak; and in the east, Ruthenian-Slovak—all purely Slavic. But in the west, on the border of Austria, one finds the German-Slovak, a more heterogeneous composition, and in the south even Magyar-Slovak. These names indicate what languages border on the Slovak country. The Serbo-Slavic dialect is not so easily explained. Safarik, a competent linguist, although ultrapatriotic, finds three chief groups of dialects: (1) The pure Slovak, (2) the Moravian-Slovak, and (3) the Polish-Slovak. He includes among Slovak dialects not only the Trpak, the Krekach, and the Zahorak, but the Hanak, the Walach, and the Podhorak of Moravia. (See article *Bohemian and Moravian* (*Czech*) for these dialects and for a general view of Slovaks themselves in their linguistic relations.) Serres, an older writer, gives the name of Charvats to the "Slovaks of Moravia," including the Walachs, who, in turn, include the Chorobats and the Kopaniczars. As explained in the article on the Bohemians and Moravians, these Walachs are considered, on the authority of Czörnig, to be Moravians. The Charvats and Chorobats of Serres are probably fragments of the old Khrovats, or Carpaths — that is, "mountaineers" — from whom the modern Croatians (see) derive their name.

In civilization "Slovakland" lies, as it does linguistically, between the east and the west of Europe—between the Teutonic and the Slavic worlds. Its culture is rather primitive. Less advanced than Bohemia, its people partake of some of the solid qualities of that admirable branch of Western Slavs. They are industrious, but they are desperately poor, partly because of the character of their mountain home. In fact they have been called the poorest people of Europe.

Their rate of immigration, 18 per 1,000 of the Slovak population in 1907, surpassed even that of the Hebrews and was double that of any other race or people excepting the Croatian-Slovenian group (13 per 1,000) and the South Italian (12 per 1,000), and treble that of most Slavic peoples, although the last named are now among the chief contributors to the movement of population from Europe to the United States. Like the Irish population, however, the number of Slovaks that remain in the old country is small. They can not long continue coming at the present rate. There are less than 3,000,000 Slovaks in all—only 2,000,000 in Hungary, according to a census that is accused of partiality. The population is smaller than that of the Irish or the Flemish, perhaps nearly half that of Holland. There are said to be already one-fourth as many Slovaks in the United States as in Europe.

Slovak emigration affects its own country more than it does America. As in Italy, some villages are becoming depopulated; others are living largely on American money. In places wages have increased 100 per cent. And, finally, the Hungarian Government is taking steps to regulate, if not to restrict, the exodus. During the twelve years 1899–1910, 377,527 Slovaks were admitted to the United States. During that period their principal destinations were as follows: Pennsylvania, 195,632; New York, 48,310; New Jersey, 35,729; Ohio, 30,785, and Illinois, 26,351. Although so small a people, the Slovak stands only eighth down the list as regards the total number of immigrants. (See article *Bohemian and Moravian* for other details, especially Slovak population statistics.)

SLOVENIAN; called also, in part, **Krainer** and **Carinthian** (**Khorutan**);

by Germans, **Wind** or **Wend**; and by Magyars sometimes, but wrongly, **Vandal**; also sometimes called, together with the Croatian (see), **Illyrian.** The westernmost branch of the Southern or Balkan Slavs; located in southern Austria between Hungary and the Adriatic, especially in the province of Carniola (Ger. *Krain*). The Slovenians or Southern Winds are, with the exception of the Northern Wends of Germany, the smallest "race" in numbers of the Slavic (Slavonic) division of Aryan peoples, and are therefore of little consequence in American immigration although their rate of immigration is high.

There is considerable confusion of thought concerning the above terms and the relation of the Slovenians to other Slavs. In the first place, the Slovenians are not to be confounded with the Slovaks, an entirely different people. They are separated from the latter by the Magyars, the Slovenians living southwest of Hungary between the Magyars and the Adriatic, while the Slovaks live on the northern border of Hungary. In language they belong to different branches of the Slavs—the Slovenians to the Southern Division, with the Servians and the Croatians, and the Slovaks to the Western Division, with the Poles and the Bohemians.

In America Slovenians are sometimes called Slavonians under the mistaken impression that they come from the neighboring province of Slavonia. The word Slavonian may be used in two senses. It may mean any inhabitant of Slavonia, but it is then a political term, denoting nationality, not an ethnographical term denoting race; and the Slavonians in this sense are Serbo-Croatians (see *Croatian*), not Slovenians, although closely related to the latter. In the second and more usual sense, Slavonian is the equivalent of Slavic, and refers to the great race of eastern Europe of which the Russians and the Poles are the northern branches and the Slovenians, Servians, and Bulgarians are the southern divisions. Of course, the words Slovenian, Slavonian, Slovak, and Slav all come from the same early name of the Slavic race. But the Slovenians are by no means to be taken as the best modern representatives of that race, although they claim to be one of the first branches of it to be introduced to western civilization in the middle ages.

It is, at the least, confusing to call the Slovenians Winds or Wends (see), as some scientific writers do. For this word is generally used to designate a distinct people of the Slavic group which belongs, with the Poles, to the Western Division, not to the Southern, as the Slovenian does. The Wend population is found only in Germany, where it is also called the Sorb, or, from its location, the Lusatian. It has dwindled to only a fragment. It is, of course, not Serb, that is, Servian. The name Illyrian is a still greater misnomer, although used in the last century by the Slavs themselves in this region. The name comes from that of the ancient province of Illyria and was given great vogue under Napoleon, when the national spirit of the Slovenians, in union with the Croatians and the Dalmatians, received a great impetus. An older name, Corutani, corresponds to that of a modern province of Austria, Carinthia, which is now more German than Slovenian. In like manner the geographical or provincial name, Istrian, signifies an Italian more often than a Slovenian. Krain, as the Austrians call Carniola, is the only true Slovenian province. Except in southern Styria, Styrian, like Carinthian, means one of German descent.

These provinces are the only ones in Austria that can be called Slovenian even in part, if we except a small district which centers in Goriz, on the Gulf of Istria, at the head of the Adriatic Sea. Here also the Slovenians extend slightly over the border into Italy, as they do on the east somewhat into Hungary. Altogether the Slovenian territory is not over 150 miles in length by 100 in breadth. The only considerable linguistic "island" in it is that of the Gottshees, a curious German stock in southern Carniola near the Croatian border.

To sum up, the Slovenian territory is bounded on the north by the German of Austria, and on the south by the Croatian, while it touches the Magyar on the east and the Italian on the west, or, rather, its sister language, the Ladin of Friuli (see *Rhæto-Romansh*). In this territory, mainly Austrian, Slovenian is spoken by about a third of the population. German predominates in Carinthia and Styria, but in the central province of the Slovenians, Carniola, Slovenian is spoken by 95 per cent of the population. It is the language of only 32,000 inhabitants of northern Italy and of 95,000 in Hungary.

The linguistic position of the Slovenian is probably evident from the foregoing. Its nearest relative is the Serbo-Croatian speech. Together they constitute the Southern Division of the Slavic. Although distinct, they shade into each other on the border. Thus the language of a large portion of western Croatia, called the "Provincial," is considered by some to be Croatian, by others Sloveno-Croatian. The dialects of the Slovenian are numerous, and are differently named by different writers. Those spoken by the largest number are the literary dialect of the Krainer, of Carniola, together with the Gorenci and the Dolenci; next, the dialects of the so-called "Winds," eight in number, found in Styria. Then come the dialects of the smaller Istrian groups, the Berkins, Savrins, and Poiks, and those of the so-called "Vandals" of Hungary. The Resian is spoken on the Italian border.

In physique the Slovenians mediate between the Germans north of them and the Croatians on the south. Perhaps the tall, broad-headed, and dark type to which the most of them belong should be called "Illyric," rather than Slavic. Deniker gives it a separate name, the "Adriatic." Broad-headed as the Slavs, the Illyrians are of greater stature than the latter. Their features often suggest an ancient Mongol element.

Their position on the western Slavic vanguard has not led them to as high a development as it has the Bohemians or the Poles, perhaps because they are weaker and have had a greater burden to share with the Serbo-Croatian in defending the marches against the Turk. Their literature has been overshadowed by that of the greater body of Serbo-Croatians. Being Catholics, they use the Roman alphabet, like the Croatians, not the Cyrillic of the Orthodox Servians. In early days they were quite unique in the use of the Glagolitic letters, which were somewhat like the Cyrillic or Russian.

Perhaps the Slovenians are more distinct in character and custom than they are in physique; but these subjects lie outside the limits of these dictionary articles. One of their marked traits is sociability, which leads them to reside in villages more than on separate farms. They are said to have become Germanized and denationalized more rapidly than any other Slavic people of Austria. Even the use of the spoken Slovenian has been largely exchanged for German as a mark of progress. Literature and science are at a low ebb. This is perhaps because of their weakness as a people. The population of about 1,200,000 is one of the smallest in Europe, less than one-third that of Bohemia or one-fifth that of Holland.

The rate of Slovenian immigration to the United States is probably very high, even for a subject Slav people. It can not be measured exactly, because in immigration statistics the Slovenians are counted with Croatians. Together the Slovenians and Croatians sent 335,543 immigrants to the United States in the twelve years 1899–1910, placing them eleventh on the list of immigrant races or peoples. (See *Croatian* for destination in America and further discussion.) Measured by the rate per 1,000 of population, the immigration rate of the Slovenians with the Croatians (13 in 1907) is surpassed only by that of the Slovaks and the Hebrews.

SORB or **SORABIAN**. Same as **Wend** (see). (See *Slav*, *Croatian*, and *Slovenian*.)

SOTAK. (See *Slovak*.)

SOUTH AMERICAN. Any immigrant born in South America, except Spanish Americans (see), is classified in the statistics of the Bureau of Immigration according to race or people, as Negro, Spanish, etc. (see these).

SOUTH ITALIAN. (See *Italian*.)

SOUTH MEDITERRANEAN race. (See *Caucasian*.)

SOUTH RUSSIAN. (See *Ruthenian*.)

SPANUOLI. Same as **Sephardim**. (See *Hebrew*.)

SPANISH. The principal people of Spain, a branch of the Romance group of the Aryan family; in general usage and in the practice of the Bureau of Immigration, the people of Spain and their descendants of pure blood in other countries, with the exception of the Spanish Americans, Mexicans, West Indians, and Cubans (see these). Even Basques and Moors (see) who have lived in Spain a long time are considered as Spanish for convenience. The national language, Spanish, is native to only a part of the Kingdom of Spain. Other native languages spoken by considerable numbers in Spain are the Basque, the Catalan, and a dialect of the Portuguese. As an ethnic group the people of Spain present a remarkable unity. They are descended from the ancient Celt-Iberians, with considerable infusion of other stocks, including perhaps even Teutonic elements (Visigothic) dating back to the middle ages. They resemble the South Italians in head form and in many psychical characters. They are for the most part Catholic in religion.

The term "Spanish language" may be used in a broad or generic sense to include several closely related native dialects of Spain—Castilian, Asturian, Leonese, Aragonese, and Andalusian. In a restricted sense it is the Castilian dialect which has been crystallized in literary form and is the cultured and court language of Spain. It is considered to be more closely related to Latin than is Italian, but contains a number of Teutonic and Moorish elements. It is the native language throughout Spain, with the exception of a narrow strip on the eastern coast (Catalan), the small Basque provinces in the north, and the provinces lying north of Portugal. It is the prevailing language in Cuba, Mexico, Central America, and the countries of South America, excepting Brazil, and among the cultured in the Philippines. In these islands, however, it is being rapidly replaced by English. It is estimated that Spanish is the mother tongue of about 50,000,000 persons, more than two-thirds of whom live outside of Spain.

Of the other linguistic groups of Spain, the Basques (see), although smallest in numbers (500,000), are perhaps the most interesting. They are one of the most ancient stocks in Europe, if not the most isolated. They occupy a small district in the northern part of Spain in the Pyrenees on the French border. They speak a non-Aryan tongue totally different from any other in Europe. Although once thought to be related to the Mongolian Finnish, their language is now known to resemble the Berber of North Africa. They present a peculiar face form, very wide at the temples and narrow at the chin.

The Galicians and the Catalans have much larger populations. The former, also called "Gallegos," live in the provinces in the northwestern part of Spain north of Portugal. They speak a dialect of Portuguese (see) which is quite closely related to Spanish. Even Portuguese was once considered a dialect of Spanish, although it has now attained recognition as an independent idiom. The population of the Galician provinces is about 2,000,000. The Catalans (see) occupy a narrow strip along the eastern coast of Spain and the Balearic Isles. Their language is unintelligible to the Castilian-speaking peasants. It is considered by some to be a separate Romance tongue on an equal with Spanish and Provençal, by others as an offshoot of the latter, which it resembles much more than it does Castilian, the neighboring dialect of Spanish. It has quite a rich literature of its own which is especially fostered by the people of Barcelona. It is the language of over 3,500,000 persons of eastern Spain and the Balearic Isles. Moors (60,000) and Gypsies (50,000) are scattered throughout Spain but are comparatively unimportant. The total population of Spain is nearly 20,000,000.

Physically the Castilians, Catalans, Galicians, and even Basques and Moors, of Spain, are quite homogeneous. The entire Iberian Peninsula is, in fact, one of the most uniform in physical type of any large region in Europe. The head form of the people of to-day is apparently that of their prehistoric ancestors, the ancient Iberians. They are among the most long-headed of all Europe. They resemble the South Italians more than the French, but are taller and less brunette than the former. The Catalans are the tallest of Spaniards and the Galicians are the heaviest. The typical Spaniard is long-headed, of medium stature (average, 5 feet 5 inches), rather brunette, and spare. Ripley places him in the "Mediterranean" group along with the South Italian, the Greek, and the Berber of North Africa. The Spanish are put in the "Iberic division" by the Bureau of Immigration.

The Spanish have long been an emigrating and colonizing people, but seem to have reached their zenith in this direction. Less than 100,000 emigrate annually. Most of these naturally go to Spanish-speaking countries. Immigration to the United States from Spain has never been large, only about 69,000 for the entire period 1819–1910. A total of 51,051 immigrants of the Spanish race were admitted during the twelve years 1899–1910. One-third of these came from Cuba. The race ranked twenty-sixth in point of numbers admitted during the period. Immigration to the United States from Spain has increased somewhat since the Spanish-American war, 5,784 persons from that country having been admitted in 1907, while before the war the number rarely reached 1,000 annually. It is said that the Basques form one of the most important groups of workmen in the Canal Zone. The principal destinations of Spanish immigrants during the twelve years considered were: New York, 16,278; Florida, 11,355; Porto Rico, 5,222; California, 4,324, and Hawaii, 2,283. Of the total number destined to Hawaii 2,251 were admitted in the fiscal year 1907. None went there in 1906. (Cf. *Portuguese.*)

SPANISH AMERICAN. Defined by the Bureau of Immigration, "the people of Central and South America of Spanish descent." Those of Negro or of Indian descent (see) are listed separately, as are also Mexicans, West Indians, and Cubans (see). The definition apparently excludes the chief people of Brazil, the Portuguese, as it does the Italians, Germans, and the like, of all South American countries. Like other terms applied to immigrants from the Americas, it does not connote, strictly speaking, a race, but a geographical subdivision set apart for practical convenience. The race, of course, is Spanish (see), although the language may have changed, as in Brazil, to Portuguese.

Among the 2,779 emigrants from South America to the United States in 1907, only 430 were Spanish Americans. Six hundred and sixty were Italians. In the twelve years 1899–1910, 10,669 Spanish American immigrants were admitted to the United States, a number exceeded by every other race or people except the Koreans, East Indians, and Pacific Islanders. Their principal destinations during the period were: New York, 5,382; California, 1,833; Porto Rico, 946, and Louisiana, 836. So far as the immigration law is concerned, the Canal Zone is a part of Central America. Aliens coming from it are not offered the same facilities as those entering from Cuba, Mexico, and Canada or from the insular possessions of the United States.

Their immigration being so small, no extended discussion of the Spanish Americans is necessary at this point. The South American countries are immigrant receiving rather than emigrant furnishing nations. In fact, if the migration from European Russia to Siberia be excepted, South America, next to the United States, receives more immigrants than any other part of the world. In this respect the Argentine Republic stands far in the lead of other South American republics, with an oversea immigration of approximately 250,000 annually, about one-fourth as great as the movement to the United States. Italians and Spaniards predominate in immigration to Argentina. Brazil comes next among the immigrant-receiving countries of South America, with 67,787 in 1907. Among these, Italians, Portuguese, and Spanish predominate. Chile receives a much smaller number of immigrants per year. The races mentioned are the chief elements in the population of the Argentine Republic and Chile. The population, about 5,700,000 and 3,400,000, respectively, is almost entirely white. In Brazil, on the contrary, less than one-half of the total population of 17,000,000 is white, about 30 per cent being of mixed blood, 15 per cent or more of Negro blood, and 8 per cent (1,300,000) of Indian blood.

STEPOVIKI. A subdivision of the Ruthenians (see) living in the plains (steppes) of Russia.

STYRIAN. A geographical term, not the name of a race. A native of Styria, a duchy of Austria. The population of Styria numbers 1,356,000, of whom about 68 per cent are Germans and the remainder Slovenians (see these).

SUDANESE. (See *Semitic-Hamitic* and *Negro*.)

SULU. A language of the southern Philippines. (See *Filipino*.)

SUOMI or **SUOMALAISET.** Finns of Finland. (See *Finnish*.)

SWABIAN. Same as **Alemanni.** A division of the Germans (see). A native of Suabia, a former duchy of southwestern Germany.

SWEDISH. (See *Scandinavian*.)

SWISS. The term Swiss simply means a native or inhabitant of Switzerland. It has no significance as to race. There is no Swiss race in the sense in which we use the terms Frenchman, German, Italian, but only a Swiss nation. The Swiss are represented by four linguistic groups, one Teutonic (German) and three Italic (French, Italian, and Romansh). Two-thirds of the population of Switzerland are German, about one-fourth are French, and only one-fifteenth are Italian. Besides these large populations of German, French, and Italian there are about 40,000 Romansh (see these). The total population of Switzerland is 3,465,000. The Romansh live in the sequestered valleys of the canton of Grisons, the Italians in the valley of the Ticino, and the French in the western part of Switzerland. In the greater part of Switzerland the speech is German. About two-fifths of the Swiss are Catholics and three-fifths Protestants.

SYRIAN (not **SIRYAN**). The native Aramaic race or people of Syria. Not Arabian, although practically all Syrians to-day speak Arabic and a considerable part of the present population of Syria is Arabian. Most often distinguished from Arabs by their religion, Syrian immigrants generally being Christians, although many of their kinsmen in Syria are Mohammedan. The influence of American missionaries and schools in Syria evidently explains in part why our immigration from that country is of Syrians rather than of Arabs. Physically the modern Syrians are of mixed Syrian, Arabian, and even Jewish blood. They belong to the Semitic branch (see) of the Caucasian race, thus widely differing from their rulers, the Turks (see), who are in origin Mongolian.

Linguistically they are not so closely related to the Aryans or Indo-Europeans as are their fellow-subjects of Turkey, the Armenians. Their ancient language, the Syriac, a form of the Eastern Aramaic, has Hebrew for its nearest relative. A little more distant is the Arabic tongue. Even the Abyssinian speech is more closely related to it than is the ancient Assyrian, with which it is sometimes confounded. These, with the Coptic dialects of Egypt, are the chief languages of the non-Aryan, Semitic-Hamitic stock (see) of Syria. Chaldee, Chaldaic, and Syro-Chaldaic are other names applied to the form of this language which was spoken by Christ and His disciples. The Neo-Syriac, Palmyrene, and Nabatean dialects are said to be the only modern forms of the Aramaic, and are spoken by only a small population of villagers under the stimulus of missionary zeal. These reside for the most part east of the main population of Syria (see *Ayssore* in article *Assyrian*).

Syria is an ancient rather than a modern term, although used, in a narrower sense, by the Turkish Government. It properly comprises all the region lying between the eastern end of the Mediterranean and the desert and is about 430 miles long by 100 wide. Palestine constitutes only one-tenth of it. Of the 3,000,000 (estimated) population of Syria, the Syrians probably outnumber the Arabs, Turks, and Jews, although there are more Mohammedans than Christians in Syria. The Christians number 900,000. The population of Palestine, 800,000, consists mainly of Arabs (see), notwithstanding the recent colonization of Jews in the Holy Land.

Among other inhabitants of Syria closely related to the Syrians, if not of the same blood, are descendants of the Phœnicians, inhabitants of the coast districts; the Maronites, Christians of the Lebanon; the Druses, half pagan and unfriendly neighbors of the Maronites; and the Nusarieh or Ansarieh, descendants of the Nazarini, who are called Fellahin in Syria, and who do not seem to be orthodox in their Mohammedanism.

The Syrian immigration to the United States for the twelve years 1899–1910, was 56,909. Their principal destinations in the United States during the period were: New York, 18,370; Massachusetts, 8,652; Pennsylvania, 7,318, and Ohio, 2,780. About 1,000 annually come from European Turkey. They stand twenty-fifth in rank among immigrants, smaller in number than the Russians, Roumanians, or Portuguese, but more numerous than the Spanish, Armenians, or Welsh.

SYRMIAN. (See *Croatian.*)

SYRO-CHALDEAN. Same as **Chaldee** language (see). (See also *Ayssore* in article *Assyrian.*)

SZEKLER. A subdivision of the Magyars (see) living in Transylvania.

T.

TAGALOG. (See *Filipino.*)

TAJIK. (See *Persian.*)

TAKTAJI. A name given certain Yuruk Turks. (See *Turkish.*)

TALYCH. A small Iranian (Aryan) people living in the Caucasus. (See *Caucasus peoples.*)

TAMIL. A branch of the Dravidians (see) living in southern India and northern Ceylon. (Cf. *Sinhalese.*) It has a population of over 16,500,000.

TAT. A Tajik or Persian living in the Caucasus. Sometimes improperly called Tatar. (See *Caucasus peoples.*)

TATARIC (TARTARIC), TURKIC, or **TURKO-TATARIC.** One of the six linguistic groups which constitute the Sibiric or Ural-Altaic branch of languages spoken by Mongolians, as divided by Brinton. The group includes the Turks, the Tatars in the narrower sense of the word, the Kazaks or "Cossacks" (Kirghiz), the Turkomans, the Huns of history (not the Magyars), and less important tribes still living in Asia, such as the Yakuts and Uzbegs. (See all these terms.) All these are supposed to have had their origin in Chinese Tartary.

Their importance to the student of immigration consists in the fact that they constitute more than 6,000,000 of the population of eastern Russia who, if they are not at present coming to the United States under the name of "Russian," are of interest as a possible source of immigration. They may fairly be said to be the most backward in civilization of any large population of Europe. Although filling the best portion of eastern Russia from north to south, they are but little known and their strength and possibilities but little suspected by the ordinary reader.

They are perhaps the largest body of non-Caucasians in Europe, about equal in numbers to the Magyars or the Jews. The only other European populations of Mongolian origin are the Ugro-Finnic stock (Magyars, Lapps, etc.) and the Kalmuks or "Calmucks" (see these). The latter is only a small, isolated tribe of Mongols near the Caspian, in close contact with Tatars and not greatly unlike them. Joined with the Mongol hordes of Genghis Khan, the Tatars have written their name large on the history of the Eastern world.. Indeed, these Mongol founders of dynasties have generally, but wrongly, been known to history as Tatars. Their descendants still possess Turkey and dominate the Mohammedan world.

As has been explained in the article on the Ural-Altaic stock, of which they form a part, the Tatars, Kazaks, and Turks are closely related in language to the Magyars and Finns, and more distantly to the Japanese and Koreans. All these have agglutinative "Turanean" languages, as contrasted with the monosyllabic Chinese and the inflected Aryan speech of India and western Europe. The dialects of Turkey are very closely related to those of the eastern Russian people who call themselves "Türki", that is, Turks, but who are more properly called "Tatars." Physically and socially the Tataric group have not become so fully Europeanized as the Finnic. As a rule the Turks are the farthest advanced of the group, and are thought of as much like ourselves; but they by no means so closely resemble Western Europeans as the blond Finns, or even the darker Magyars, the Finnic stock of Hungary. The greater part of the Tataric populations of Russia are Mohammedan in faith, although Shamanism still persists among them, as it does among their kinsmen of Asia. Some are still polygamists.

Since the Turks are discussed in a separate article, it remains to speak here only of the more backward Tataric stock, and especially of the 6,000,000 Turko-Tatars of eastern Russia. Geographically they all live south of the Finnic stock of Russia. With the latter they give one the impression of being simply a part of Asia that has everywhere pushed over the line and settled upon European soil. In some provinces the competing Russian stock has entirely surrounded them. The Mordvinian and Bashkir communities dot the map like little islands in the Russian flood. It is in such districts that the Tataric populations are becoming most rapidly Christianized and Russified by intermarriage.

The relative numerical importance of the Tataric peoples of the Russian Empire, both in Europe and in Asia, will be seen from the following table, taken from the census of 1897.

Distribution of Turko-Tatars.

Race (by language).	European Russia.	Poland.	Caucasus.	Siberia.	Central Asia.	Total.
Tatar	1,953,155	4,336	1,509,785	210,154	60,197	3,737,627
Bashkir	1,316,764	80	948	924	2,647	1,321,363
Mestcheriak	53,799	....	....	40	8	53,847
Tepyak	117,734	3	5	14	17	117,773
Chuvash	837,872	929	411	4,232	311	843,755
Karatchai	....	....	27,222	1	....	27,223
Kumyk	....	....	83,389	13	6	83,408
Nogai	....	....	64,048	2	30	64,080
Osmanli-Turk	68,807	156	139,419	172	268	208,822
Karapapakh	....	....	29,902	....	....	29,902
Turkoman	7,938	6	24,522	124	248,767	281,357
Kirghiz-Kazak	264,059	123	98	32,637	3,787,222	4,084,139
Others	693	....	159	227,826	2,519,277	2,747,955
Total	4,620,821	5,633	1,879,908	476,139	6,618,750	13,601,251

The total Turko-Tataric population of the world is about 25,000,000, if we include the 10,000,000 Turks of Turkey, about 2,000,000 of Persia, and 1,000,000 Tataric subjects of China in Eastern Turkestan.

As is evident from the foregoing table, the most important division by far of the Turko-Tatars of the Russian Empire is that of the Tatars proper, using this term in the narrow sense. They call themselves "Türki," not "Tatars," but they are distinct from the Turks of Turkey. They are scattered widely throughout Russia, especially in the large cities, but are most numerous on the Volga (700,000 in Kazan province) and about the Caspian Sea, in southeastern Russia. Only about 270,000 live in Asia. About 200,000 others live north of the Black Sea. This number probably includes the "Nogai" Tatars of the Crimea, still Mohammedan, who are mentioned by various authorities. The census shows none there, but 64,000 in the Caucasus. About 17,000 Tatars located north of the Crimea have embraced the Greek faith and are Caucasian rather than Tataric in physical type, no doubt because of intermarriage with the surrounding Little Russian population.

The Karaits, some of whom come to the United States, are a small group of 5,000 or 6,000 people, also in the Crimea. They are said to be Tatar in origin, but to have been long ago converted to the Jewish faith. They speak a Tatar dialect.

Leaving the better-known Kazaks to a separate article (see *Cossacks*), we need to consider here only the Bashkirs, the Chuvashes, the Turkomans, and a few less familiar tribes, mainly of Asiatic residence. Of these the Bashkirs (1,300,000) are by far the most numerous. They do not extend over the line into Asia in such numbers as do the Tatars, although they live on both sides of the Ural Mountains, in the easternmost province of Russia, Orenburg, and in Ufa, which joins the latter on the west. They therefore are located farthest toward the northeast of all the Tataric peoples of Russia, with the exception of a small group called "Mestcheriaks" (50,000). The Tepyaks (117,000) lie close to these in Ufa and the province of Samara, next to Asia.

There remains to be noted in eastern Russia the more important branch known as the "Chuvashes," 800,000 strong. They extend farthest west of the Tataric populations, into Central Russia, being quite surrounded by Great Russians and Eastern Finns (Cheremisses and Mordvinians). Like the Bashkirs, they are really a mixed Finno-Tataric stock. The Kazan Tatars live on the eastern bank of the Upper Volga, opposite the Chuvashes.

The Turkomans proper (280,000), closely related to the Osmanlis of Turkey, live for the most part east of the Caspian, in Central Asia. Less than 8,000 are found in eastern Russia. They are for the most part a wild population of nomads. The name Turkoman is sometimes used in a wider sense to include the related peoples of Persia (such as the Aderbaijani Turks, Kajars, and Afshars) and of Asia Minor (Kizil-Bashis, Yuruks, and Götchebes—"Seljuk Turks," as the peasant classes are called). Some of these, as the Kizil-Bashis, are largely Aryan (see) in descent rather than Mongolian. The Kazaks (see) live north of the Turkomans in Russian Asia.

Passing now to the Tataric peoples of the Caucasus provinces, the most numerous and important are the Osmanlis, the proper name of the Turks of European Turkey (see *Turkish*). They number 200,000 in Russia, living mainly near the Black Sea and including some 68,000 scattered throughout southern and eastern Russia. Neighboring them are the Nogais, already mentioned, and the small populations of the Karatchais and the Karapapakhs. More numerous are the Kumyks (83,000), who live on the Caspian side of the Caucasus. They, like the Nogais, are no doubt a blend of Tatar and Caucasian. Most of the Caucasus peoples (see) are not Turko-Tataric, that is, of Mongolian origin, but are Caucasians who generally speak non-Aryan languages.

The remaining Tataric tribes, numbering 2,700,000, are confined to Asia and need no especial notice here. Among them are the Kara-Kirghiz, or "black" Kirghiz, the Kara-Kalpaks, the Sartes, and the Uzbegs, all of Central Asia, and the Yakuts of Siberia.

Although, as above indicated, Tatar immigrants to the United States may be an important factor in the future, but few of them are known to come as yet. Such as do come are probably counted as "Russian" or "Ruthenian," because they speak these languages. If any speak the old "Türki" dialect they may be counted as "Tatars" and go to make up the column of "Other peoples" in the tables of the Bureau of Immigration.

TAVASTIAN or **TAVAST**. A division of the Western Finns. (See *Finnish*.)

TCH-. (See "*Ch-*" for words beginning with "*Tch*.")

TELUGU. A subdivision of the Dravidians (see) living north of the Tamils, in southern India. They have a population of over 20,000,000.

TEPYAK. A Tatar people (see) in eastern Russia.

TEUTONIC. A great branch of the Aryan (see) family of languages and "races," including all those of northwestern Europe excepting the Celtic (see). Its many subdivisions are shown in the following table from Keane, with the exception of Dutch and Flemish, which are variously classed as Low Frankish or Low Saxon:

The Teutonic group.

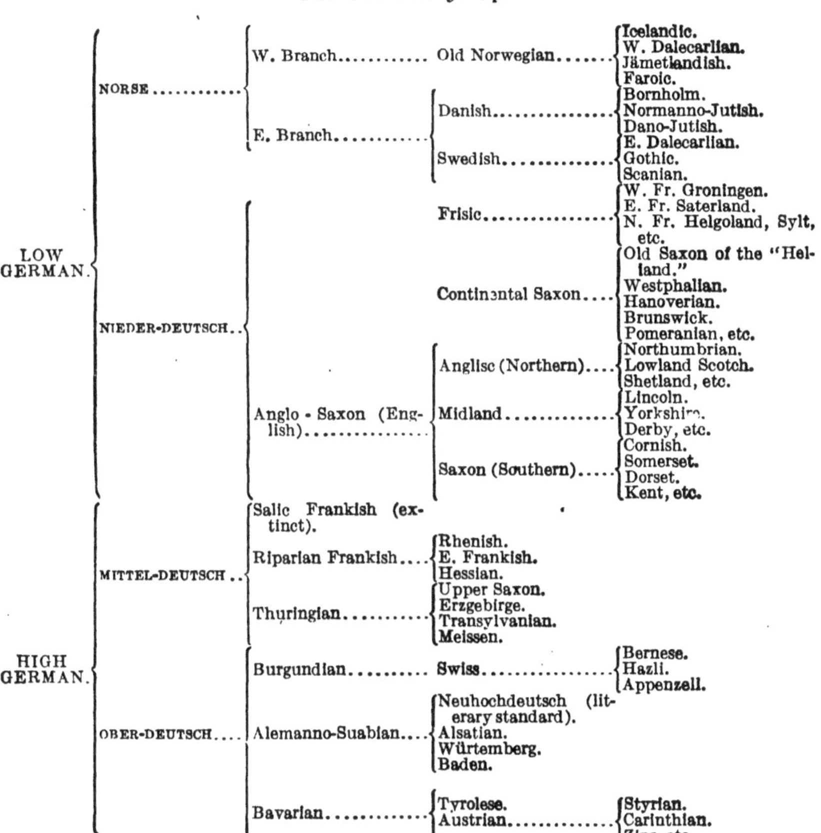

LOW GERMAN	NORSE	W. Branch	Old Norwegian	Icelandic. W. Dalecarlian. Jämetlandish. Faroic.
		E. Branch	Danish	Bornholm. Normanno-Jutish. Dano-Jutish.
			Swedish	E. Dalecarlian. Gothic. Scanian.
	NIEDER-DEUTSCH		Frisic	W. Fr. Groningen. E. Fr. Saterland. N. Fr. Helgoland, Sylt, etc.
			Continental Saxon	Old Saxon of the "Heliand." Westphalian. Hanoverian. Brunswick. Pomeranian, etc.
		Anglo-Saxon (English)	Anglisc (Northern)	Northumbrian. Lowland Scotch. Shetland, etc.
			Midland	Lincoln. Yorkshire. Derby, etc.
			Saxon (Southern)	Cornish. Somerset. Dorset. Kent, etc.
HIGH GERMAN	MITTEL-DEUTSCH	Salic Frankish (extinct).		
		Riparian Frankish	Rhenish. E. Frankish. Hessian.	
		Thuringian	Upper Saxon. Erzgebirge. Transylvanian. Meissen.	
	OBER-DEUTSCH	Burgundian	Swiss	Bernese. Hazli. Appenzell.
		Alemanno-Suabian	Neuhochdeutsch (literary standard). Alsatian. Würtemberg. Baden.	
		Bavarian	Tyrolese. Austrian	Styrian. Carinthian. Zips, etc.

THURINGIAN. (See *German.*)

TIBETAN. A group of peoples inhabiting central Asia, and therefore of no importance in an immigration study. They are Mongolians and closely related to the Chinese (see these).

TONKINESE. Annamese (see) living in Tonking. (See *Indo-Chinese.*)

TOSK. A division of the Albanians (see) living in Epirus.

TOUHOLTS or **TUKHOLTSI.** A Little Russian of Galicia. (See *Ruthenian.*)

TRIPOLITAN. Any native of Tripoli. About three-fifths are of Arabian stock (see) and two-fifths are Berbers (see).

TSEKH or **TSHECK.** Same as **Czech.** (See *Bohemian and Moravian.*)

TSINTSAR. Same as **Kutzo-Vlach** (see).

TSRNAGORTSI. Same as **Cernagorian** or **Montenegrin.** (See *Croatian.*)

TUNISIAN. Any native of Tunis. About equally divided between the Arabs and the Berbers (see these).

TURANIAN. A discredited term equivalent to Ural-Altaic (see).

TURKISH. In the narrow sense, the people now dominant in Turkey; called by themselves "Osmanlis," that is, Ottomans. Immigration statistics are to be understood in this popular sense of the word, although some ethnologists define the word "Turkic" in a much broader sense to include all the Tataric group (see) of the Sibiric branch of the Mongolian division of mankind. In this sense it includes not only the Osmanlis of Turkey, but other peoples of eastern Russia, such as the Tatars, the Kirghiz-Kazaks, and the Turkomans, and also the older relatives of this group stretching across Asia from Turkey to central Siberia, such as the Yakuts. While we apply the name "Turks" only to the Osmanlis, they themselves apply it only to provincials; and we do not apply it to the Tatars, although the latter call themselves "Türki." With all the foregoing may be combined the Lapps, Finns, Magyars, and other non-Caucasian Europeans to make up the larger group variously known as the "Finno-Tatar," the "Turanian," or the "Ural-Altaic." (See these.)

The linguistic relationship of all these peoples is much closer to-day than the physical. The languages are agglutinative, like the Japanese, not inflected like the speech of the Arabs, Syrians, Armenians, and Hebrews subject to Turkey. Physically and in culture the Turks have become Europeanized, though to a less degree than the related Finns and Magyars. Instead of becoming blond, as the Finns, they have approached the brunette type of southern Europe, probably in part through their frequent intermarriages with the Circassion and other Mohammedan peoples of the Caucasus. In fact, to-day they are not so much Turkish by blood as Arabian, Circassian, Persian, Armenian, Greek, and Slavic. They prefer to be considered as Arabo-Persian in culture rather than as Turkish. In religion they are almost universally Mohammedan. They are not included in one of the five grand divisions of the Bureau of Immigration, but are put under the term "All others," along with the Magyars and Armenians. We may put under the term "All others" also the Tataric peoples of eastern Russia and other races of the Caucasus, who are rarely found among our immigrants. (See *Russian.*)

The Turks are in the minority in their own country, especially in the European part of Turkey, where the Turks, Greeks, Albanians, and "Slavs" (Bulgarians and Servians) are said by some writers to be found in nearly equal parts. The first three named have been estimated to constitute 70 per cent of the population. No census of Turkey has ever been taken. The following estimates are compiled from various sources. The entire Ottoman Empire, excluding States practically independent, has a population of about 24,000,000. Of these, 10,000,000 are Turks. In European Turkey, 1,500,000 out of a population of 6,000,000 are Turks. Here they are without doubt decreasing in numbers. In Macedonia, the geographical center of European Turkey, the Turks number about 500,000 out of a population of 2,200,000. Of the latter number, however, only about 1,300,000 are Christians. In the capital itself, Constantinople, the Turks constitute only about one-half of the population of 1,200,000.

In Turkey in Asia, on the other hand, the Turkish race is in the majority. The Mohammedans number perhaps 10,000,000 in a total population of 13,000,000 in Asiatic Turkey and Armenia. There are about 500,000 Turks in Bulgaria out of a total population of 4,000,000. The Mohammedan population of Bosnia and Herzegovina—550,000 out of a total of 1,600,000—is mainly Slavic rather than Turkish. In Servia and Greece there is practically no Turkish population.

Only 1 out of 5 of our Turkish immigrants comes from Turkey in Asia. The total immigration of this race is very small—only 12,954 during the twelve years 1899–1910. They stand thirty-fourth in point of numbers, or lower than the Armenians, Chinese, or Welsh. Their principal destinations in the United States during the period were: Massachusetts, 3,073; New York, 2,632, and Pennsylvania, 1,412. Occasionally an immigrant from Macedonia may insist that he is not a Turk, Bulgarian, Greek, or Albanian, but a Macedonian; he may be Tsintsar, Vlach, or Aromun, names applied to those who speak a Macedonian dialect of the Roumanian. The Tsintsars number about 90,000, of whom about 3,000 are Mohammedans.

TURKOMAN. An important Tataric people of Asia closely related to the Osmanli Turks. (See *Tataric* and *Turkish.*)

TURKO-TATARS. (See *Tataric.*)

TUSCAN. (See *Italian.*)

TYROLESE. Not the name of a race and not used by the Bureau of Immigration. Any native or inhabitant of the province of Tyrol, Austria. There is no Tyrolean race in the sense that we use the terms French, German, or Slovak race. Tyrol has a population of about 831,000. The Tyrolese represent two very different linguistic divisions of the Aryan family. Teutons and Latins. About 55 per cent of the population are German. Of the remainder, about three-fourths are Italian and one-fourth Ladin (see these) or Rhæto-Romansh (see). There are some 2,000 Czechs and Slovenians.

The inhabitants of Tyrol show marked differences physically. Ripley says that rarely is so close a relationship found between physical characters and language. The Germans are long-headed, tall, and light, the majority being above 5 feet 6 inches, while the Italians and Ladins to the south are broad-headed and brunette, and less than one-fifth of them attain the height of their Teutonic neighbors. Most of the Tyrolese are Catholic in religion.

It is not known how many come from Tyrol to the United States, as the Tyrolese are listed according to the language they speak.

TZINTZAR (TSINTSAR). (See *Roumanian.*)

U.

UGRO - FINNIC, UGRIAN, UGRO-SCYTHIAN, FINNO-UGRIC, sometimes **FINNIC.** The equivalent of "Finnish" when used in the widest sense to include both the Finnic and the Ugric branches of the Ural-Altaic division of Mongolian languages. The chief immigrant peoples speaking Finnic languages are the Magyars and the Finns. (See all the above terms, especially *Ural-Altaic,* for further details.)

UIGURIC. A branch of the Tataric (see) group of languages, including the Turkoman (see) and the **Jagatai.** From the ancient Uigurs is derived the name of the great Ugro-Finnic (see) group of northern Mongolians.

UKRANIAN. A geographical term; a name applied to the Little Russians of Ukraine. (See *Ruthenian.*)

URAL-ALTAIC; synonyms, **Finno-Tataric, Mongolo-Turkic, Sibiric, Scythian, Turko-Ugrian, Altaic, Uralic,**

Ural-Altaic.

Mongolo-Tataric, Ugro-Altaic (in widest sense), and formerly **Tataric** or **Turanian.** (See *Ugro-Finnic* for narrower terms.) The family of agglutinative languages, which distinguishes the Sibiric division of the Mongolian race from the remaining or Sinitic division (Chinese, etc.), the latter possessing a monosyllabic speech. (See Classification of Races, in Introductory, *Mongolian* and *Finnish.*) These are more properly linguistic than ethnical terms, although "Finno-Tataric," which is used in both senses, might well be reserved to designate the peoples and "Ural-Altaic" to designate the languages they speak.

This is a subject of which the ordinary student of immigration may know but little, and yet it is indispensable to a proper understanding of important immigrant peoples like the Magyars, Finns, Turks, and Japanese. (See articles on these peoples.) It is not commonly known that these all derive their origin from the same primitive Mongolian stock of northern Asia, and that, although the western members of the stock have become more or less Europeanized in blood, they still have languages of absolutely different origin and type from our own. They are thus cut off from participation in our literature, and necessarily, to a certain extent, from our ideals and institutions. The Ural-Altaic languages are agglutinative, while our Indo-European languages are inflected and the Chinese is monosyllabic. The only remaining primary division or family of languages in the world is that of the American Indians, the polysynthetic. The term "Turanian," now generally discarded, was applied by Max Müller to nearly all Old World languages that are neither Indo-European nor Semitic. It was soon loosely applied to all poorly understood languages and ethnical stocks of Europe. Nor is the term "Scythian" in common use, although carefully limited by Whitney to the group now under discussion. The remaining terms suggest localities and peoples of which the relations will be made clearer by the following classification from Keane (somewhat condensed in Asiatic portions):

Classification of Ural-Altaic languages.

Language.[a]	Continent.	Location.
I. SAMOYEDIC.		
Yurak and Yenisei	Europe and Asia.	White Sea to the Yenisei.
Tavghi	Asia	Between lower Yenisei and Khatanga rivers.
Kamasin	do	Upper Yenisei.
II. FINNIC.		
Finnish	Europe	Finland, part of Norway, Lakes Onega and Ladoga.
Lapp	do	Russian and Scandinavian Lapland.
Esthonian and Livonian	do	South side of Gulf of Finland.
Mordvinian and Tcheremissian	do	Middle Volga.
Permian, Votyak, and Siryenian.	do	Between the Vyatka and Petchora rivers.
III. UGRIC.		
Ostiak	Asia	Middle and Upper Obi and its eastern affluents.
Vogul	do	East slopes of the Ural Mountains.
Magyar	Europe	Central and southeastern Hungary.
IV. TURKIC.		
Uigur or East Turki, including Uigur proper.	Asia	Kashgar, Kulja, and Yarkand.
Jagatai	do	Bokhara, Ferghana, and Khiva.
Kara-Kalpak	do	Southeastern side of Aral Sea.
Turkoman (Turkmenian)	do	West Turkestan, north Persia, and Asia Minor.

[a] See articles on the more important of these terms.

Classification of Ural-Altaic languages—Continued.

Language.	Continent.	Location.
IV. TURKIC—continued.		
Seljuk or West Turki or Osmanli.	Europe and Asia.	Asia Minor and the Balkan Peninsula.
Tchuvash	Europe	Southwest of Kazan and about Simbirsk.
Kipchak (Kapchak) Coman	Europe and Asia.	Extinct, formerly current throughout the Kipchak Empire from the Altai Mountains to the Black Sea.
Kazan Tatar	Europe	Middle Volga.
Kirghiz	Europe and Asia.	West Siberian steppes, lower Volga, the Pamir, and west slopes of the Altai, Thian-Shan, and Kuen-Lun Mountains.
Nogai with Kumuk	Europe	Bessarabia, Crimea, Volga Delta, Daghestan, Terek Valley.
Yakut	Asia	Middle and lower Lena and northern slopes of the Sayan Mountains.
Siberian Tatar, Teleut, Koibal, Soyot, Kotta, Bashkir, Mescheryak.	do	Spoken by Tatarized Finn populations from the Altai to the Urals.
V. MONGOLIC.		
Sharra or East Mongolian	Asia	Mongolia.
Kalmuck	Asia and Europe.	Dzungaria and lower Volga, thence to lower Don.
Buriat or Siberian Mongolian	Asia	East and west of Lake Baikal.
VI. TUNGUSIC.		
Tungus proper	Asia	From the middle Yenisei to the Pacific.
Lamut	do	Western coast of the Sea of Okhotsk.
Manchu	do	Manchuria.
VII.		
Japanese	Asia	Japan and Riu-Kiu (Lew-Chew) Islands; doubtful.
VIII.		
Corean	Asia	Corea; doubtful.
IX AND X.		
Accad and Etruscan	Asia and Europe.	Both doubtful and extinct.

The foregoing classification will be found to agree fairly well with that of Brinton, adopted in this dictionary (see Introductory), which runs as follows: (1) Tungusic, (2) Mongolic, (3) Tataric, (4) Finnic, (5) Arctic, and (6) Japanese. By Castren the first three were called the "Altaic" branch; the fourth, the "Uralic." Others divide the Ural-Altaic into the Northern division (groups 3 and 4) and the Southern (1 and 2). Brinton follows the French authors Lefèvre and Hovelacque, as well as Whitney, in combining the Finnic and the Ugric, while he probably improves upon all these in putting the Samoyedic also into this group. The connection of the Japanese and the Arctic groups with the remainder is not now considered by Keane to be so doubtful as when he made the above classification. It is but fair to say that this doubt was formerly expressed by the other authors mentioned. While the agglutinative speech of the Japanese differs very widely, like the rest, from the monosyllabic Chinese, it is by no means so closely related to the Ural-Altaic languages of Europe in vocabulary or in its grammar as are the other Sibiric languages.

The physical differences existing today between the Finno-Tataric peoples can be best discussed in separate articles. (See *Japanese* and the rest.) Their geographical extent is immense, being second only to that of the Indo-European stock. As will be seen from the foregoing table, they extend from the Atlantic (the Lapps of northern Norway) to the Pacific (the Japanese), filling not only all of northern and western Asia down to India, but much of eastern and southeastern Europe (the "Hungarians," Turks, Finns, and various peoples of eastern Russia).

The population of this stock is nevertheless small, perhaps 60,000,000, not counting the 60,000,000 Japanese and Koreans. They are very thinly spread out over 10,000,000 square miles, largely in frigid and desert regions of Siberia and central Asia. Their migratory instinct threatened to submerge Europe in the middle ages, but their numbers now count for little even when the proportion that leave their homes is abnormally large, as in the case of the Magyars and the Finns to-day (see). The entire Finnish population numbers less than 6,000,000; the Magyar population about 8,500,000.

URALIC. Same as **Ugro-Finnic**, a division of the Ural-Altaic (see these).

URUGUAYAN. (See *Spanish American.*)

V.

VEDDAH. A primitive branch of the Dravidians (see) living in southeastern Ceylon.

VELIKO-RUSSIAN. Same as **Great Russian** (see).

VENETIAN. (See *Italian.*)

VENEZUELAN. (See *Spanish American.*)

VEP or **SOUTHERN CHUDE.** A division of the Finnish (see).

VICOL or **BICOL.** (See *Filipino.*)

VISAYAN or **BISAYAN.** (See *Filipino.*)

VLACH. Same as **Wallachian.** (See *Roumanian.*)

VLAH or **WLACH.** Same as **Morlak.** (See *Croatian.*)

VOGUL. A Finnish people (see) living partly in Siberia.

VOT, VOD, or **VATJALAISET.** A Southern Chude. (See *Finnish.*)

VOTYAK. (See *Finnish.*)

W.

WALACH. A division of Moravians. (See *Bohemian.*) Not the Wallachians of Roumania. (See *Roumanian*).

WALLACHIAN. Same as **Roumanian** (see). (Cf. *Walach.*)

WALLOON. A name applied to French Belgians and to their language, a dialect of French (see). They number over 3,000,000 in the southeastern provinces of Belgium and the neighboring district of northern France. They are supposed to be descended from the ancient Belgian Gauls of Cæsar. Walloons do not emigrate in large numbers, although colonies are to be found in the large cities of Holland, and the first permanent settlement of New Amsterdam contained a number of them. They are counted as French in immigration statistics. Only 964 "French" came from Belgium to the United States in 1907. Most of these were, no doubt, Walloons.

WALSER. A name applied to certain Germans (see) living in Austria.

WELSH. The principal people of Wales; linguistically, a division of the Cymric branch of the Celtic group of Aryans (see); physically, a mixed race. The term "Welsh" is also used to mean any native or naturalized inhabitant of Wales, but thus used it is a term of nationality, not an ethnical one.

The Welsh language is the most important member of the Cymric division of Celtic tongues (see). It is an ancient and distinct tongue so far as history carries us, and since the eighth century has had a literature nearly, if not quite, as rich as that of the Irish, which is the most important division of the other branch of Celtic tongues, the Gaelic. In modern literature the Welsh excels all other Celtic languages, for there are several quarterlies, monthlies, and weeklies printed in it, some of which have thousands of subscribers. It is the freside speech of nearly half the population of Wales, and is used in the churches and the church schools. The Welsh eisteddfod, or musical and literary meeting, is very popular, not only in Wales, but in large Welsh colonies in the United States and in Australia. Nevertheless, the Welsh language, like all other Celtic tongues, is losing ground. Its nearest kinsman, the Cornish (see), became extinct a little over a century ago. Ravenstein says that 70 per cent of the population of Wales for 1871 could speak Welsh. The census of 1901 shows only about 50 per cent of the population able to speak Welsh.

Yet, as compared with other Celtic tongues, Welsh is still quite vigorous. For, while less than 1 per cent of the populations of Scotland and Ireland can speak a Celtic tongue only, 15 per cent of the population of Wales speak Welsh only. Only in Brittany, France, is another Celtic language, the Breton, so extensively used.

Physically, the Welsh are anything but homogeneous, for Beddoe finds at least two physical races in Wales not yet thoroughly amalgamated. One is the "Northern," whose representatives are tall, long-headed, light-eyed, darkish haired—a type that reminds one of the Irish (see). The other presents quite a contrast. It is short, compactly built, broader-headed, of dark complexion, with dark eyes. This type is thought to belong to the "Alpine" race, called by some, perhaps hastily, the "Celtic" (see) physical type. Here again is a difference between the Cymric people of Wales and the Gaelic peoples of Ireland and Scotland, for in the latter physical anthropologists fail to find evidence to warrant an "Alpine" origin. In religion the Welsh are, for the most part, Protestants, dissenters from the Church of England.

Geographically, the Welsh are found in Wales and in that part of England immediately adjoining Wales, especially in Monmouthshire. The population of Wales in 1901 was 1,720,600 and that of Monmouthshire was 230,-800. Not all of these, however, are Welsh, for many of English blood now reside in Wales. Nearly 1,000,000 persons speak the Welsh language.

The Welsh do not form numerically an important element in American immigration. Only 20,752 came to the United States in the twelve years 1899–1910. This places them near the end of the list of immigrants. Their rate of movement is low, 1.4 per 1,000 of the population of Wales, in 1907. This is but little more than that of the Germans or of the English, about one-sixth that of the Irish or of the Norwegian, and one-thirteenth that of the races which stand at the head of the list, the Slovak and the Hebrew. Their chief destinations in the United States during the twelve-year period referred to were: Pennsylvania, 6,779; New York, 4,119; Ohio, 1,440, and Illinois, 955.

WEND, LUSATIAN, or SORABIAN. A small branch of the Western Slavs living in Lusatia, a name formerly applied to a part of Germany, now forming parts of the provinces of Silesia and Brandenburg (Prussia) and of the Kingdom of Saxony. The Wends call themselves "Serbs." They are now restricted to a region about 40 by 75 miles in extent and are entirely surrounded by Germans, by whom they are being rapidly absorbed. They number about 115,000. Their language, which has two dialects—a High and a Low—is called "Lusatian" or "Sorabian." It was nearly extinct as a literary language when revived by the efforts of a society about the middle of the last century. The Wends are peasant farmers and for the most part Lutherans. Only a few thousand are Catholics.

The term "Wind" is sometimes improperly used to apply to Slovenians (see). "Wend" was formerly used by Germans to mean any Slav (see).

WENDIC. A term given by Max Müller to the Letto-Slavic (see) group of languages. Not **Wend** (see).

WERCHOWINCI. A geographical term applying to mountaineers of different stocks ethnically in the Carpathians, in eastern Austria; it includes the Boikos, the Tuholtses, and the Huzuls. (See these in article *Ruthenian.*)

WEST INDIAN. Defined by the Bureau of Immigration thus: "'West Indian' refers to the people of the West Indies other than Cuba (not Negroes)." Those of Indian blood also are counted separately. (Cf. *Indian, Negro, Cuban, Mexican, Spanish American.*) "West Indian" is therefore rather a geographical term than strictly ethnological. It does not include the original West Indian aborigines but only the native whites or "creoles" of the island, and does include such dissimilar ethnical elements as Dutch, English, French, and Spanish colonists. The last named have given the dominant character to the civilization of this tropical country, and have left their language not only in the islands which until recently belonged to Spain, as Cuba and Porto Rico, but also in Santo Domingo and portions of the Lesser Antilles. English, French, and Dutch are spoken in some of the smaller islands. Reclus says that three-fifths of the population of the West Indies are mulattoes. Excluding the 3,000,000 inhabitants of Cuba and Porto Rico, the rest of the West Indies contain about 3,000,000 Nearly one-half of these are in the three English islands of Jamaica, Trinidad, and Barbados. Naturally the white immigration to the United States from these populations is small. Only 11,569 West Indians were admitted to the United States as immigrants in the twelve years 1899–1910. They ranked thirty-fifth among the various races or peoples in point of numbers. Of the number admitted during the period specified, 6,238 were destined to New York, 1,503 to Porto Rico, 1,490 to Florida, and 638 to Massachusetts. The number of Cubans and Negroes (see) arriving from the West Indies was nearly six times greater than the number of "West Indians" admitted.

WESTPHALIAN. (See *German.*)

WHITE RUSSIAN. (See *Russian.*)

Y.

YEZIDI. A branch of the Kurds (see).

YIDDISH. A modern language of the Hebrews (see).

YUGO-RUSSIAN. Same as **South Russian.** (See *Ruthenian.*)

YUGO-SLAVIC. Same as **South Slavic.** (See *Croatian.*)

YURUK. A section of nomadic Osmanli Turks living in Asia Minor. (See *Turkish* and *Tataric.*)

Z.

ZABECACI. (See *Bohemian.*)

ZIGEUNER. A name by which Gypsies (see) are known in Germany.

ZINGARO. A name by which Gypsies (see) are known in Italy and Spain.

ZINZAR. Same as **Tsintsar.** (See *Kutzo-Vlach* and *Bulgarian.*)

ZIP. A name applied to Germans (see) in northern Hungary.

ZULU. (See *Negro.*)

ZYRIAN, ZIRYENIAN, SIRYAN, or **SIRYANIAN.** A division of the Eastern Finns (see ***Finnish***) of Russia. (Not **Syrian.**)

www.ingramcontent.com/pod-product-compliance
Lightning Source LLC
LaVergne TN
LVHW021402110826
845150LV00007B/1757

* 9 7 8 1 4 2 5 5 7 2 2 2 8 *